RAPE WITHIN MARRIAGE

A Moral Analysis Delayed

Edward J. Bayer, S.T.D.

Wipf & Stock
PUBLISHERS
Eugene, Oregon

Wipf and Stock Publishers
199 West 8th Avenue, Suite 3
Eugene, Oregon 97401

Rape Within Marriage
A Moral Analysis Delayed
By Bayer, Edward J.
Copyright© January, 1985 by Bayer, Edward J.
ISBN: 1-59244-248-X
Publication date: May, 2003
Previously published by University Press of America, January, 1985

There is true love,
And then there is its counterfeit.

This book is dedicated to
JENNIFER SILER,
She taught us to seek only the real thing.

— Uncle Eddie
August 19, 1984

Nihil Obstat:

Rev. Lorenzo Albacete, S.T.D.

IMPRIMATUR:

Rev. Msgr. John F. Donoghue,
Archdiocese of Washington

Romae, apud Pont. Universitatem S. Thomae

Vidimus et approbavimus ad normam Statutorum Universitatis

Romae, apud Pont. Universitatem S. Thomae
die 19 mensis Novembris anno 1982
Philippus F. Mulhern, O. P.
Urbanus Voll, O. P.

IMPRIMATUR

Nihil obstat quominus imprimatur
E Vicariatu Urbis, die 24 Novembris anno 1982
  + Giovanni Canestri, Vicegerente
    Arciv. tit. di Monterano

ACKNOWLEDGEMENTS

There are many without whom this work would not be, and I here render a word of thanks to all:

To William Cardinal Baum, who formerly as Archbishop of Washington and later as Prefect of the Sacred Congregation for Catholic Education, encouraged me both by his hospitality and by his efforts on my behalf;

To Rev. Philip Mulhern, O.P., whose wisdom and faith made this work an experience in Christian discipleship, friendship, and scholarship;

To my mother and other family members, and to personal and parishioner friends who have offered me every support and encouragement;

To my brother priests with whom I have served in the Archdiocese of Baltimore, Washington, and St. Louis; to those of the Casa Santa Maria, especially those who supported my work by their friendship, questions, challenges, and example;

To my colleagues at The Pope John XXIII Medical-Moral Research and Education Center, to the secretarial staff who made room for my work in a very busy schedule, and in a special way to Miss Sherry Horton whose generosity helped me bring the final editing, writing and typing to completion; and to the Reverend Joseph Brennan, C.S.Sp., for proofreading the gallies.

To the married couples and their children who have made me part of their life; and especially to the couples and priests of the Worldwide Marriage Encounter who have enabled me to see the presence and power of Jesus in their Sacrament as theological treatises never could;

And, finally, to the Sisters of St. Francis of Philidelphia who in my first years as now in my later years, and to the Little Sisters of the Poor, their residents, all of whom have shown to me the reality of the love of Christ in the service of the Christian community;

To all, my deep thanks and a prayer that God may bless them as they have blessed me.

TABLE OF CONTENTS

Acknowledgements v
Abbreviations ix

Chapter

I: FACING AND FOCUSING A NEGLECTED PROBLEM 1
    Introduction 1
    A. The concept of "Sexual Oppression within Marriage" 1
    B. "Contraception" vs. "Prevention of Pregnancy" 4
    C. Artificial Means of Defense Against Unjust Impregnation 7
    D. Doctrinal Presuppositions of the Present Study 10
    E. The Division of the Book 12

II: THE QUESTION OF RAPE WITHIN MARRIAGE RAISED --
    FOR A WHILE 13
    Introduction 13
    A. Representative Writers of the Period 1600-1749 15
        Thomas Sanchez 15
        Basilius Pontius 18
        Lopez de Texeda 19
        Other authors 21
        John Bossius 21
    B. The Decrees of Innocent XI 22
        Commentators on the Decrees 23

III: 1750-1880: SORTING OUT THE BEST AND SURVIVING THE WORST 25
    Introduction 25
        The Influence and Status of St. Alphonus Ligouri in Moral Theology 25
        Intellectual and Social Uprisings Hobble Theological Life 26
        The Leonine Revival of Theology 27
        A New Chapter in Embryology 27
    A. Authors from 1750 to 1880 28
        1. Authors who Accepted Sanchez' Position 28
            Claude La Croix 28
            Nicholas Mazzotta 30
            Edmund Voit 31
        2. Authors Who Oppose Sanchez' Position 32
            St. Alphonsus Ligouri 32
            Marc Strüggl 33
            Other authors 34
        3. Authors Who Did Not Take Sides Regarding Sanchez' Position 34
    B. Church Magisterium 35
        Response of the Sacred Penitentiary, 1822 35
        A Hermeneutic Principle for Magisterial Documents 37
        Response of the Holy Office, 1853 38
    C. Conclusions for the Period 1750-1880 40

IV.	1880-1960: PROGRESS AMIDST GREAT PROBLEMS	42
	Introduction	42
	Turmoil in Society and the Church	42
	Progress in Church Doctrine and the Theological Enterprise	43
	A. Authors: 1880-1960	
	1. A Single Author Moves to Develop Our Thesis During the Period 1880-1960	44
	2. Two Writers Specifically Reject Our Thesis	
	Marcellinus Zalba	47
	Godfrid Heinzel	47
	3. Writers Who Do Not Treat Our Thesis Specifically	48
	a. Writers Who Accept Sanchez' Position	48
	b. Writers Who Reject Sanchez' Position	55
	4. Summary of Theological Writers 1880-1960	56
	B. The Teaching of the Magisterium 1880-1960	56
	1. Specific Points of Papal Teaching Pertinent To Our Teaching	57
	Leo XIII: Arcanum Divinae Sapientiae	58
	Pius XI: Casti Conubii	58
	Pius XII's Discourses	63
	a. Pius XII on Contraception	64
	b. Pius XII on Sterilization	65
	c. Pius XII on Totality	67
	2. Teaching of the Roman Congregations	74
	C. Summary of the Period 1800-1960	80
V.	SEXUAL OPPRESSION IN MARRIAGE AND A WIFE'S RIGHT TO DEFENSE AGAINST IMPREGNATION	82
	Introduction	82
	A. Authors 1960-1980	83
	Joseph Fuchs	84
	Hermes Peeters	84
	Bernard Haring	85
	Jan Visser	86
	Marcellinus Zalba	88
	Christopher Derrick	96
	Anselm Günthör	97
	Bertrand de Margerie	100
	B. The Magisterium: 1960-1980	102
	John XXIII	102
	Paul VI	104
	The Second Vatican Council	105
	Humanae Vitae	108
	Quaecumque Sterilizatio: Response of the Sacred Congregation for the Doctrine of the Faith to the National Conference of Catholic Bishops in the United States	113
	Human Life in Our Day	115
	John Paul II	115
	Familiaris Consortio	116
	The Irish Episcopal Conference	121
	C. Summary	122

VI.	AN ENDING AND A BEGINNING	
	A. Development of Theologians' Doctrine Regarding Sexual Oppression Within Marriage	124
	Development of Doctrine: An Ecclesial Reality	124
	Development on Sexual Oppression Has Taken Place	126
	B. A Solidly Probable Opinion Today	126
	Intrinsic Reason	127
	Extrinsic Reason	128
	C. Elements To Be Abandoned	128
	Physicalism	129
	A Distorted View of the Conjugal Right	130
	A False And Timid Interpretation of The Principle of Totality	131
	D. Elements For A More Adequate Theology of Marriage	133
	A Procreational Act	133
	An Act of Justice	136
	A Kind of Speaking	140

ABBREVIATIONS

AAS: *Acta Apostolicae Sedis.*

DISCORSI: *Pio XII, Discorsi Ai Medici,* a cura di S. E. Mons. Fiorenzo Angelini, Edizioni *"Orizzonte Medico",* Romae, 1959.

E.S.: *Enchiridion Symbolorum Definitionum et Declarationum De Rebus Fidei et Morum,* ed. H. Denzinger. A. Schonmetzer, Romae, 1974.

E.V.: *Enchiridion Vaticanum,* Edizioni Dehoniane, Bologna, 1981.

G.S.: *Gaudium et Spes,* "The Constitution on the Church in the Modern World" of the Sacred Vatican Council (E.V., *supra,* Vol. I, p. 770-967.)

H.V.: *Humanae Vitae, Encyclical Letter of Paul VI, 1968 (*E.V., *supra,* Vol. 3, pp. 280-319).

L.G.: *Lumen Gentium,* "The Dogmatic Constitution on the Church" of the Sacred Vatican Council (E.V., *supra,* Vol. 1, pp. 120-266).

N.C.E.: *New Catholic Encyclopedia,* Washington, D.C., 1967.

P.H.: *Persona Humana,* Sacred Congregatio Pro Doctrina Fidei, Dec. 29, 1975 (*E.V., supra,* Vol. 5, pp. 1126-1157).

CHAPTER I:
FACING AND FOCUSING A NEGLECTED PROBLEM

Christian people who truly seek to understand the Gospel, and Christian pastors who dedicatedly seek to lead them to such an understanding will often draw out of that Gospel challenges which fly in the face of some of the world's most cherished habits of thought. This type of Gospel challenge we all saw, for example, when Pope John Paul II, in 1980, called our attention to the clear implication of the Gospel that a married man could be adulterous in his heart, not only towards a woman not his wife, but even towards his very own wife herself, - - and indeed that a wife could fall into an adulterous attitude in her sexual desires towards her own husband.[1]

A. The Concept of "Sexual Oppression Within Marriage"

If this thought of "adultery within marriage" (even if only "in the heart") strikes so unfamiliar a note as to incite honest shock or even angry rejection,[2] one can expect that, at least for many, the concept of "sexual oppression within marriage" may very well need some explaining and some getting accustomed to. For we here intend that "sexual oppression" retain the meaning Catholic moral theology has assigned to it throughout most of its history, namely "rape". What we shall be discussing in this study, then, is "intra-marital rape", a concept at least as challenging to the world's thought patterns as "adultery towards one's own wife."

Whether or not such a concept is *de facto* rooted and implicit in the Gospel as the Church has been given to hold and understand it, especially in the living teaching ministry of her bishop-shepherds today, is, of course, another issue. As this study proceeds, we shall defend the thesis that it is at least a probable opinion that such is indeed the case. But for now we must define more precisely what we mean by this apparently foreign new concept which seems to be invading the familiar old landscape of our moral theology today.

For the purposes of this present treatment of "rape within marriage," we stipulate by this phrase *any complete genital copulation or any other sexual act* which is *capable of impregnating a wife* and which *is forced upon her by her husband at a time or under circumstances when she justifiably refuses her consent.*[3] Throughout this study, we will speak directly only of *complete* genital copulation in the sense in which the conjugal act is defined in the classic moral treatises, e.g.:

---

[1] John Paul II, Wednesday audience talk, October 22, 1980. cf. *Osservatore Romano*, October 23, 1980, p. 1.

[2] For a review of public reactions, cf. *Time*, October 27, 1980, p. 106, and *Newsweek*, November 3, 1980, p. 75; cf. also Novak, Michael, in *National Review*, November 14, 1980, p. 1401.

[3] We do not wish to discuss in the present study the moral situation of a woman who *should* (e.g., because of her serious heart condition) refuse sexual relations, but does not.

> The pressing of the male organ into the vagina of the wife with insemination then made directly into the vagina.[4]

It is understood, however, that although we are speaking directly of complete copulation in this sense, the thesis we propose applies equally to *other* sexual acts which can cause pregnancy.[5]

We are dealing, moreover, only with cases where a wife's right to refuse sexual actions is truly a *substantial* right. A merely *incidental* right to refuse sexual actions, however serious such a "right" might be both subjectively and objectively, is not under consideration here, e.g., as when a husband has failed to live up to some reasonable expection of his wife, but one not essential for the overall good of the marriage. An example of such an expectation might be his arriving home on time for dinner on a given night. Such minor infractions of the exigencies of family life and spousal love are part of the human condition and of the vocation to patience, tolerance, and forgiveness which are basic to married life. In contrast to such an accidental "right" (really not a right, but a motive) for a wife's refusing sexual actions, we consider only a *substantial* right so to refuse. It would be beyond the scope of the present study to do more than state that there is indeed such a right to refuse, and that it is clearly recognized within reasonable bounds by moral theologians.[6] Besides, at least a basic consideration of this right to refuse the conjugal act has been developed by many standard moralists who include, e.g., immoderate frequency of sexual requests, basic irresponsibility in supporting a wife and family, and a clear and serious threat to the wife's life or basic health should be a pregnancy ensue.[7] Moreover, especially since the Encyclical Letter of Pius XI, *Casti Conubii*,[8] increasingly clear recognition of the obligation of "responsible parenthood"[9] has been developed both in the teaching of theologians[10] and that of the Magisterium, the latter notably in the Pastoral Constitution of the Second Vatican Council, *Gaudium et Spes*.[11] Obviously, with the *obligation* of responsible parenthood comes the *right* to carry out that obligation. Any unilateral, clear, substantial refusal of a husband, therefore, to abide by this obligation which is mutual

---

[4]Zalba, M., *Theologiae Moralis Summa*, BAC, Madrid, 1954, V. III, p. 832. "Immissio membri virilis cum inseminatione directa in vaginam." We are here accepting the purely physical definition which the manualists generally agree upon for the *conjugal act* as an adequate definition only for *copulation between husband and wife*. As will become obvious, however, later in the thesis, we have serious misgivings about considering every act of copulation between husband and wife as necessarily and substantially "the conjugal act."

[5]Cf. Billings, John, Dr., *Natural Family Planning*, 4th ed., Collegeville, Minn. 1978, *Amplexus reservatus* or any other genital-to-genital contact, according to Billings, can indeed cause pregnancy, especially if the "mucus symptom" of the woman is at its "peak".

[7]Cf. Noldin-Schmitt, *Summa Theologiae Moralis, Supplementum de Sexto Praecepto*, ed. 31, 1940, Oeniponte, n. 91-92. Merkelback, *Summa Theologiae Moralis*, Parisiis, 1931, vol. III, n. 961; A. Ballerini D. Palimieri, *Opus Theologicum Morale in Busenbaum Medullam*, Prato, 1893, vol. VI, n. 406 and 410-411

[8]AAS, vol. 22, (1930), 565

[9]Thomas Sanchez, in his *De Matrimonio*, (Venetiis, 1626 edition, 1.9, d. 25, n. 3) is only one of a number of examples of development of this subject long before *Casti Conubii*.

[10]Zalba, *op. cit.*, n. 998.

[11]n. 50, *E.V.*, vol. 1., pp. 869, #50

to both spouses would be a serious injustice to his wife because an interference with her right to carry out her basic vocation as wife and mother, as well as a member of society and of the Church.[12]

We do not wish to enter into the question of whether, in theory, *any* basic refusal of *any* kind whatsoever on the part of a wife would make a true conjugal act *impossible* for a husband.[13] For instance, we are not here considering the case of a husband who forces copulation on his wife when she is seriously and substantially refusing her consent out of mere whim or selfishness, and therefore unjustifiably; we are not considering here whether copulation forced by a husband under such circumstances could or should be considered in some true sense "intra-marital rape." We are considering "intra-marital rape" only as a justified category for a forced sexual act which a wife has objectively *serious* and *substantial* reasons for refusing.

Finally, it may be helpful to note that the "force", as we are considering it here, need not be only of a physical kind, but quite conceivably might be psychological, i.e., *absolutely* overwhelming psychologically (as when a husband will not hesitate even to wake up the children in the middle of the night with his loud ranting about his sexual desires) or only *relatively* so (as when the woman is in such an undeveloped or devastated emotional condition that she does not have even normal psychic ability to withstand the attempts of her husband to bully her with unreasonable sexual demands).

It must be noted here also that intra-marital rape as we have defined it above is described by some writers as only "analogous to rape" or "quasi-rape". Howevermuch the predications "analogous" and "quasi-" might tend to weaken the force of the expression "intra-marital rape," it is the intention of this study to show that these qualifications do not cast any doubt on the fact that there is solidly probable opinion, or even something can indeed be applied to "intra-marital rape," namely 1) the right of a woman so victimized to avoid an impregnation from this act, and 2) the liceity even of artificial means to do so. As in the case of extra-marital rape, of course, as we shall more fully explain later in this chapter, the right we affirm for a wife in such cases is to prevent a pregnancy in the first place, - - not to terminate a pregnancy once begun.

In summary, then, "intra-marital rape", - - sexual oppression within marriage -- as the phrase is used in this study, means any sexual act of a husband, which is capable of impregnating his wife, and which is at the same time forced upon her by her husband against her objectively justified and serious refusal of consent.

---

[12]Cf. *Humanae Vitae*, nn. 10 and 16 (*E. V.*, vol. 2 pp. 291 and 299) where Pope Paul VI indicates that it is part of the vocation of Christians qua *Christians* to take into consideration economic and social conditions of *society at large*, as well as their own domestic limitations, in deciding the number of children which they should seek to have.

[13]The present writer does not wish to insinuate that this question should not be examined or that it is closed. It is interesting to notice, for instance, that the *wording* of the Guidelines for Marriage issued by the Irish Bishops (*America*, Feb. 7, 1981, p. 89) speaks only of lack of consent on the part of the woman as an element of "quasi-rape," but not of a *justified* lack of consent. Cf. *infra*, pp. 6 and 121-122.

B. "Contraception" Vs. "Prevention of Pregnancy"

This age has seen the Church suffer greatly as, in the Magisterium of her bishop-pastors, and notably of her supreme pastors, she has stood against the prevailing *mores* of the times, and even against the tenaciously held opinions of many of her own sons and daughters, regarding a number of issues, but especially that of contraception. Our thesis speaks positively, however, of the use of *artificial* means beforehand to prevent pregnancy from beginning. One would naturally be led by this formulation to think of the anovulants, diaphrams, spermicidal foams, etc. which are usually categorized simply as "contraceptives" when one is speaking of agents whose use for preventing pregnancy stands condemned by the Church. It might at first appear, then, that the thesis includes an opinion clearly in opposition to the position of the Magisterium. As will be seen in section C of this chapter, however, nothing could be further from the truth or from the purpose intended by the writer. It will be necessary, therefore, to stipulate for purposes of our thesis quite different meanings for two expressions: "contraception" and "prevention of pregnancy". The reason for this stipulation is that a general conventional use of the term "contraception" has grown up in Magisterial and in many theological writings, as well as in common parlance.[14] It is true that the word "contraception" is, by way of exception, used also in a sense quite different from this general, conventional use to mean simply "periodic abstinence" and other practices not condemned by the Church. Nonetheless we will use it here in its generally accepted sense of acts which are authentically discerned by the Church as being beneath the human person, and especially the Christian. Here it means, therefore: *The substitution of what the Catholic Church*[15] *considers a substantially deformed physiological act in place of the authentic conjugal act*[16] *and for the purpose of avoiding pregnancy.*[17] Contraception in this sense is, of course, widely and correctly known to be repudiated by the Catholic Church in her Magisterium. "Contraception", then, will refer here to a deliberate *physiological* substitution of one kind of act for another, that is, of what is in the judgement of the Church a basically deformed sexual act for the true sexual act which we call "conjugal".

---

[14]*Baltimore Catholic Review*, April 17, 1981.

[15]We do not wish here to enter into natural law arguments regarding the intrinsic evil of such contraceptive substitutions for the conjugal act, though we hold that such arguments can be presented with at least objective validity. We here wish simply to acknowledge that official Catholic teaching on this point does indeed substantially meet the requirements of a morality "based on the nature of the human person and of his acts". (*G.S.* n. 51)

[16]Paul VI in *Humanae Vitae*, Par. 11 does not say simply that the sexual act of *copulation* must remain open to the transmission of human life, but that the *actus conjugalis* must so remain open. "Quilibet matrimonii usus ad vitam humanam procreandam per se destinatus permaneat." It does not seem possible from the text to see simply *any* act whatsoever of copulation as *included, even if, for example, the copulation takes place outside of marriage;* nor is it clear at all *from this key passage* that the Holy Father considers every possible act of copulation within marriage to be an *usus matrimonii*.

[17]In using the qualifying phrase "for the purpose of avoiding pregnancy," we do not intend to insinuate that it is *only* this purpose which makes these substitutions illicit. Even when, for example, these substitutions are done simply out of some sexual anomaly or for any other reasons, actions which substantially depart from the physiology which the Church recognizes as coming from the creative wisdom of God would be beneath the human being because they would be a contradiction of the image of Himself which God has built into him or her. Indeed, acts which seem to substantially depart from the natural physiology of the conjugal act and therefore to offend against its *entire* significance, but make this departure precisely in order to *achieve pregnancy* also are repudiated by the Church. This it would seem is the strongest objection brought against *in vitro* fertilization. Whether or not this objection may at some later date be overcome to the satisfaction of the Magisterium remains to be seen; but the physiological sacredness of the conjugal act is certainly a datum for any further theologizing of these problems.

Derivative of this concept of an illicit physiological substitution of an unnatural and evil act for a natural and good one is the concept of "contraceptive intention,"[18] which here indicates an *interior* rejection (including therefore an act of the will) of the substance of one's sexuality in its procreational dimension. It should be pointed out that this contraceptive intention may dominate one's mind and heart,[19] even though the person may *de facto* no longer be *physiologically* substituting illicit acts for licit ones. The person may, to the contrary, *de facto* be giving physiologically all that he/she here and now possesses of a complete sexuality in the genital, i.e., the procreational sense.[20] An example would be that of a person who has had his/her basically healthy reproductive system[21] sterilized by vasectomy or tubal ligation in order to avoid pregnancy, and now makes full physiological use of what is left of the mutilated generative system, but without any substantial repentance for the illicit operation.[22] Such a person is still clinging to an immoral "contraceptive intention". So much for the meaning which we here stipulate for the word "contraception."

"Prevention of pregnancy", however, in this study, shall mean something quite different from contraception as we have stipulated its meaning above. "Prevention of pregnancy" here means to prevent impregnation from sexual actions which the Church cannot consider as authentic conjugal acts because of the justified refusal of free consent on the part of the wife. The essential difference of this "prevention of pregnancy" from "contraception" as we have defined that word above involves, then, *a justified withholding of free consent.* Such a withholding, we maintain, makes it impossible for a given sexual act to be the authentic conjugal act, even though the said act is *per se* quite capable of impregnating the wife. It is this *justified withholding of free consent* which in some way renders a forced sexual act within marriage less than the conjugal act, *at least with the effect* that such a forced sexual act does not fall within the scope of the Church's defense of the "conjugal act" against the abuse of contraception, as that abuse is rejected, for example, in *Humanae Vitae.*

As will be seen as the study develops, a significant number of moral theologians who unquestionably seek to draw their inspiration from the teaching of *Humanae Vitae* believe that our distinction between "contraception" and "prevention of pregnancy" is at least implicit in the teaching of Paul VI in *Humanae Vitae.* Whether or not they are objectively correct in that assessment and can produce con-

---

[18]Cf. The United States' National Conference of Catholic Bishops (hereafter NCCB) *To Live in Christ Jesus,* 1976, United States Catholic Conference, p. 18.

[19]ibid.

[20]M. Zalba, *Theologiae Moralis Compendium,* 1958, BAC, (Madrid BAC, 1958) (hereafter: Zalba ... *Compendium)* Vol. 1, n. 1511 and n. 4; Cf. also, Noldin-Heinzel, IV, GG and Vermeersch, IV. GO, *ibid. cit.*

[21]We here use the phrase "basically healthy reproductive system" in order not to enter into the disputed question as to whether a womb utterly traumatized, e.g., by repeated caesarean sections, may be "isolated" by cutting the fallopian tubes, but then left *in situ* so as to avoid adhesians and other possible complications which might result should the womb actually be removed. Cf. O'Donnell, T., *Medicine and Christian Morality,* 1976, Staten Island, p. 133-134.

[22]As has been pointed out both implicitly and explicitly in both theological writings and in Magisterial documents, even natural methods of avoiding pregnancy can fall victim to the "contraceptive mentality". Cf. Pius XII, "To Midwives", in DISCORSI, p. 163-165.

vincing arguments for it remains to be seen. It will suffice at this point to maintain that what most people consider the key passage of *Humanae Vitae* is in no obvious way closed to this distinction.

> The conjugal act must remain *per se* open to the transmission of life.[23]

The Pope, in this passage, does not further define "the conjugal act". Our understanding of that phrase, then, will have to come from other sources which the Church deems valid, such as the common and healthy sense of mankind, the teaching of theologians recognized as attempting to teach in union with the contemporary papal Magisterium (including *Humanae Vitae* itself in passages other than the one we have just cited), teachings of local episcopates, and the Scriptures. All of this will point to the possibility that there are indeed sexual acts within marriage which are capable of impregnating, but which, in a truly basic sense, cannot be called "conjugal". Against such "non-conjugal acts" the condemnation of contraception would not necessarily be aimed. Clarification of the concept of "conjugal act", then, we contend, founds a distinction between "contraception" as opposed to "prevention of pregnancy."

But in addition to our own clarification of the concept "conjugal act", it might be that also some extrinsic authority will help justify the distinction between "contraception" and "prevention of pregnancy". Such would be the case, if, for instance, official episcopal documents themselves would begin to use this distinction implicitly or even explicitly. Such indeed now seems to be the case. For in marriage morality guidelines issued by the Irish Episcopal Conference in November, 1980, we read:

> It sometimes happens that the use of contraceptives does not have the real meaning of a contraceptive act. The situation may be one of "quasi-rape", in which the husband forces intercourse on the wife, thereby contradicting the very meaning of married love. In these circumstances recourse to contraceptives by the wife would not appear to be an act of contraception *in the moral sense,* since this presupposes that intercourse is free, i.e., possesses the minimum degree of freedom necessary for a human act.[24].

Obviously the Irish Bishops here are making a distinction between "the conjugal act", which *Humanae Vitae* defends against any contraceptive act whatsoever, and "quasi-rape", which "contradicts the very meaning of married love". Equally obviously, the same Bishops are making a distinction between acts which

---

[23] *Humanae Vitae,* n. 11.

[24] The guidelines are of unquestionable authenticity, this having been verified to the present writer by two leading members of the Irish Episcopate, as well as by a number of Irish clergy who received them in mimeograph form from their Ordinaries. The Irish Bishops, however, have, for whatever reasons, not put them into printed form, and the present writer has been requested not to quote directly from the mimeographed copies which he has obtained. Cf. *supra,* p. 3, footnote 13, and *infra,* p. 121-122.

do "have the real meaning of a contraceptive act", and "acts which do not appear to be an act of contraception," i.e., acts which are a "contraception", as contrasted with mere "prevention of pregnancy".[25]

The reason for this terminological distinction, it should be noted, is by no means merely etymological. Etymologically, both expressions could easily be taken to mean the same thing, since etymologically both expressions signify only an act which aims at heading off a human conception which otherwise may occur from a physiological genital act.

C. Artificial Means of Defence Against Unjust Impregnation

In raising the question of whether a wife may make use of "artificial means" in order to avoid pregnancy from a seriously unreasonable sexual act substantially forced upon her by her husband, we must now limit our discussion considerably. First of all, it must be made clear that we are considering only *"ante-factum"* means which a wife might use *before* an unjustly imposed copulation is forced upon her by her husband, and precisely *in view of* such a prospect. Confining ourselves to these *ante-factum* means, we will not enter into a consideration of *post-factum* means of preventing pregnancy, such as vaginal, uterine, or tubal spermicidal douches, dilation-and-curettege (D-and-C), and surgical and pharmaceutical sterilization (after the forced copulation, but before fertilization is likely to have taken place). We exclude consideration of these because 1) some of them are not considered at all medically effective in actually preventing pregnancy (the douches, and the D-and-C.)[26]; 2) others are considered impracticable and not justified by a proportionately serious reason (surgical sterilization)[27]; 3) and at least one must be considered immoral because basically abortifacient (D-and-C).[28] Furthermore, all of the above *post-factum* means of dealing with the problem of rape were studied at length by Charles Curran in his doctoral dissertation in 1961,[29] and we do not wish to cover that ground again.

The one remaining means mentioned above which could be used *post-factum* is diethylstilbestrol (DES), which has been judged by some to be effective in preventing ovulation and thus pregnancy, but also has a *de facto* abortifacient effect, even

---

[25]*ibid.*

[26]C. Curran, *The Prevention of Pregnancy After Rape*, Pontificia Universitas Gregoriana, Roma, 1960, p. 40; Ashley, Benedict, O.P., and O'Rourke, Kevin, O.P., *Health Care Ethics,* 1st edition, (The Catholic Hospital Association, St. Louis, 1978) p. 295.

[27]Curran, *loc. cit.*

[28]Ashley and O'Rourke, *op. cit.* p. 295-296.

[29]Curran, *op. cit.*

if only in 2.5% of cases.[30] We choose not to treat of DES here, however, because neither *the scientific evidence of its ovulation-inhibitory effects nor the moral arguments used to justify* it on the basis of its double-effect are convincing to all, even in the case of extra-marital rape. It would be beyond the scope of this present study to enter into whatever controversy remains regarding this drug.[31]

Our consideration, then, is of *ante-factum* means of preventing pregnancy for a wife substantially victimized by her own husband. We include the *standard barrier methods* of preventing pregnancy: diaphrams, cervical cups, spermicidal foams, etc. We include also artifically induced sterility,[32] be it quasi-permanent by surgery[33] or temporary by truly anovulant (i.e., non-abortifacient) drugs.[34]

All of the above methods for a victimized wife to avoid pregnancy obviously can with good reason be categorized "artificial". And it is precisely here -- in the word "artificial" - - that we find one of the most thought-provoking aspects of the theological development which we are studying. In the minds of many - - which perhaps too often includes the minds of pastors and even theologians - - to defend what is "natural" to man seems to demand a rejection of anything "artificial" as immoral. In the process of this study, we must, however, give consideration to this identification of what is "natural" with what is "non-artificial", - - an identification we find misleading because too facile.

For now, however, we need to distinguish the pregnancy-prevention which we are defending for the sexually victimized wife from certain other practices which we in no way would defend: 1) actions superficially deemed pregnancy-prevention, but

---

[30] Cf. Ashley and O'Rourke. *op. cit.*, pp. 295-296, and McCarthy, Donald, "Medication to Prevent Pregnancy After Rape," in *Linacre Quarterly*, 1977, 44: 210-222. The presumption of these authors who defend the use of DES is always: 1) that there is the strongest moral certainty that no pregnancy already exists; and 2) that the intention of the doctor, and even more so of the rape victim, is directly to the *prevention* of ovulation and pregnancy, and only indirectly to the tolerating of the termination of a pregnancy which statistically may possibly occur in only 2.5% of rape cases. Ashley and O'Rourke cite O'Donnel, *op. cit.*, p. 247, as condemning "outright" the use of DES. O'Donnell's actual wording, however, does not bear this out as the only possible interpretation of his opinion, since he condemns the use of DES "when there is suspicion of contraceptive failure". It would seem that "contraceptive failure" is the equivalent of "pregnancy", and thus O'Donnel's opinion may very well basically coincide with McCarthy's. In their 1982 2nd edition, however, Ashley and O'Rourke abandon McCarthy's position. Cf. also W. Walsh's objections to McCarthy's position in *Linacre Quartly, op. cit.*

[31] Ashley and O'Rourke. *loc. cit.*

[32] We use the term "artificially induced sterility" here and throughout this study, and avoid the term "direct sterilization," because it is evident that the Magisterium, at least in the instance of the Sacred Congregation for the Doctrine of the Faith, is using currently this latter term to repudiate only "contraceptive sterilization". Cf. *Quaecumque sterilizatio*, a letter to the U.S. National Conference of Catholic Bishops, March, 1975, *E.V.*, Vol. 5. As we shall show in Chapter V, the "direct sterilization" to which the Congregation here refers is limited to sterilization to prevent pregnancy from sexual actions *clearly foreseen and freely willed.*

[33] We do not enter here into "uterine isolation", as that term is used by some for cutting the fallopian tubes, but leaving in situ a uterus which has been basically ruined by repeated caesarean sections or other pathological conditions so that it cannot carry another pregnancy to term. For such authors, it is clearly illicit on the one hand to de-activate a basically healthy reproductive *system* by destroying one of its basic and healthy components in order to alleviate problems being caused by another *system* of the body (v.g., the renal or vascular system). Not illicit, they would hold on the other hand, is the de-activating of one healthy surviving component (e.g., the fallopian tubes) of a reproductive *system* which has otherwise *substantially deteriorated* as a *system* through the pathology of one of its most important parts, i.e., the uterus. Cf. O'Donnell, *op. cit.* pp. 133-134 for a slightly different argument in defense of "uterine isolation".

[34] Whether the present-day typical composition of anovulant pills is such as truly to prevent ovulation, or whether it merely camoflauges a true ovulation and actual fertilization by disrupting the endometrium and causing a *de facto* abortion is a much disputed question into which we do not wish to enter here. It would be beyond the scope of this study also to enter into an evaluation of the effects of anovulant drugs on the health of the woman or of offspring whom she might conceive at a later time.

actually abortifacient; 2) sexually perverted actions which require a wife's positive, formal cooperation; 3) pregnancy-prevention procedures which seriously threaten the wife's life or health; 4) and pregnancy-prevention procedures which are provenly useless.

First of all, in spite of much loose use of the word "contraception", we wish in no way to justify certain practices which do not actually prevent conception, but in fact destroy the conceptus. We do not include them in our study because: 1) they do not *prevent* pregnancy and thus fall outside of our thesis; and 2) they involve a *much more serious issue* than the mere abuse of one's sexual faculties (profoundly devasting as this latter is to man and to the image of God in man), namely the taking of innocent human life.

Secondly we do not attempt in any way to justify in any "situation" a wife's resorting to specifically sexual actions which the Church in her moral tradition considers *in se mali,* in themselves perversions. Thus no consideration is given in this study to, for example, a wife's masturbating her husband or engaging in any similar distortions of the physiology of the conjugal act in order to avoid being unjustly impregnated by a husband. Rather we are concerned with a physiologically complete copulation which a husband has already perverted, not physiologically, but by making it an act of true violence. From such an act a woman can, in our view, justifiably seek to avoid pregnancy, not in positively performing a perverted act, but in negatively withholding a dimension of her sexuality, namely her fertility, lest in surrendering that fertility she compound the violence to which she is being subjected.

Thirdly, we do not wish to consider means which in the present state of medical science are *predictably* and *gravely* injurious to the woman's health. This limitation is admittedly a somewhat relative one, involving as it does different degrees of danger for different women in different conditions of health. There has certainly been sufficient documentation, however, of the negative side-effects of anovulant drugs, even in their present mitigated dosages, to cause a victimized wife to weigh carefully the risks she takes in using such drugs as compared to the risks she takes in resorting to less "sure" ways of avoiding impregnation. In excluding consideration of these dangerous means of pregnancy-prevention, the present writer does not wish to deny that, just as a woman in the case of extra-marital rape may indeed be justified in allowing herself to be killed (though she has no strict obligation *per se* to allow this) rather than to be degraded sexually,[35] so also a wife in an analogous situation within her marriage might very well be justified in certain cases in risking her health in order to avoid pregnancy. We simply do not want to treat this refinement of moral application here, since it requires more maturation than the present status of the development of doctrine may allow for.

Finally, we do not wish to discuss means which are provenly useless for prevention of pregnancy. This is one reason why we choose to study only *ante-factum*

---

[35]Cf Zalba . . . *Compendium, op. cit.,* Vol. I, n. 1573-b. For a summary of risk possibilities in artificial pregnancy prevention, see *Handbook of Critical Sexual Issues,* ed. D. McCarthy and Edward Bayer, St. Louis, The Pope John Center 1983.

methods of avoiding pregnancy; as other have pointed out, most *post-factum* methods of avoiding pregnancy are generally recognized by medical experts as futile, impracticable, or dangerous, or all three of these.[36]

D. Doctrinal Presuppositions of the Present Study

The presuppositions of the present study are doctrines fundamental to the Catholic moral Tradition as that Tradition is upheld, implied, explained, and applied in the contemporary Magisterium of the Bishops teaching in collegial unity with the Bishop of Rome.[37]

Among the more important of these doctrines are, in our judgement, the following:

1. Moral imperatives are rooted in certain abiding elements of created nature, specifically the nature of man and his acts, and in the exigencies which flow from the ever varying circumstances of human life at any stage of its development in the individual or in society.[38]

2. Among the abiding elements which are morally significant, some elements, notably those in the nature and actions of the individual as a body-soul being, are the matrix of moral norms which are absolute: a) Some of these absolute moral norms are of a *positive* character and require of us that we work to actualize these norms to the greatest degree possible for the greatest number of cases possible (*ut in pluribus*), given the limitations of an imperfect world.[39] b) Other absolute norms are of a *negative* character and indicate an evil action which one may never licitly choose to perform, even as a means to a good end. Nonetheless, one may in some case and for proportionately serious reasons have to tolerate, *not* personally *performing* such an action, but such an evil action's *happening*. This is the case where the evil action is the inevitable result of the performance of some justifiable deed which is *per se* good or at least not *per se* evil.[40]

3. *Per se*, that is, by a natural capacity and thrust, man is called by his Creator to grasp both the abiding absolute elements of moral judgement and the moral meaning of the variable circumstances which also affect

---

[36] Cf. Curran, *op. cit. pp. 40-41*

[37] *Paul VI, Humanae Vitae, E.V.*, Vol. 3, p. 280-318; "Address to International Congress of Equipes Notre Dame", May 4, 1970 (U.S.C.C., Washington, D.C.).

[38] *Vatican Declaration on Certain Questions Relating to Sexual Ethics, E.V.*, p. 1129; Vatican Council II, G.S. n. 51; H.V., n. 11.

[39] May, Wm. E., and Harvey, John F., *On Understanding Human Sexuality*, Franciscan Herald Press, 1977, pp. 28-29; Armstrong, R.H., *Primary and Secondary Precepts of Natural Law Teaching*, (Hague, 1966), pp. 142-179. St. Thomas Aquinas, *Summa theologiae*, I-IIae, q 94, a. 4.

[40] Grisez, Germain, "Catholic Faith and Intrinsically Evil Acts", in *Proceedings of the Fellowship of Catholic Scholars*, 1978, p. 33 ff.

such judgements.⁴¹ As a matter of fact, however, *per accidens* (the *accidens* being original sin), an adequate grasp of these elements of moral judgement easily eludes man, and he stands in need of the moral pedagogy which Christ gives through His Spirit in the discernment of the whole Church and ultimately of her pastor-bishops.⁴²

4. Even when man with special help of the Spirit grasps in his thinking the moral implications of the Christian Revelation for a situation with which he is faced, various non-rational factors may interfere with his freedom so as to diminish or even destroy any personal culpability in failing to do what is objectively the right thing to do.⁴³

5. The Church in her Catholic unity is charged with the mission and aided by the Spirit, even to the point of being able to speak with infallible certainty, in keeping before her members fundamentals of a truly human and Christian moral doctrine and its application to concrete instances of human life.⁴⁴

6. This call of the Spirit for the Church to speak with the confidence that she is being infallibly guided in her understanding of the ethical implications of the Christian Revelation does not rule out a genuine growth in her moral teaching, but actually aids and forces such development.⁴⁵

7. The root of the Church's competency in natural law is not in defending a moral philosophic system as such, but in her understanding of the Incarnation and of the sacramentality of the Christian life.⁴⁶

Given these seven points of the doctrine which undergirds Catholic moral teaching, it is outside the scope of this investigation to consider the opinions of writers of the various schools which are consequentialist in principle or method. The purpose of this study is, however, not to refute such opinions, but simply to explore the solutions offered by theologians who are working within the traditional classical understandings of fundamental moral, and to see how those solutions have been received by the Church in her Magisterium.

---

⁴¹*P.H.*, nn. 3-4

⁴²*P.H. ibid.;* Vatican Council I, "De Revelatione", in *E.S.*, n. 3004.

⁴³*P.H.* n. 9

⁴⁴Vatican Council I, *E.S.*, n. 3074, Vatican Council II, *G.S.* art. 25; art. 51; *H.V.*, n. 4; Pius IX, Encyclical Letter, *Qui pluribus:* Pius IX, *Acta,* 1, pp. 9-10; St. Pius X Encyclical Letter, *Singulari quadam,* AAS, 22, 1930, pp. 579-581; Pius XII, Allocution, *Magnificate Dominum,* to the Bishops of the whole world, AAS, 46, 1954, pp. 671-2; John XXIII, Enclyclical Letter, *Mater et Magisra,* AAS, 53, 1961, p. 457. The present writer recognizes that the *infallibility* of the Church's competence in areas of natural law is not admitted by all. See Levada, *infra cit.,* footnote 46. It is my own position, however, that the Church can teach points of natural law not only bindingly but infallibly, and indeed has done so.

⁴⁵Grisez, *op. cit.,* p. 28

⁴⁶*P.H.,* n. 3, Par. 3
For the intent of *"fides et mores"* in the First Vatican Council's Dogmatic Constitution "Pastor Aeternus", see Gasser's responses as chronicled in William Levada's doctoral dissertation, *Infallible Church Magisterium and Natural Law,* (Gregorian University, Rome, 1972). Cf. also La Commission Theologique Internationale, *Principes de Morale Chretienne,* 1974, I: "Neuf Theses pour Une Ethique Chretienne" in *E.V.,* Vol. 5, especially in nn. 1012-1029; and Grisez, *op. cit.,* p. 27.

F. The Division of the Book

After this introductory chapter, we shall study whatever teaching we find in the doctrine of the Magisterium and of theologians regarding both any *right* and any *licit means* a wife might use to prevent pregnancy from copulation unjustly forced upon her by her husband. These two points - - the *right* and the *means* to pregnancy-prevention -- will be studied in their history over the past 380 years in four chapter sections:

a) The period 1600-1749 (Chaper II). This period represents one of the eras most prolific in moral theology writings. The subject of our thesis was first raised in this period, with an almost universal rejection of the liceity of any effort of a wife to prevent pregnancy from a copulation forced on her by her husband.

b) The period 1750-1879 (Chapter III). This era marks a notable standardization of moral theology largely through the influence of St. Alphonsus Ligouri, as well as a certain stagnation as the theological enterprise found itself hindered by the social and political storms which affected the Church in all aspects of its life. The subject of our thesis simply disappeared from the agenda of discussion for theologians during this period.

c) The period 1879-1959 (Chapter IV). This era shows the beginnings of a theological fruitfulness rooted in the efforts of Leo XIII to re-institute Catholic theological life. The subject of our thesis re-appears, at least at the end of the period, and finds only one theologian recognizing, in a very limited way, the right of a wife, in cases of true sexual oppression, to interrupt artifically the generative process.

d) The period 1960-1980 (Chapter V). This era of the Second Vatican Council shows an extraordinary acceleration of theological activity closely preceeding, then accompanying, and finally following upon the Council. In this same period, certain widely publicized cases of moral dilemma, such as that of Catholic missionary Sisters caught up in the revolutionary disorders of the Belgian Congo, as well as an effort to formulate a comprehensive theology of marriage based on the Council itself, stimulated both popular interest and professional re-examination of the implications of Catholic moral teaching regarding pregnancy-prevention measures.

e) Finally, in our closing Chapter VI, we shall summarize the history of theological teaching and Magisterial overview regarding sexual oppression within marriage and the theoretical and practical right of a wife thus oppressed to take steps to ward off the danger of pregnancy. We shall show that 1) there has been, in our time, among a significant number of theologians of unquestioned adherence to papal Magisterium, a complete repudiation of the dominant theological opinion on this issue in the 17th and 18th Centuries; 2) for both intrinsic and extrinsic reasons, it is, at this point in the Church's life, solidly probable opinion that a wife victimized by intra-marital rape may have recourse to artificial methods of preventing pregnancy, without being in conflict with Magisterial teaching.

CHAPTER II:
THE QUESTION OF RAPE WITHIN MARRIAGE IS RAISED - FOR A WHILE

To study the roots of any emerging concept of sexual oppression, i.e., rape within marriage, it is necessary to begin first with the period 1600-1749. For 1600 represents the appearance of a new age in moral theology, an age often controversial and harshly so; and 1749 in many ways marks the end of this era.

It was in 1600 that the Jesuit, John Azor, introduced the first of what came to be known in the history of theology as *Instutiones Morales,* a new genre of theological literature and one which allowed for a concentration and elaboration such as had not previously been given to moral questions.[1] It was in the first wave of these new systematic concentrations on specifically moral questions that Thomas Sanchez in 1606 and others later on raised, for the first time in the history of the Church, and treated the question of 1) whether there is any such thing as sexual oppression i.e., rape, within marriage, and 2) if so, what rights a wife might have in such a situation to attempt to ward off a pregnancy which might otherwise ensue.

The year 1749, coming at the close of the period, follows by one year the appearance of the first major work of St. Alphonsus Ligouri, his *Medulla Theologiae Moralis R.P. Hermanii Busenbaum.*[2] With this commentary on Busenbaum, Alphonsus began his great project of discerning the best fruit of the at time exuberant disputations of the previous 150 years. As a result of this and his subsequent works, however, Alphonsus' prestige so developed that his opinions to a large extent preempted any very adventurous thinking after his death.[3] 1749 thus marked an end of an era of almost uninhibited moral controversy (and at times extremist positions which the Church had to repudiate) which after 1600 had raised, among other issues, the one which we are studying: rape within marriage and its significance for the use of artificial means to prevent pregnancy.

In this period beginning in 1600, two questions were the source of a certain amount of attention from the moralists of that age, and affected the topic we are studying. One was the question of the *bimestre;* the other, that of a woman's *expulsion of the semen of a rapist.*

The *bimestre* was a period of two months protected by Canon Law since the days of Gregory IX.[4] During this period, a newly married wife had a right to hold off sexual consummation of her marriage in order to avail herself of an option to enter the convent for the sake of eventual religious profession. If she chose this path during this two month period, her marriage, as *ratum et non consummatum,* would then be dissolved by her solemn religious profession, thus leaving her husband free

---
[1] Vereecke, Louis, CSSR, in *N.C.E.,* Vol. 2, p. 118, and "Moral Theology Today," *ibid.,* vol. 9, p. 121.
[2] Napoli, 1748.
[3] Vereecke, *loc. cit.*
[4] Gregorius IX, *Decretalia,* 1616, Lugdunesi, Lib. IV, Tract. XXXII, Cap. VII.

to enter into another conjugal union. This right to refuse the conjugal act was, of course, a right *extrinsic* to the marriage union itself, because it was granted purely by an act of positive law, in this case Canon Law.

The moralists of this period did treat of other bases, intrinsic to the marriage, for a wife's justly refusing copulation, such as drunkeness, insanity, serious disease, certain death from a possible childbirth, non-support etc.; there was even the beginning of a discussion of "responsible parenthood" in the sense of that term as it would be treated over 300 years later in the era of the Second Vatican Council.[5]

In treating these situations *intrinsic* to the very marriage itself, however, no comparisons were made between the right of a wife in these circumstances to refuse copulation and the right of a woman victimized by *extra-marital* rape to do so. No one asked the questions: What of the wife who has a right to refuse copulation by reason of circumstances *intrinsic* to the marriage, but who, in spite of this, has copulation forced upon her by her husband? Is she in effect being raped by her own husband? May she avail herself of whatever remedies are morally appropriate for the victim of extra-marital rape? But while no one raised the question of the implications of a wife's rights *intrinsic* to marriage itself, many did raise the question regarding a right *extrinsic* to the marriage, i.e., the right granted by the positive provision of Canon Law in its legislation regarding the *bimestre*. Here, as we shall see, in the question of the *bimestre*, the comparison *was* made during this period between the violation of a wife's right by her own husband *inside* marriage and the violation of a woman's right by a rapist *outside* marriage.

It was in making this comparison that moralists had to enter into the second question which much occupied theology during this period: the *expulsion of the semen of a rapist after an attack*. And in entering into this question of the expulsion of semen they showed quite clearly either that they did not see the violation of the *bimestre* as even analogous to extra-marital rape, or that, if they did see such an analogy, it was not strong enough to justify a victimized wife's attempting to remove the semen of her oppressive husband. Even those who like Sanchez conceded the right of the rape victim outside marriage to attempt to rid herself of the semen were, one author excepted, adamant in refusing to recognize any such right to a wife victimized by her own husband. Even those who, once again like Sanchez, recognized that the violation of the *bimestre* was a serious injustice (serious enough, according to many, to entitle a wife to leave her oppressive groom forever) forcefully denied to the victimized bride any right to take steps to stop the deposit of semen from moving towards a pregnancy. *A fortiori*, of course, those who recognized no true right of a wife even to refuse the conjugal act during the *bimestre*, and those who denied even to the victim of extra-marital rape the right to expel the semen of her attacker, recognized no right of a victimized wife to avoid pregnancy from a copulation unjustly forced on her by her own husband.

---

[5] Cf. Busenbaum, H., *Medulla Theologiae Moralis, Romae*, 1676. Lib. VI, Tract. VI, Cap. II, Dub.II, p. 477.

As we examine this beginning of these questions which will affect the subject of sexual oppression within marriage, we must note what several representative writers of this period say, and, eventually, what, if anything, the contemporary Magisterium says on these two points:

1) Is it possible for a serious injustice, equivalent to rape, to be inflicted on a woman by a husband who forces her to copulation against her express will and in violation of her basic rights?

2) Granted the hypothetical possibility in general and the actual presence of such a serious injustice in a concrete case, are there steps which a woman may licitly take physiologically in order to avoid being impregnated from such a violation of her rights?

A. Representative Writers of the Period 1600-1749

Thomas Sanchez in his classic *Disputationes de Sancto Matrimonio,* poses the question:

> May a wife forcefully violated by her husband before the two-month *(bimestre)* period is up expel the semen? It seems that she may *not* do so, because it is intrinsically evil and against nature, which orients the semen towards the propagation of offspring. But if we are speaking of a woman who has suffered violence, but *not from her husband,* I consider it certain: 1) that if she *delays* in expelling the semen, then she may not do so at all; but 2) if she expels the semen *without delay,* then it is strongly probable that she may licitly do this.[7]

In this passage, Sanchez is raising the question of 1) whether *ever* some intervention to prevent a deposit of semen in the vagina from issuing in a pregnancy can be justified, and 2) whether the wife oppressed by her own husband may do this. But, as far as we can tell, he is raising these questions for the first time in the history of Catholic moral theology. For, contrary to his constant references to past and contemporary writers as corroboration for his own positions on other points, in this case he gives no references whatsoever to past writers. Nor do the many authors who comment (pro- or con-) on Sanchez' position indicate that any authors prior to him had treated the subject.

It is obvious, moreover, that although he is taking a position on extra-marital rape victims which is truly innovative and will be the cause of much opposition, he is careful to clearly distinguish this position from one which would attempt to justify expulsion of the semen for a wife unjustly violated by her own husband. He makes the point several times:

---

[6] Venetiis, 1606; *ibid.;* Sanchez Thomas, SJ, *Disputationes de Sancto Matrimonio,* Antuerpiae, 1624

[7] *ibid.,* Lib. II, n. 17 "Quaestio quinta, utrum sponsa per vim oppressa a sponso ante bimestre, possit, semen expellere? Videtur *non* posse, quia est intrinsice malum, et contra naturam ordinantem semen ad sobolis propagationem. Sed si loquitur de foemina, quae *non a sponso* vim passa est, certum reputo, *nisi incontinenti* semem expulerit, non posse postea: *incontinenti,* autem valde probabile est mihi posse." (emph. add.)

Concerning, however, this case which we are considering of the wife who is carnally known by her husband through force, I would not recognize such a right to expel the semen, because the injury done to her is a much lesser one, nor is she subject to loss of reputation, nor is the damage so grave (as in the case of the victim of extra-marital rape).[8]

It must be said that the husband sins mortally because he takes away her bodily integrity when he has no right to do so until the *bimestre* is over. Besides this, he imperils the woman's obvious right to enter the religious life, and her profession (as a religious) is held up until the litigation is brought to a conclusion. There will be great expense to all this; and the outcome of it is in doubt, for perhaps the judge will go by the more probable opinion, which is that she cannot enter the religious life. Besides, perhaps a child will be conceived, and then she will indeed be impeded from entering the convent.[9]

For this reason, all of the great teachers we have cited in number 6 consider the injury done to the wife so serious that, the true consummation of the marriage notwithstanding, they believe the husband's crime to be sufficiently grave that the wife could leave him for good and make her religious vows, while the husband remains bound by the marriage.[10]

From Sanchez' own words, then, the following conclusion can be drawn as to his teaching: It is indeed possible for sexual relations to be forced upon a woman within marriage with a basic and serious injustice to her. Sanchez' conviction on this point is manifested: a) in his use of the words *damnum* and *injuria* in referring to the wife's plight; b) in his championing of her right, after such a violation of her rights, to leave the husband for life and enter the convent, while the husband remains bound until death in the marriage which he has consummated by violence; c) in the detailing of the wrongs done to the wife; and d) finally, one might argue, in the very treatment of this case in the context of extra-marital rape and therefore as one in some way parallel to extra-marital rape itself.

About the presence of a genuinely serious right and its violation by the husband, then, there can be no doubt in the mind of Sanchez. But is there any licit means available for relieving the wife of this injustice? One effective means would

---

[8]*ibid.* "De sponsa autem de praesenti per vim cognita, id non affirmarem, quia injuria est multo levior, nec infamiam patitur, et damnum non est adeo gravis."

[9]*ibid.*, n. 14 - 15.
"Sed dicendum est peccare lethaliter: primo quia suffert corporis integritatem, cum non habet jus, donec bimestre transeat. Praeterea, quia jus certum sponsae transeundi ad religionem, reddit dubium, et litigiosum, et lite mota impedietur professionem usque ad litis conclusionem, magnisque sumptibus opus erit, et dubius erit litis eventus, forte enim judex amplectetur probabilissimam sententiam docentem non posse ingredi. Praeterea, quia forte ex ea copula sequetur proles, ob quam sponsa impedietur ab ingressu."

[10]*op. cit*, n. 17 *in fine.* "Deinde quia omnes doctores allegati, nu. 6. adeo gravem hanc injuriam reputant, ut non obstante matrimonii consummatione, credant esse sufficientem, ut sponsa possit perpetuum facere divortium, profitendo religione, manente sponso ligato matrimonii vinculo."

be the wife's physical resistance against her husband, to the point of even forcing him to withdraw the male organ with the result that he ejaculates outside the vagina. This is a solution which Sanchez recognizes as licit for the woman attacked outside her marriage, but which he does not mention as a moral option for the beleaguered wife. As a matter of fact, he seems to allow this *only* for the rape victim outside of marriage, since he uses this option as an argument that the rape victim, should her physical resistance not succeed in avoiding ejaculation within her vagina, may licitly expel the semen immediately after the attack. Sanchez, of course, as we have seen does *not* allow this option to the wife, an option which he would logically have to allow were the physical resistance allowable for her.

We should note also that it might appear from Sanchez' wording that this expulsion of the semen is also not allowed to the wife for any *other* reason either, e.g., non-support, danger of death from pregnancy, etc. True, Sanchez' reasoning here appears at first to be that such expulsion of the semen on the part of the wife is "intrinsically evil" in our contemporary sense of that category; indeed he uses the very phrase *intrinsice malum*.[11] On further examination of his treatment, however, Sanchez seems to use only an argument of proportionality, not one of exclusion for any absolute reasons. For him, the frustrating of the semen by having it expelled outside the vagina through a douche or any other means the woman might take is a truly *tragic* event, a *malum* in that sense. It is not, however, one outside the ambit of legitimate human action *if there are proportionately serious reasons* for doing this. The proportionately serious reasons, in Sanchez' mind, are present in the case of the unmarried woman (or even a married woman) attacked *outside* of marriage, e.g. loss of reputation, inability to support an illegitimate child by herself, etc.; but such reasons cannot be argued in the case of the wife violated within her own marriage.[12] It may indeed be that in Sanchez' mind the concept of *intrinsice malum* with all the basic clarity of later moral teaching may have developed; it may indeed be that he included the expulsion of a husband's semen by a wife in the *bimestre* case under this category. But if this is his thought, it is not at all clear in what he writes here.

It should be noted also that our present study is concerned with *ante-factum* the means of preventing pregnancy, not with the one *post-factum* means (expulsion of semen) which Sanchez treats. Nonetheless, his logic would seem to exclude any type of physical intervention on the part of the wife to avoid pregnancy.

In the 17th century controversy which follows, both most who supported Sanchez' views which we have just discussed, and those who opposed them, at times vehemently, agreed with him on the one point we are concerned with: a wife has no right to take steps to avoid impregnation from a forced sexual act with her husband, no matter how unjustly that act may have been imposed upon her. Often times, as we shall see exemplified in the next author we examine, certain opponents of

---

[11] *supra* note 7

[12] *Tractatus de Sacramento Matrimonii*, Venetiis, 1645.

Sanchez' views on the right of the victim of *extra-marital* rape to expel the semen did not realize that Sanchez did not differ with them on the issue of the abused *wife*. They had a false notion of Sanchez' position in this regard, and show it quite plainly by misrepresenting him as allowing the wife to expel the semen.

Basilius Pontius writing in 1645, completely rejects Sanchez' views regarding the victim of *extra-marital* rape. He also rejects Sanchez' contention that the wife violated by her husband in the *bimestre* may leave him and enter the convent, the valid consummation of their marriage notwithstanding and providing she has no child to care for. Pontius then goes on to ascribe erroneously to Sanchez and then to reject personally the teaching that the wife thus oppressed may take steps to expel the semen.

> But even less (than Sanchez' opinion regarding the right of this wife to enter the convent) can one tolerate in this author what he asserts in the end of his discussion, (namely), that a woman who suffers violence in that case (of the *bimestre*) can (licitly) attempt immediately to get rid of the semen which now she has received, because then, says (Sanchez), the semen does not yet have peaceful possession of the (female) organ . . . (I say) that once the semen has been released and received, since it has no other use except to be destined to generate (offspring), it is a corrupt act to get rid of it.[13]

In this passage, then, Pontius rejects *in globo* the position erroneously attributed by him to Sanchez: that a wife victimized in the *bimestre* may expel her husband's semen. Thus, in spite of Pontius' mistaken idea of Sanchez' position, Pontius' own position is clearly negative.

There is another measure this beleaguered wife might take without actually expelling the semen, namely to fight off the aggressive husband even though she thus (indirectly, as we would say today) cause his semen to be spilled outside the vagina. Pontius does not seem to deny this right of the wife in the *bimestre* while the marriage is still only *ratum,* but not yet *consummatum.*

> If while the woman is resisting (her violent husband), it happens that the semen pours out outside the vagina, I would judge her free of guilt.[14]

It is obvious from this that Pontius recognizes that the wife has a serious right to refuse the conjugal act; otherwise he would never approve her forceful resistance. In the following passage, he clearly asserts this right to refuse.

---

[13]*Tractatus De Sacro Matrimonio,* Venet. 1645; Caput X, n. 4 . . . "sed multo minus ferendum est in eo auctori quod asserit in ejus disputationis fine posse feminam, quae in eo casu vim patitur, incontinenti conari ad semen emittendum jam receptum, quia tunc inquit semen non habere pacificam possessionem . . . Semel effusum semen atque receptum cujus nullus alius usus est, nisi in ordine ad generationem emittere turpissimum est. . ."

[14]*ibid.,* "si dum reluctatur foemina, evenerit ut semen effunderetur extra vas, illam ego a peccato liberam judicarem."

> From what has been said you will conclude that a husband does indeed sin mortally if before the *bimestre* (is over) he violently forces copulation, because he inflicts a grave injury, since he prevents or renders his wife incapable of entering the religious life[15]

Then he seems to assert that this right to resist vanishes the instant a drop of semen is deposited.

> It is not true that, just because the woman, while she is undergoing this violence, could (licitly) get the mail organ out of her body, she could therefore (licitly) also get rid of the semen once it is in her. For it is one thing to place an obstacle in the way of a violent aggressor when he is on the way to consummating (his violence); it is quite another thing to get rid of the semen, when it has *already reached its goal* and the *marriage has been consummated,* as it plainly has been.[16]

Another opponent of Sanchez also misrepresented Sanchez' position on the right of a wife violated in the *bimestre* to prevent the deposit of semen from making her pregnant, and, of course, in the process of making this mistake, shows his own rejection of such a right. *Franciscus Lopez de Texeda, O.P.,* writing in 1646, not only denies the right of such a wife to expel the semen, but even denies that the husband has done her any significant injustice. Lopez first denies Sanchez' position that such a wife may abandon her violent husband and enter the convent.

> It is not forbidden to the couple that either one of them make use of their marriage right. And so the man in approaching his wife (during the *bimestre)* does not sin, at least not mortally, for, since, the marriage has been legitimately contracted, he brings no violence upon his wife, *but (simply) takes what is his,* and does not want to use the dispensation which has been granted to him (of not consummating the marriage for two months). Wherefore the position of this modern writer (Sanchez) must be abandoned. Both in teaching and in counselling it cannot be followed. . . If copulation is had once, then the wife is rendered unable to enter religious life against the will of her husband, because they have already become one flesh.[17]

---

[15]*ibid.* "Ex praedictis inferes peccare quidem lethaliter conjugem qui ante bimestre exigit violentam copulam. quia gravem irrogat injuriam, cum impedit vel impotem reddat conjugem ad transeundum ad religionem."

[16]*ibid.* "neque vero quia foemina posset, dum vim patitur, virile membrum extrahere, ideo potest et semen jam receptum emittere. Nam aliud est impedimentum ponere, dum quasi in via est ad consummationem violentius aggressor; aliud vero est semen ejicere, cum *jam ad finem perventum est,* et *consummatum matrimonium,* ut satis constat."

[17]*Controversiae theologiae Moralis,* Neapoli, 1646, n. 112. ". . . non tamen illis interdicatur positive quod unusquisque utatur jure suo: vir autem accedendo ad uxorem suam non peccat saltem mortaliter, nam matrimonio legitime contracto nullam infert uxori vim, *sed accipit quod suum est,* et non vult uti dispensatione juris sibi concessa, quare a sententia hujus moderni recedendum neque in docendo, neque in consulendo potest sequi. Resp. 2 quod etiam si vir comprimendo uxorem intra bimestre illi faciat injuriam, dum privat eam libertate ad deliberandum de meliori statu, tamen si semel copula habita impotens redditur ad transeundum ad religionem invito marito, quia jam facti sunt unus caro."

Lopez later even more emphatically denies that the wife has any right during the *bimestre* to resist impregnation, or even to resist the forced copulation itself.

> Even if, in regard to a husband who would force himself (on the wife during the *bimestre*), the wife would suffer some injury (to her rights), *which however I do not admit,* she would not (suffer any injury to her rights) as far as conceiving a child from that act is concerned. I answer (also) . . . that, by the very fact that a marriage has been legitimately entered into, the man has a right to his wife's body. Therefore if he forces her within the *bimestre he does her no injury,* or, if he does, it is very slight. Wherefore, the afore-mentioned Sanchez should have realized that that husband who knows his wife (carnally) within the *bimestre* does her no violence in the formal sense, because by reason of the fact that between them there is a true marriage the man has a true right to the body of his wife, and *thus is (only) rightly taking what is his.* It is the same as the case of (a thief's) having in his possession some object of great value. The owner of (that) thing tries to take it away from him. But if the (thief) resists, and the (owner) takes it nonetheless, we don't say that obviously the act of taking the thing is an injurious act, nor that the owner who takes his own property is doing violence. Nor would it make any sense for him to give it back.[18]

It is plain, then, that Lopez recognizes that the woman who is forced into copulation by her husband during the *bimestre* has little if any right to protest, let alone actually resist; nor has she any right to then take action to render the forced act infertile.

It is helpful to compare Lopez' position with that of the authors we have previously examined. Sanchez taught that very serious rights are being violated in this case, and that the woman can licitly salvage these rights by simply leaving the oppressive husband and thus escape any further sexual violation. She should leave him especially to escape further risk of impregnation which, because of her duty to any child she might conceive, would render her ineligible for many years, if not forever, from entering religious life. The only other remedy which could conceivably ward off even this latter damage to her rights is, however, in Sanchez' view, not a morally available one i.e., the expulsion of the semen. Pontius, though disagreeing with Sanchez about the violated wife's right afterwards to abandon her oppressive husband and enter religion, nonetheless recognized that the husband has sinned gravely against her, and that she had the right to struggle physically against him

---

[18]*ibid.,* n. 128, *emph. add.*

". . . etsi respectu mariti opprimentis passa sit injuriam, *tamen non admitto,* non tamen respectu prolis ex eo generandi. Resp. . . quod eo ipso quod in matrimonium sit legitime initum, vir habet jus in corpus uxoris, et ideo etiam si intra bimestre illam vi comprimat *nullam injuriam ille infert,* vel si infert, satis levis. Quapropter debebat praefatus Sanchez advertere quod maritus ille qui intra bimestre cognovit uxorem formaliter loquendo nullam vim ei intulisse quia ex quo inter illos matrimonium verum stetit, vir habuit verum jus in corpus mulieris *atque rite accepit quod suum erat;* sicut si quis haberet rem aliquam apud se pretiosam, et dominus rei intentaret illam ab eo auferre; atque eo invito illam ab eo abstulit, non dicitur profecto illa actio auferendi rem illam actio injuriosa, neque auferentem rem propriam vim inferre alteri, esto repugnaret restituere illam . . ."

even if in the struggle he should ejaculate outside the vagina and "lose the seed." Regarding the wife's right to avoid pregnancy during the *bimestre*, then, Pontius drew the line exactly where Sanchez drew it: at the expulsion of the semen.

All other authors we were able to examine, with, as we shall see, one exception, were unanimous in rejecting any right of a victimized wife to attempt to expel the semen of her husband. These authors include supporters of Sanchez' views on the expulsion of the rapist's semen, such as James Marchant,[19] George Gobat,[20] Thomas Tamburinus,[21] and Vincent Trancred.[22] Other authors who reject Sanchez' views on the moral option open to the victim of *extra-marital* rape *a fortiori*, of course, reject any thought of a *wife's* being able licitly to resort to expulsion of her own husband's semen. Among this latter group are Anthony Diana,[23] Gabriel of St. Vincent,[24] Leander of the Blessed Sacrament,[25] and Matthew Renzi[26].

One 17th century author who presents quite a different picture from all the above authors is unique among his contemporaries in the role which he gives to *consent* in sexual actions, and will remain unique for several centuries. He is John Angel Bossius, a Barnabite. Bossius strongly reaffirms the evil of "onanism", which he condemns as worse than fornication.[27] He then goes on to describe the position of Sanchez and his defenders regarding the expulsion of the semen immediately after rape. He points out that Pontius misrepresents Sanchez as accepting such expulsion as a remedy for the wife unjustly forced to copulation by her husband during the *bimestre* period. Bossius then proceeds to go beyond Sanchez and his defenders, and, at least implicitly, to hold that copula forced on a woman unjustly and against her will gives her a right to expel the semen, no matter what her marital status, or who the oppressor.

> However, in both of these cases- - that of the wife physically forced in the *bimestre* period, and that of the unmarried woman induced by fear to consent to fornication - - a grave injury is done; for the wife during the *bimestre* period is not bound and cannot be forced to the rendering of the debt; she has a right to enter the convent, a right of which she will be deprived if by copulation, forced though it may be, she should conceive a child . . . Even the (unmarried) woman who has relations out of fear, though she does sin by consenting (because such relations are intrinsically evil), nonetheless does not thereby cease to suf-

---

[19]*Resolutiones Morales*, Coloniae, 1650, Pars. I, Cap. VI. Qu. 21, p. 178 179.

[20]*Opera Moralia*, 1670, Venet., Vol. I, Lib X De Matrimonio, Disp. XVI. Gobat at first rejected Sanchez' position regarding expulsion of the semen of the rapist, but in a later edition accepted it. (*ibid.*, Appendix II).

[21]*Theologia Moralis*, 1726, Venetiis, Vol. I, Lib. II, Disp. XXII, no. 5.

[22]*De Sancto Matrimonii* Sacramento, Panormi, 1640, Tom I, Lib. II, Disp. XXII, n. 5.

[23]*Resolutiones Morales*, Venetiis, 1650, Resol. XLI, n. 1.

[24]*De Sacramentis*, Roma, 1657, Pars. IV, De Matrium, Disp. II, Qu. VI, n. 52.

[25]*Quaestiones Morales theologicae in Septem Ecclesiae Sacramentis*, Lugduni, 1644, Tr. IX, Disp. V, q. 35.

[26]*Encyclopedia Universae Theologiae Moralis*, Neapoli, 1671, Lib. II, Tract. V, Caput I.

[27]*De Effectibus Contractus Matrimonii*, Lugduni, 1655, no. 5.

fer grave injury and to be unjustly exposed to loss of reputation if a child should be conceived. This kind of copulation, forced on her by fear, is a violation of her rights because it is not out-and-out willed by her, but is willed only as a means of escaping another evil which is unjustly threatened. Wherefore in both these (latter) cases the reasoning brought forth in our previous section (concerning rape victims in the strict sense) seems to apply, and the immediate expulsion of the semen, as soon as the sexual desire (of the man) has been consummated by physical force or fear, has the nature of self-defense.[28]

Thus Bossius expressed a view which not only diverges from that of his contemporaries, but one also which, as we shall see, will not appear again until the 20th century.

B. The Decrees of Innocent XI

All of the authors whose works we have been examining above were part of a scene of doctrinal controversy, at times tumultuous, within the Catholic Church during the 17th century. No less than in the famous questions regarding the interplay between God's grace and man's free will, controversy raged also around issues of moral theology, whose doctrine was being tested and developed in a special way by various conflicting theories regarding probabilism. Inevitably this controversy produced extremes and errors on the side of laxism and on the side of rigorism; and popes such as Alexander VII and Innocent XI judged it necessary for the Holy Office to intervene.[29] These interventions were aimed primarily at laxist extremes rather than rigorist ones. The decrees issued under Innocent touched in a special way upon laxist opinions regarding sexual morality.

While a number of the authors whom we have examined above are identified by scholars in our time[30] as having held (or at least seeming to have held) various positions condemned in these decrees of the Holy Office, no mention was made of the one position (Bossius') which favored a wife's being able licitly to take steps to avoid being impregnated by a sexual act which had been forced upon her by her husband during the *bimestre*. The controversial doctrine of Sanchez regarding extra-marital rape was also left by the Holy Office to further free dispute among theologians, for, again, no mention was made of it in the decrees.

---

[28]*ibid.*, no. 6
"Cum tamen in utroque casu et tam sponsae per vim cognitae intra bimestre, quam foeminae per metum cognitae gravis injuria inferatur; nam sponsa intra primum bimestre non tenetur, nec cogi potest ad redditionem debiti, et habet jus ingrediendi religionem, quo privatur, si per copulam licet violentam proles concipiatur . . . Foemina autem per metum cognita, licet peccet consentiendo, eo quod copula sit intrinsice mala, tamen ex hoc non desinit pati gravem injuriam et injuste exponi periculo infamiae, si proles concipiatur; sicut et ipsa copula metu gravi expressa est injuriosa, quia non est simpliciter volita, sed solum ad malum quod injuste comminatum evadendum. Quare in utroque casu videntur precedere rationes numero praecedente adductae, et expulsionem seminis incontinenti, et statim ac libidinis consummationem per vim, aut metum intervenerit, factam habere rationem justae defensionis."

[29]*E.S.*, 2021-2065 and 2102-2167.

[30]*ibid.*, footnotes, pp. 457-465.

Thus the Magisterium in these major interventions, especially those under the authority of Innocent XI, takes no position whatsoever on: 1) any absolute and universal inviolability of the act of *effusio veri seminis in vaginam,* as a *merely physiological* act, i.e., considered separately from the presence or absence of a woman's *consent.* (As we have seen, this inviolability was alleged by the more restrictive theologians of the time as a most fundamental objection to Sanchez' and Bossius' position); 2) the specific inviolability of such an *effusio* in an act of rape outside marriage (an inviolability which Sanchez denied); 3) the specific inviolability of such an *effusio* in the case of a *wife forced* to it with *grave injustice* by her husband during the *bimestre* (an inviolability which Sanchez affirmed, but Bossius denied); and 4) the specific inviolability of such an *effusio* in the case of any woman who *consents* to it, but out of *fear* which is both grave and unjustly imposed upon her (again, an inviolability which Bossius denied, again alone among all writers). In short, whatever might come in the future, the Magisterium at this point in time was simply not prepared to speak on issues central to the subject of the present study: rape within marriage and its consequences for prevention of pregnancy by artificial means.

After the Decrees of the Holy Office under Innocent XI, representative writers such as Raymund Lumbier,[31] John de Cardenas,[32] Claude LaCroix,[33] Cassian Of St. Elias,[34] Dominic de Viva,[35] and Thomas Milante[36] explored the implications of the Decrees. In their commentaries on the Decrees, all consciously note that certain opinions previously defended by some can no longer be held by Catholics. (A notable example is that abortion of the "inanimate" fetus would be a licit way for a rape victim to avoid being ostracized or even killed by members of her family or community.) At the same time, one commentator after another admits that Sanchez' doctrine regarding rape outside marriage simply does not fall under any of the condemned propositions. On our question of the *bimestre,* on which Bossius took an affirmative position, however, the commentators are simply silent. The only exception is Cassian,[37] who specifically condemns expulsion of semen by the wife oppressed during the *bimestre* and presumes that this is Sanchez' opinion.[31] The reaction of theologians prior to the Decrees of 1679 substantially continues, then, in those who comment on the Decrees, namely, a generalized unwillingness to accept the idea, if not its outright rejection, that a physiologically complete act of copulation within marriage could *ever* licitly be interfered with in order to prevent a consequent pregnancy.

---

[31] *Observationes Theologicae Morales,* 1682, IX, n. 300, p. 169.

[42] *Crisis Theologicus,* Venetiis, 1724, Lib. III, Pars. I, Tract. III, Dubium IV, Quaest. 182, no. 2.

[33] *Theologia Moralis Antehac ex Probatis Auctoribus Breviter Concinnata a R.P. Herm. Busenbaum,* Parisiis, 1867, Lib. III, Pars. I, Tract. IV, Dubium IV, Quaest 182, n. 2.

[34] *Arbor Omnium Opinionum Moralium,* Ferrariae, 1705, Abortus, n. 25.

[35] *Cursus Theologico-Morales,* Patavii, 1723, Tomus Posterior, Quaestio VII, Art. I; and *Damnatae Theses,* Patavii, 1737, Propositis XXXIV, n. 11. Innoc. XI.

[36] *Exercitationes Dogmatico-Morales in Propositiones Praescriptas,* Neapoli, 1739, XVII, II

[37] *loc. cit.*

The Decrees of 1679 mark a real milestone in the development of the Church's moral teaching. The next great milestone, it is generally recognized, came not from the public ecclesial charism of the Magisterium, represented as it had been in the office of men such as Alexander VII and Innocent XI, but in the individual and personal charism of St. Alphonsus Ligouri (1697-1787). His opinions, formulated in the 18th century, were to become by the time of the First Vatican council in the 19th century the generally common doctrine of Catholic moralists.

It is to this era of the ascendancy of Alphonsus' influence (1750-1880) that we must address ourselves in the next chapter. For Alphonsus' rejection of Sanchez' view on *extra-marital* rape, as we shall see, was accompanied by his total silence on the plight of the wife unjustly forced to copulation by her *own husband*. That silence was, for the time being, to end all discussion of this issue which, as we have seen, was the object of a universally negative reaction from 1600 to 1749, with the exception of John Bossius' favorable position and the tolerant silence of the Magisterium.

CHAPTER III:
1750-1880: SORTING OUT THE BEST AND SURVIVING THE WORST.

The period from 1750 to 1880 is bracketed in medico-moral history by two events of major important. The first event was in the area precisely of moral theology, namely the ascendency of St. Alphonsus Ligouri as the Church's leading moralist. His first moral treatise appeared in 1748.[1] Alphonsus' was a more than merely adequate effort to bring to practical pastoral effectiveness the myriad of discussions, controversies, and opinions of previous centuries of moral theology, and especially of the 150 years immediately prior to his life.[2]

The second event was in the area of medicine itself. A new era in embryology was consolidated in the last quarter of the 19th century by the discovery and acceptance of some of the most basic facts of human reproduction. The establishment of these facts was a new beginning, not only of medical progress, but also of a realistic *engagement* of Catholic moral tradition with the best of modern medical science.[3]

In the internal life of the Church itself, three characteristics mark this period (1750-1880). It is precisely these three characteristics of the Church's own life that will contribute to the development - - or, more correctly, to the lack of development -- of our topic: rape within marriage and its moral implications for the use of artificial measures to prevent pregnancy. These characteristics are: 1) A great degree of stabilization and even standardization of moral thinking largely through the influence of St. Alphonsus; 2) A great deal of social upheaval and organized hostility against the Church, phenomena which militated against sound theological development in all fields, including moral; 3) A "Second Spring" in the second half of the 19th century in which the religious orders, long suppressed (or at least oppressed), were revived, and Catholic university life began to flourish once again.

The first of these characteristics, then, is a noticeable stabilization of moral doctrine within the Catholic Church. Indeed, St. Alphonsus' great service to the Church at this time was 1) *to take the discussions,* often fiery ones, of theologians of the previous 200 years (and even further back into medieval and patristic writers); 2) *to judge* them in light of the interventions of the Magisterium under such popes as Alexander VII, Alexander VII, and Innocent XI in the 17th century; and 3) with the insight of a saint and scholar, *to commend* what, in his judgement, were the best and soundest opinions for the ever pressing and always on-going pastoral work of the Church. Thus, Alphonsus contributed by his own personal influence to a large degree of resolution of controversy, at least on the practical level of pastoral work, i.e., in the Confessional.

---

[1] *Medulla theologiae Moralis R.P. Hermanii Busenbaum, SJ, theologi, cum adnotatione per Rev. P. Alphonsum Ligouro Rect. Maj. Cong. SS Salvatoris,* Napoli 1748.

[2] Vereecke, L., "Alphonsus Ligouri, Saint," *N.C.E.* Vol. 1, pp. 340-341.

[3] Jordan, Harvey Ernest, and Kindred, James Ernest, *Textbook of Embryology,* 4th edition, New York, 1942, pp. 1-5.

Moreover, without further development being at all excluded, and without rigidly canonizing either the Saint's systematic speculations on certain fundamentals of moral theology or his position in every concrete application of principles, the Church was moved, in a declaration of the Holy Office in 1831,[4] to commend Alphonsus' evaluations of moral theology, both that previous to him and that contemporary with him, as an established guide to sound moral doctrine. By the time of the First Vatican Council, in 1870, Alphonsus' influence was universally accepted by reason both of his personal charism and persuasiveness as a theologian, as well as of the great esteem accorded him by official doctrinal agencies of the Church. Alphonsus' ascendency thus helped immensely to establish an era of stabilization and even standardization in moral teaching with the Church.[5]

This will notably affect the subject of our study. It is true, on the one hand, that Alphonsus was quite willing and effective in breaking away from many mistakenly rigid doctrines of certain theologians prior to and contemporary with himself. On the other hand, as we shall see, Alphonsus could not bring himself to accept the doctrine of Sanchez regarding the expulsion of semen by the extra-marital rape victim. True, he never so much as discussed specifically the question of whether such measures taken after a forced sexual contact (or measures taken prior to and in view of such a forced act) would be licit for a *wife* who is sexually oppressed by her own *husband*. Nonetheless, we can conclude only that *a fortiori* his logic would have to reject such measures also for the wife. While it is too much to attempt to hold that Alphonsus explicitly rejected our thesis, nonetheless his monumental influence simply cannot be totally discounted in explaining why our question never surfaces anywhere among theologians from 1750 to 1880.

The second characteristic of this period, 1750-1880, was a growing indifference and even outright hostility from the rising atheistic and deistic philosophical movements of the late 18th century. The eventual political expression of these movements[6] in the French Revolution in 1797 and the subsequent Napoleanic era and Bourbon Restoration period seriously hampered the work of those agents and agencies upon which the Church has relied most heavily for stimulation to theological development, namely, the religious orders and the Catholic universities.[6] The papal suppression of the Jesuits with the decree *Dominus ac Redemptor* in 1773 began the paralysis by eliminating from the theological community one of the religious communities most prolific in moral thinking.[7] The same *ancien regime* which worked for the suppression was, of course, itself to fall or at least be radically modified by the events beginning 1797.[8] But with that regime fell also many of the

---

[4]*E.S.*, nn. 2725-2727; *Pii IX Acta*, I/V, 296 ss., cited *ibid.* p. 548.

[5]Vereecke, L., "Moral Theology, History of, *N.C.E., op. cit.,* Vol. 9, p. 1121-d.

[6]Hughes, Philip, *A Popular History of the Catholic Church,* New York, 1968, pp. 221-222; Billmeyer, Karl, and Tuckle, Herman, *Church History,* Westminster, USA, 1966, pp. 245-253. Church historians generally point out that the naturalistic tendencies of the "Enlightenment" in the 18th century, which century we are considering in this chapter, infected and debilitated the thinking even of those who, as clergy, were professionally associated with the Church. cf. Billmeyer-Tuckle, *ibid.,* p. 251-253: "The study of the theological sciences, which reached a high standard during the 17th century, was superficial and woefully neglected."

[7]Hughes, *op. cit.,* pp. 223-228.

[8]*ibid.,* pp. 230-232

religious orders and the Catholic universities. Struggling against entrenched hostility for the next hundred years, the Church began the slow work of rebuilding. And until this rebuilding could be substantially achieved, much of the truly critical groundwork necessary for any development in theology and doctrine had to wait. The theology and doctrine of marriage was no exception to the rule, nor, therefore, was the point of our present study: rape within marriage and its implications for the use of artificial pregnancy-prevention.

The third characteristic of this period from 1750 to 1880, and the one which is evident especially at the end of the period, is the very notable Catholic revival as it particularly affects Catholic theology, moral theology including. The "Second Spring" of John Henry Newman's famous sermon was not limited to England; nor was the need for it any less in "Catholic" countries whose Faith had been devitalized and whose organizational life had been mangled by the movements and events we have mentioned above. This "Second Spring", in the form of a newly found freedom from the restricting alliances with the *anciens regimes* showed itself, as a beginning, in the dramatic restoration of the Society of Jesus by Pius VII in 1849.[9] Religious orders such as the Dominicans and Benedictines slowly found a place in the new constitutional world of the European nations. The Catholic University of Louvain was re-opened in 1830[10] and marked the beginning of the establishment of theological faculties where issues of theology could once again be examined in dialogue among various "schools", a dialogue which offered hope of challenge, convergence, and consensus.[11] There were blunders and false starts, of course; and there was a loss of political power under Pius IX in 1870. This latter notwithstanding (and perhaps largely because of it), by the time Leo XIII began his reign in 1878, scholars in the Church - - both clergy and laity - - were looking for leadership in renewing the theological enterprise; and with that pope the renewal began in a clearly visible way. In moral theology, interest is revived in the great moralists of the 17th and 18th centuries, as it is also in the works of Ligouri; and here in moral questions, as in all theology, the thought of St. Thomas Aquinas is sought out once again to give coherence and comprehensiveness.

Most happily too for moral theology as the "Second Spring" broke forth, medicine inself emerged from the influence of a number of erroneous conceptions which had been working hypotheses centuries. These erroneous conceptions within medicine itself had led to moral speculation which was to prove, in the long run, as useless for ethical consideration as for medical practice. In particular, in 1861 the ovum was discovered; and by 1871 it was generally accepted that only with the union of the nuclei of sperm and ovum could a new human life truly begin.[12] These newly discovered facts would prove extremely important in theologically evaluating measures which a rape victim might licitly take in avoiding pregnancy after an

---

[9]*ibid.*, pp. 240

[10]*ibid.*, pp. 238-239

[11]*ibid.*, pp. 248-249

[12]Speert, Harold, *Obstetrics and Gynecological Milestones*, New York, 1958, pp. 161-167; Fordan and Kindred, *loc. cit.*

attack; and that question was re-examined.[13] Also re-examined eventually, but only in the 20th century,[14] was another question which theologians had ceased discussing altogether for 150 years: our question. Is there such a thing as a sexual oppression within marriage so basically unjust as to allow for a licit use of artificial means for a wife to avoid pregnancy? Until the reorganization and reorientation of the Catholic theological enterprise could get off the ground, as it did only with Leo XIII's accession to the papal throne in 1878, development on this point could not be expected.

A. Authors From 1750 to 1880.

As we have seen, in Chapter II, there was only one discussion which had even managed to occasion, in the 18th century, any consideration of the point we are studying - - rape within marriage and its implication for the use of artificial means to prevent a pregnancy from ensuing therefrom. This one discussion had been really an *obiter dictum* of another discussion, related but distinct, namely Sanchez' newly proposed view that after a rape attack outside marriage any woman might indeed licitly take at least certain limited steps to head off a consequent impregnation. Logically, one could look for a less rigid view regarding a *wife* abused by her husband only from authors who favored Sanchez' position regarding a non-wife. From those who held a more rigid view of this latter matter and thus rejected Sanchez' basic position, one could *a fortiori* expect only a more rigid view regarding the case of intra-marital sexual oppression. Considering these two schools, then, one accepting Sanchez' opinion and the other rejecting it, we now search - -fruitlessly, as it will turn out - - for further consideration of the plight of the wife who, against her will and unjustly, has copulation forced upon her by her own husband.

1. AUTHORS WHO ACCEPTED SANCHEZ' POSITION

Among these authors who accepted Sanchez' comparatively lenient views regarding remedying the injustice of extra-marital rape, the famous Claude LaCroix, SJ, (d. 1714) wrote his *Theologia Moralis Ante Hac Ex Probatis Auctoribus Breviter Concinata a R.P. Busenbaum* from 1707 to 1714.[15] His work, however, was published only posthumously in repeated editions right up to 1807 (the most famous edition being that of 1757).[16] It was, however, a standard text throughout the period we are studying, and as such represents the typical moral theology formation being given priesthood students of that time.

After re-iterating Innocent XI's condemnation of the aborting of any fetus, even an inanimate one, in order to save a pregnant woman from being murdered, LaCroix then goes on to adopt as his own the position of Sanchez regarding the rape victim. He then immediately brings up the case and condemns the action of the

---

[13]Curran, Charles, *op. cit.*

[14]As we shall see, A. Schmitt raises the question in his thirty-first edition (1940) of H. Noldin's *De Sexto Praecepto et de Usu Matrimonii.*

[15]Parisiis, 1867

[16]Somervogle, C., *Bibliotheque de la Compagnie de Jesus,* Brussels-Paris, 1890-1932, Vol. IV, 1347-54

married woman who seeks to expel her husband's semen a few moments after intercourse, not because copulation has been in any way forced upon her, but because the semen is causing her great vaginal pain. He compares such an expulsion to the (illicit) expulsion of semen by a rape victim who, contrary to Sanchez' stipulation (which LaCroix makes his own), has *delayed* the effort at expulsion and has *not* attempted it *immediately (continuo)*.

> Even if otherwise a whole community should have to suffer a bad reputation or even be totally overthrown, it would still be illicit to directly procure an abortion of a fetus, even if it is inanimate, for the reasons given in Card. n. 32. It is true, of course, that a girl who has suffered oppression from a man could expel his semen and stop it from truly being deposited in her body, for the reason that his semen is an unjust aggressor against her virginity, as Sanchez and others teach. . . If, however, the semen has already (in truth) been deposited, it ceases to be an unjust aggressor, and by that very fact her virginity is already violated, and therefore it is illicit to expel it, Carden. n. 39 and 60.
>
> In a same way, Lugo notes . . . that a married woman sins if she takes a fetal position in order that thus the semen may flow out of her, even if she does this to prevent serious pains caused by her husband's semen, for then she directly intends the flowing out of the semen as a means to relieve the pain.[17]

Two things might be especially noted in this passage from LaCroix.

First, the whole issue of sexual oppression within marriage is simply by-passed, even as a mere *obiter dictum* to some other question. This is a change from earlier writers who had at least raised the point, even if they then usually proceeded to take a rigid position forbiding any effort of the oppressed wife to expel the semen.

Second, the expulsion of the husband's semen by a wife (because of the pain it is causing her) or of a rapist's semen by a virgin when she has delayed that expulsion and allowed the semen to take truly "peaceful possession", is treated *in globo* with the abortion of a fetus. This is not to say that LaCroix considered all three of these equally criminal, although there is nothing in the text to suggest that he does not so consider them. Be that as it may, LaCroix obviously does not consider *any* reason, even grave pain, as ever being able to justify a wife's expelling the semen. Even the violated virgin may use expulsion of the semen as a means (however regrettable) of defending her virginity, provided only that she takes this step

---

[17]LaCroix, *op. cit.,* Lib. III, Pars. I, Tract. IV, Dub IV, Quaest 182, n. 2
"Etiamsi tota aliqua communitas deberet pati infamiam vel extremam eversionem, adhuc illicitum est directe procurare abortum foetus, etiam inanimati, ob rationem datam. no. 52; hinc quamvis puella vim ab aliquo patens posset repellere semen, ne immittatur, eo quod semen viri injustus aggressor suae virginitatis uti docent Sanchez et alii . . . si tamen immissum sit, jam, desit esse injustus aggressor, et re ipsa violata est virginitas, ideoque illicitum est expellere, Carden. h. 39 et 60, similiter notat Lugo *peccasse uxoratam* quae ut impediret graves dolores a semine virili causatos componebat fetali situ quo semen efflueret, nam sic directe intendebat effusionem seminis tamquam medium levandi dolorem." (emph. add.)

immediately. Not so the married woman (*uxorata*). In contrast, she is in an entirely different moral situation; for her to remove her husband's semen, even for a grave reason, is morally "out", even if she does it immediately.

A difference (but not the only one) between the options morally open to the virgin and those open to the wife seems to be grounded in the fact that the virgin has *in no way given consent,* whereas the wife, in LaCroix' mind, has done so, at least implicitly, *in the marriage vows.* The role of this consent is seen in the fact that LaCroix, following again Sanchez, allows for a girl who has begun an act of fornication to leave off the act *in mediis rebus* out of sincere repentance for having even begun this illicit sexual liaison. This is licit for her even though her partner is now at the point of losing the seed, and indeed is beginning to ejaculate; but, says LaCroix, if the girl has *allowed* any semen whatsoever to be deposited while her *consent* has perdured, then she may *not* seek to eject that semen, no matter how penitent she may moments later become. The generative act becomes sacrosanct, i.e., morally exempt from any human intervention whatsoever, *once it has been consented to.*[18] This conviction as to a dramatic difference between the expulsion of a husband's semen and that of a rapist's semen is a pattern we have seen in moralists previously; and whenever the subject comes up (as rarely it will) we shall see the same reactions in moralists for the next 200 years.

It should be noted that LaCroix contributes to a further clarification of another element of intra-marital sexual oppression, namely, the grave injustice of copulation forced upon a wife by her husband in certain circumstances.

> A wife who knows from the judgement of doctors that, if she should conceive and give birth, there will be grave danger to her life, (nonetheless) *illicitly expels the semen,* as the certain and common teaching holds against Fagundez. Thus she may both decide to *do without* the conjugal act herself as well as *refuse the debitum* (if her husband asks it), for according to what was said in nu. 395 *she is not bound* to render him the debt under such danger.[19]

Nicholas Mazzotta (d. 1737),[20] who also follows Sanchez in the matter of extra-marital rape victims, strongly affirms the wife's right to refuse the conjugal act for serious reasons.[21] Like all writers of this period, however, he, once again, does not even enter into the case of the wife forced by her husband unjustly and against her will to copulation, either in the case of the *bimestre* or in the case where she has a right or an obligation to refuse because of circumstances intrinsic to the marriage.[22] He indeed quite explicitly says that she may *only refuse,* and that she

---

[18]*ibid.* Lib. VI, Pars. III, Tract. VI (De Matrimonio), Cap II, dub. II, Art. II, Quaer. 59.

[19]*ibid.* Resp. 1 through 7, (emp. add.); "Uxor sciens ex judicio medicorum se, si concipiat et pariat, fore per hoc in proximo periculo vitae, *illicite* ejiciat semen, uti habet communis et certa, contra Fagund, itaque vel *deprecetur* vel *neget debitum,* nam secundum dicta num. 395: *non tenetur* reddere cum tali periculo."

[20]*Theologia Moralis,* Venetiis, 1760. As in the case of LaCroix *supra,* this work was published only posthumously.

[21]*ibid.,* Tom IV, Disp. IV, Quaestio I, Cap. II, n. IV

[22]*ibid.*

may *in no wise expel* her husband's semen, even if pregnancy seems certain to lead to her death.

> May a woman get rid of the semen of a man or procure an abortion for the sake of saving her life, her reputation, etc.?
>
> I answer: If a *wife* has prudent reasons to fear that she will die in childbirth, she may for this reason refuse the debt. She may not however render the debt with the intention of immediately expelling the semen of her husband. But a *single girl* who is oppressed by force . . . may for the defense of her honor immediately and without delay expel the semen; but not if she delays.[23]

Once again, the clear distinction between the status of the violated virgin and that of the oppressed wife.

Edmond Voit, SJ, (d. 1780),[24] in contrast to this silence of the preceeding authors, does indeed speak of the *bimestre* case, and, against Lopez and Diana, clearly defends a wife's right to refuse the conjugal act during that two-month period.[25] Indeed, he articulates at length other reasons which would justify a wife's refusing the debt.[26] And, with Sanchez, he recognizes expulsion of the semen as licit for the extra-marital rape victim.[27]

When, however, he treats specifically the illiceity of the semen expulsion by a *wife*, his position is stated in such absolute terms as to seem to preclude such expulsion (or, logically, any other artificial interventions) even in the case where the wife is force unjustly to copulation.

> Wives (sin gravely) if they deliberately get rid of the deposited semen *for whatever reason,* because any such flushing out *whatsoever* is intrinsically evil and a sin against nature because directly opposed to the end of marriage and of physical copulation, namely the begetting of children.[28]

Voit, then, seems not to even consider directly, either here or elsewhere, the case of the wife unjustly forced to copulation. But, given the absolute nature of his terminology in a passage such as above, it is difficult to see, had he considered the case of

---

[23]*ibid.* "An liceat faeminae ob conservationem vitae, famae, etc., semen viri receptum effundere, aut abortum procurare? Respondeo: Si *uxor* prudenter timeat se morituram in partu, licet ex hoc non teneatur reddere debitum, tamen non potest eo animo reddere, ut semen mariti statim expellat; Si autem *foemina soluta* per vim sit oppressa Sanchez 1:2 d. 22 n. 17 autem posse ob defensionem honoris statim et incontinenti semen receptum expellere, at non postea; . . . " (emph. add.)

[24]*Theologia Moralis,* Bassanesi, 1766.

[25]*ibid.* Pars. secunda, n. 1213, Resp. 1.

[26]*ibid.* Resp. 2-6; cf. also no. 1215, 1216, 1218, 1220.

[27]*ibid.* Pars. Prima, n. 669

[28]*ibid.,* n. 1224; " . . . item si uxores semen jam receptum voluntarie ejiciant, *quacumque de causa;* quia *qualibet* talis effusio est intrinsice mala, et peccatum contra naturam, utpote directe opposita fini conjugii et copulae carnalis, scil. generationi prolis." (emph. add.)

the oppressed wife, how he could logically have made room for a wife's expelling the semen or for any other deliberate disruption of the physiological process which would begin with physiologically completed copulation within marriage.

2. AUTHORS WHO OPPOSE SANCHEZ' POSITION

In contrast to the authors such as those whom we have treated in Chapter II who reject Sanchez' position regarding the victim of extra-marital rape, we find among opponents of Sanchez from 1750-1880 not even a mention of unjust force in the *bimestre* case or in any other instances where a wife has a basic right to refuse copulation. Moreover, the stand taken by the opponents of Sanchez is absolute 1) as to the moral inviolability of the physiological generative process, inside or outside marriage, no matter what the duress experienced by the woman, and 2) as to the precise point in time when that inviolability begins (namely the instant at which there is any deposit whatsoever of semen in the vagina). It is therefore inconceivable that, had they even raised the question, they would have admitted the liceity of a wife's ever using artificial means to prevent pregnancy.

St. Alphonsus Ligouri (d. 1787)[29] is not only representative of this negative view regarding artificial interventions to prevent pregnancy, but, of course, because of his unique status as *the* moralist of this period 1750-1880, stands out in his opposition. He does, indeed, recognize and clarify various reasons which could justify a woman's refusing the marriage debt to her husband.[30] He gives no consideration, however, to the case where she rightly refuses, but, nonetheless, has copulation forced upon her. Thus the element of the woman's *consent*, which figures so largely in the consideration of other theologians (e.g., LaCroix), means nothing to Alphonsus as far as this question of ours is concerned. Consent adds nothing to the substantially sacrosanct nature of the generative process which begins with the physiological ejaculation of semen into the vagina. At that instant, in Alphonsus' mind, nature immediately begins something in which man has no right to intervene for any reason whatsoever.

This same absolute inviolability of the physiological process itself shows itself again as Alphonsus cites with approval the "common teaching":

> Never, no matter what the danger she is in, is it licit for a mother (who already has some children) to take a drug to prevent (another) conception.[32]

The irrelevancy of the woman's consent or lack of it, in Alphonsus' thought, is obvious even more clearly in the one case where Alphonsus treats of force, namely in the case of extra-marital rape, as he comments on Sanchez' opinion:

---

[29]*Theologia Moralis,* Torino, 1846, Lib. III, Tract IV, De V Praec Decal, Cap. I, Dub. IV (De Occisione Innocentis) n. 394

[30]*ibid.,* Lib. VI, Tract. VI, Cap. II (De Matrimonio), Dub. II, Art. II, nn 940-955

[31]*ibid.,* ". . . sic *nunquam* licitum est expellere semen, etsi ex eius abundantia mors timeatur."

[32]*ibid.* "Nunquam licitum esse matri ob quodcumque periculum sumere potionem ad conceptionem impediendam."

> I am not able to be at peace with this opinion of his . . . For *immediately* when the man ejaculates his semen (into the vagina) the matrix of the woman takes this semen up and encloses it within itself.[33]

Moreover, it is not the mere ejaculation of the sperm, but its simultaneous deposit in the vagina which commences the inviolable physiological process, since, Alphonsus teaches, a woman being violated is justified in fighting to interrupt the copulation, even though she knows for certain that her attacker will, as a result of her resistance, lose the semen outside of her body.[34]

Alphonsus, in summary then, explicitly recognizes the right of a woman to refuse the debt, and thus at least implicitly recognizes the injustice of her husband's forcing copulation on her in certain instances. He does not, however, directly treat the question we are concerned with: the predicament of a wife *forced* thus unjustly to copulation by her own husband, and its implications for her possibly resorting to artificial interventions to prevent pregnancy from ensuing. Given, however, his absolute stand against any such intervention even in the case of extra-marital rape, we must conclude that there is no way logically that he could have allowed such intervention for a wife, no matter under what duress she might find herself.

Marc Strüggl (d. 1760)[35] also recognizes a number of instances of the *right* of a wife to refuse copula, and even goes on to argue for a wife's *obligation* at times to refuse the debt for the sake of her own good or that of the children she already has; but he then immediately compares any expulsion of the genital materials ("*duplex semen*", that is, the male and female genital products, now mingled within the vagina) with abortion of an *in*animate fetus, which abortion he equates is seriousness with the abortion of an *animate* fetus:

> Procuring an abortion for a fetus which has (yet) to be animated is equivalent to homicide and is against the nature of generation. Moreover, a direct pollution is never licit because it too is against the nature of the generation; therefore also (there can be) no direct aborting of the fetus which has yet to be

---

[33]*ibid.* "Sed huic opinioni acquiescere nequeo; nam si mulier posset tunc expellere semen tanquam aggressorem sui honoris, posset etiam postea. . .; Statim ac vir semen effundit, feminae matrix illud recipit et clauditur." Alphonsus is, or course, here using the physiology widely accepted in his day to buttress his moral opinions, that is, that the tissues (*matrix*) of the female generative tract immediately absorb the semen and that the cervix immediately contracts so as to prevent any substantial loss of semen deposited. The presence of the ovum and the necessity of its union with the sperm were, of course, unknown in his era. Cf. also *ibid.*, Lib. VI, Tract. VI, Cap. II (De Matrimonio), Dub. II, n. 954, Resolv 2, where Alphonsus once agan rejects Sanchez' opinion because: "numquam licet ejicere semen effusum atque receptum in utero, ubi statim ac recipitur (quod puto quidem statim recipi) habet suam pacificam possessionem, unde non potest mulier ab eo expellere quia injuriam irrogaret naturae sive speciei humanae, cujus propagatio impeditur."

[34]*ibid.*

[35]*theologia Moralis,* Venetiis, 1758, Tr. VII, Quest. II, Art. III. n. 14, cf. also *ibid.*

animated, for such an abortion destroys the twofold semen (*duplex semen*) and the beginning of the generation of a human being. Wherefore Innocent XI condemned this proposition...[36]

It is highly questionable, as we shall see in the next section of this chapter, that Innocent's condemnation had such a wide implication as Strüggl here maintains. Nonetheless, Strüggl considers any destruction of the "duplex semen" as falling under Innocent's intended condemnation, and thus almost seems to put himself squarely in the anti-Sanchez camp. What is more to our point, however, is that, like Alphonsus, he never even raises the question of the wife who is unjustly forced to copulation by her own husband.

Other opponents of Sanchez' position follow the same pattern: they reject his opinion regarding extra-marital rape victims, and never even mention the possible case of a wife's being sexually oppressed by her own husband during the *bimestre*. This is in contrast to many of their own camp who in the 17th century *did* at least raise the point, as we saw in Chapter II. Nor do they discuss the right of artificial intervention in any other circumstance where the wife has a right and even a duty to refuse the debt. Among these other opponents of Sanchez' position who exemplify this silence are Daniel Concina[37] (d. 1756), Joseph Bruschi[38] (d. 1851), Anthony Konigs (d. 1861).[39]

3. AUTHORS WHO DO NOT TAKE ANY SIDES REGARDING SANCHEZ' POSITION

A number of writers do not refer to the debate regarding expulsion of the semen after extra-marital rape. As we might expect, then, *a fortiori* they do not treat the issue of expulsion of semen after intra-marital sexual oppression. Anthony

---

[36] ... "quia procuratio abortus foetus animandi est *homicidium aequiparenter* tale, & repugnat naturae generationis. Ergo. *Praeterea* pollutio directa numquam licita est eo quod repugnet naturae generationis; ergo neque procuratio directa abortus foetus animandi. Nam talis abortus destruit *duplex semen*, & generationem hominis jam inchoatam. Unde Innocentius XI damnavit sequentem propositionem..."
ibid. Tr. XII: De Sacramento Matrimonii, "Quaest. II, Art. VII, "De obligatione Reddendi Debiti". Strüggl argues here for an obligation to refuse the debt where the copulation would threaten the wife with death or grave illness, remarking that in the marriage contract the spouses grant each other the mutual right to the body, *"except where it would be harmful to them"* and insists that spouses "are not owners of their bodies (*non habent dominium proprietatis in sua corpora*) and therefore cannot promise to one another a use of the body where danger of death or grave illness would be present." (emph. add.) He respects the man's need to be relieved of the danger of masturbation, but (unlike most writers up to this time) focuses on the man's responsiblity to seek and exercise the gift of self-control through grace. He speaks clearly of the need even of chaste abstinence, should regular access to marital intercourse not be reasonably available to the man. For instance, Strüggl does not accept the fact that a couple already has a large family as justification in itself for a wife's refusing the debt; but he does recognize their being on the brink of economic disaster as truly excusing for the wife. If the husband, however, is basically negligent, abusive, or dangerous, then all obligation ceases on the part of the wife, according to Strüggl, regardless of the size of the family or the husband's problems with pollution or other unchastities. "This is entirely to be ascribed to his own negligence."
While our present thesis is not concerned directly with the grounds for a wife's right to refuse the *debitum*, nonetheless Strüggl's commentaries on this are a good example of how insight into the personalist aspects of the conjugal act were beginning to develop. By 'personalist', we mean what is characteristic of a 'person', that is, the characteristic of cultivating a freedom in himself which will enable him to generously respect his own sexual dignity, even at the physiological level, and that of others.

[37] *Theologia Christiana Dogmatico-Moralis*, Romae, 1751

[38] *Cursus Theologiae Moralis*, Camerini, 1790

[39] *Theologia Moralis Sancti Alphonsi*, New York, 1778

LeCompte, Charles Cappellman, John Gury, and D. Neyraguet are among those who might be cited in this category.[40]

B. Church Magisterium: 1750-1850

As we noted in Chapter II regarding the period 1600-1749, the Church in her Magisterium was silent during those years regarding our topic: rape within marriage and its moral consequences regarding artificial means of avoiding pregnancy. The Magisterium was silent also regarding the related issue of pregnancy prevention after extra-marital rape. The only 17th century Magisterial statement which even touched on any effort to undo the effects of a complete copulation was the Decree of the Holy Office under Blessed Innocent XI in 1679. This, however, touched directly on *abortion* after rape, not the mere expulsion of the male fluids (or the commixture of the male and female fluids as a *duplex semen*) where no new life had yet begun. Theologians generally recognized that Sanchez' position regarding the rape victim was left untouched by the Decree; and neither the Decree nor the theologians of the era mention at all Bossius' opinions regarding the wife oppressed sexually within her own marriage.[41]

This silence of the Magisterium extends itself for the next 130 years, and, indeed, as our study will show in Chapters IV and V, into our own times. The reason for the silence may very well lie in the fact that no one ever really took up discussion on Bossius' position. This may have been for the very good reason that, with Sanchez' position on *extra-marital rape* being so hotly contested, no one was ready to give consideration to what, on the face of it, would seem an even more obvious challenge to theological assumptions of that era regarding sexual acts *within marriage itself.* Indeed as we have seen, the *bimestre,* the one example of clear sexual oppression within marriage previously dealt with, was for all intents and purposes dropped from theological discussion during the latter part of the 17th century. By the 18th century, writers are not discussing it at all, at least as to the liceity of a wife thus abused in the *bimestre* taking artificial steps to head off a pregnancy from the forced copulation. It is not surprising, therefore, that the Magisterium in the 18th and 19th centuries has no reaction, positive or negative, to our question.

One Response of the Sacred Penitentiary on April 23, 1822 might, however, at first give the appearance of in some way challenging this latter observation. The Response regarded wives whose husbands insisted on "natural onanism", i.e., withdrawal.

> May a good wife permit that her husband approach her after it has become obvious to her from past experience that he will conduct himself according to the forbidden act of Onan?

---

[40]LeCompte, *L'Ovulation Spontanee*, Louvain, 1873; Cappellman, *Medicina Pastoralis*, Aquisgrandi, 1892; Gury, *Compendium Theologiae Moralis,* Romae 1866; Neyraguet, *Compendium Theologiae Moralis S. Alphonsi,* Ratisbonae, 1841

[41]Cf. *supra,* Ch. II, pp. 21-22.

Especially if, by denying him, the wife expose herself to the danger that he will beat her, or if she fear that he will go to prostitutes?

Since in the case as proposed the woman on her part does nothing against nature and deliberately does only something which is good and licit, the entire disordering of this act comes from the malice of the husband. He it is who, instead of consummating the act, withdraws and ejaculates outside the vagina. Therefore if the woman, after raising due objection, sees that it is doing no good, and if the husband is insistent (on copulation) and threatens a beating or death or other cruelties, then she may (as approved theologians teach) without sin make herself available in a passive way, since in these circumstances she is simply tolerating the sin of her husband, and is doing so for grave reasons which leave her guiltless; for charity, by which she is indeed bound to prevent such a sin, does not bind her where she would pay so dearly.[42]

While making no mention of any explicit approval of the Pope currently reigning (Pius VII, d. 1823), the Response was the beginning of a series of interventions from the Holy See over the next 100 years on the plight of wives confronted with this specific "onanistic" practice. The Holy See will deal also with other ones deemed even more seriously vitiated than "withdrawal", e.g., condomistic copulation.[43] Despite the fact that none of these interventions of the Holy See claims explicit approval of a reigning Pontiff, this series certainly represents the ordinary teaching of the Church (though not necessarily in every instance in an infallible mode). They must therefore now be taken into consideration.

What is *explicit* in the Response of 1822 is that 1) it is possible to sin gravely by deliberately violating the integral physiological structure of the conjugal act, 2) that the onanistic husband, indeed, is doing precisely this, at least in the objective order, and 3) that his action may therefore be spoken of as a *"malitia"*. Precisely because the wife is desirous that her husband not violate this physiological structure, she is free of blame. It is explicit, moreover, that the wife must show her true will in this matter by bearing every possible witness by way of *"debitas admonitiones"* against what the husband intends to do. Finally, it is clear that the wife may only *tolerate (passive se praebere)* her husband's abuse of their conjugal act, and indeed only in order that she might escape other intolerable evils.

---

[42]*E. S.* n. 2715: "Potestne pia uxor permittere, ut maritus suus ad eam accedat, postquam experientia ipsi constiterit eum more nefando Onan se gerere, praesertim si uxor denegando se exponat periculo saevitiarum aut timeat, ne maritus ad meretrices accedat?

Cum in proposito casu mulier e sua quidem parte nihil contra naturam agat detque operam rei licitae, tota autem actus inordinatio ex viri malitia procedat, qui loco consummandi retrahit se et extra vas effundit, ideo si mulier post debitas admonitiones nihil proficiat, vir autem instet, minando verbera aut mortem aut alias graves saevitias, poterit ipsa (ut probati theologi docent) citra peccatum passive se praebere, cum in his rerum adjunctis ipsa viri sui peccatum simpliciter permittat idque ex gravi causa quae eam excuset; quoniam caritas, qua illud impedire teneretur, cum tanto incommodo non obligat."

[43]*E. S.:* nn. 2758-2760; 2791-2793; 3795; 3142-3146; 3148; 3185-3187;4; 3705; 3716; 3760-3765.

Certain other views in the Response, while not so explicit as those just mentioned, may at least *appear* to be *implicit*, given the context of theological thinking of the time. One such *possibly implicit* view might be, for example, that the man is sinning *"contra naturam"* only in the sense that he is violating the *physiological* nature of the conjugal act, and that he would not be sinning against the nature of the conjugal act if he allowed for its full physiology, even though his intentions might otherwise be quite hateful towards his wife. Another view *possibly implicit* in the Response is that, in marriage, one could *never* be justified in disrupting the physiological structure of copulation. Indeed, a later Response from the Sacred Penitentiary, treated below, will indicate that not only may a woman not herself disrupt the physiology of the conjugal act, but she may not willingly enter into a "conjugal act" whose physiology her spouse has already disrupted from the beginning e.g., when a husband is going to use a *condom* from the beginning of the act. Such is the doctrine of the *theologi probati* of the period; and there is no sign that the Responseis not influenced by this thinking. Quite the contrary.

Aside from these definite *explicit* points and perhaps some *implicit* points in the Response, the Response remains silent, however, on another point, a key one: Is the act of the husband corrupt, not *only* because of his disruption of its physiological dimension, but *also* because this physiology is being used as an expression of an exploitation basically bereft of any genuine love for the wife? Is such an *inner* attitude as much a corruption of the *nature* of the conjugal act as is the disruption of its physiological dimension? Or is there some other way (a *"modus"*) in which this egotistical attitude violates the conjugal act, without corrupting its actual nature? These questions are not raised in the Roman Response. Nor could we expect them to be, since theologians, with the notable exception of Bossius, had never seriously begun to discuss these points.

Regarding this assembly of theological points definitely explicit, possibly implicit, and simply passed over in silence, some comment is called for. Our thesis involves the principle that mere physiological copulation (*effusio veri seminis in vaginam*) even between husband and wife is not *necessarily* that sacrosanct act of which the Church intends to speak when she speaks of *"the conjugal act"*. Merely physiological copulation is not that act which, the Church teaches, must remain morally exempt from any human intervention to prevent a pregnancy from resulting.

While none of the *explicit* points of the Response of 1822 go against this principle, the possibly *implicit* points which we have listed immediately above would indeed do so. The Response speaks *only* of a *physiological* criterion for judging the compatibility of a particular genital act within marriage with the human or Christian life. Such a *merely physiological* criterion would be inadequate to defend our thesis.

To these difficulties we would respond, first, that even if arguments for the "bottom-line" decision expressed in the Response had been given *explicitly*, one would not be bound to accept the arguments themselves if one could not see their cogency. One would of course indeed be bound to accept the *substance* of the position of the Church expoused in the decree itself, according to the clear mind expressed and the degree of adherence required by the Church's bishop-shepherds, especially the Pope.[44]

Secondly, *de facto,* in the Response, comprehensive arguments are *not* given *explicitly* to support the position of the Sacred Penitentiary. One could indeed enter into an intense discussion as to what such arguments *could* be *implicit;* but even if one could come to a convincing conclusion, certainly such implicit arguments would bind one's assent even less than explicit ones would.

Thirdly, the whole possibility that the *object* (not merely the circumstances or the intention) of the husband's human act of choice might be basically vitiated even prior to his actual disruption of its physiological dimension is not envisioned in the Response. Nor had that possibility been seriously raised (except, again, long ago and only in passing by Bossius) among theologians. The following questions are not yet clearly in the mind of the Church: Is every complete copulation between husband and wife *necessarily* the "conjugal act"? Must a *genital* act between husband and wife, in order to merit the designation, "the *conjugal* act", be substantially and at least virtually an expression of a man's *love* for his wife? Must he intend it to express a love which includes a fundamental, even though imperfect respect for her reality as a *person* with *rights* and *obligations?* If the husband effectively *repudiates* such love, does a genital act *lose its identity* as "the conjugal act?" Nor is the question raised of whether a wife, thus abused, acts morally in seeking to defend herself from pregnancy, even by the use of artificial means. We would judge then that the Response of 1822 and many of its Magisterial sequels intend to answer only the limited question placed before Church authorities at that time, and that theological development was not yet mature enough for the Church to be able even to intend to deal with the point of our thesis.

The only other statement from the Holy See on the issue of onanism during this period 1750-1880, however, causes a bit more difficulty. On April 6, 1853, the Holy Office issued a Response which, though extremely brief, made a clear distinction between the plight of a wife forced, on the one hand, to an act of "natural"

---

[44]Alfaro, Juan, SJ. "La teologia di fronte al Magistero," in Latourelle, Rene, - - O'Collins, Gerald, *Problemmi e Prospettive della Teologia Fondementale,* Rome, 1981, p 427.

"The practice of Catholic theology has established the following interpretive norms which keep before one's mind the basic intention of the Magisterium in its definitory acts. That alone is defined which is found directly in the sentence of the act of defining, be that sentence affirmative or negative. Presuppositions which are subordinate to the definition and are presented as reasons justifying the definition or as mere further explanations of the definition do not have dogmatic character. Nor does anything belong to the definition simply because it is expressly called a presupposition or a foundation of the definition. It can happen that the very formula of the definition contains expressions which go beyond the problem which the definition was planned to solve, and which, therefore, have to be considered simply as further explanations belonging to the theology of that particular era. In the case where, serious research notwithstanding, some doubt arises about the act of definition or some aspect of its content Canon Law itself provides (c. 1323): "Nothing is to be understood in matters dogmatically declared or defined except what is manifestly there." This retrospective phase for a theological understanding of dogmas seeks only the exact delimitation of the defined content which requires the assent of faith."

Alfaro is speaking of the non-dogmatic character of arguments used in *ex cathedra* definitions; the definitions themselves require the assent of faith, but the probative force of the Scriptural, patristic, and theological reasoning used to explicate them does not. This would have to hold not only for dogmatic definitions, but also for teachings of the ordinary Magisterium even in the infallible mode, and *a fortiori* certainly where the teaching is not clearly irrevocable, but rather provisional and tentative, though binding. Cf. Vatican II, *Gaudium at Spes.* n. 25

onanism (i.e., an act of *withdrawal* on the part of the husband), and, on the other hand, to a "condomistic" copulation.[45] The Sacred Penitentiary, as we have seen above, allowed for a merely passive resistance on the part of a wife who foresees that, after beginning the copula in a physiologically normal way, her husband will later withdraw and ejaculate outside the vagina. In contrast (but not in contradiction), the Holy Office, in this 1853 Response, indicates that a woman who sees that her husband is going to vitiate the physiological dimension of the act *ab initio* by using a condom may not give mere passive resistance. What kind of resistance she is bound to give is not at all clarified in the Response, though it will be in another Response in 1916 (Chapter IV).[46]

> May a wife knowingly involved in condomistic copulation maintain a merely passive attitude?
>
> No, for she would be consenting to a thing intrinsically evil.[47]

This is the first authoritative Church document which teaches *explicitly* that condomistic intercourse, at least in some basic sense, is intrinsically evil when it take place between husband and wife. (No stand was taken here regarding extra-marital acts, especially forced ones. The opinions and disputes of Sanchez and other *probati auctores* were allowed to stand.)

Implicitly, one might speculate, the principle underlying the *explicit* position of the Response is that the physiological dimension of any act of copulation between husband and wife may never, under any circumstances, be disrupted by human intervention. Were this the case, then, of course, our thesis could not stand: that when a man unjustly forces copulation on his wife, then this forced act is in no way what the Church wishes to defend as morally inviolable. Such speculation, however, as to the principles *possibly* implicit in the Response is, as in the Response of 1822, of no serious weight theologically. The only thing this Response of 1853 says is: 1) That the husband's act is intrinsically evil; 2) That the wife may not willingly be involved in it.

The Response does not say *why* the husband's act is intrinsically evil. Nor does the Response ask, let alone answer, questions such as the following: Was there an intrinsic sexual evil in which the husband had involved himself *prior* to the actual use of the condom, e.g., a decision to cease accepting, respecting, and loving his wife as a procreational being? Was the use of the condom simply an explicitation of a contraceptive mentality already embraced by him i.e., a non-acceptance of his own and his wife's procreational character? Does such a contraceptive mentality substantially corrupt the conjugal act so that even physiologically complete copulation between husband and wife is no longer the conjugal act? In the case of "natural" onanism, there was at least a slight chance that the husband might have a change of heart, decide to accept his marital union for the procreational reality it is,

---

[45] *E.S.*, n. 2795, Q. 2, and ad 2).

[46] *ibid.*, n. 3638

[47] "An uxor sciens in congressu condomistico possit passive se praebere?. . .
Negative; daret enim operam rei intrinsice illicitae."

and carry through with the physical act he had begun, *not* subverting its structure by withdrawing. There is no such possibility with the use of the condom (or of anal or oral copulation); this course of action must be *physiologically reversed* before a couple can express in it any true acceptance of the procreational character of their union. A sexual act headed towards "natural" onanism has at least *some* intrinsic possibility of being "converted" into a true conjugal act, whereas the condomistic act has no such possibility and must simply be physiologically reversed if there is to be the "conjugal act" which God created. Is this the reason (slender though it is) why a wife may "go along with" "natural" onanism, but not with condomistic onanism? And when a husband does not internally basically accept his wife in all her reality, including her human rights and obligations and procreational nature, and yet never physiologically violates the act of copulation, is he necessarily being sexually "moral"? Is not such a man harboring a contraceptive mentality which can vitiate even the use of natural family planning?

Thus, as in the case of the Response of 1822, so also in this of 1853, we invoke the same basic principle of hermeneutic: Magisterial responses say what they say, nothing more. They do not raise questions or give answers for which the Church in a given era is not prepared either in her theologians or in her episcopal Magisterium. They do not canonize the valid, but the limited theological vision of any one era. When questions of the type we have mentioned above begin to be raised in the 20th century, as we shall see in Chapters IV and V, the Magisterium will allow discussion of them to go forward unimpeded.

C. Conclusions for the Period 1750-1880

The period 1750-1880 was not conducive to any real progress in the study of our subject of sexual oppression within marriage and of the means to which a woman might have licit recourse in order to defend herself from the further injustice of actually becoming pregnant from such an abusive act. It is true that there was a continued and even developing understanding of the right of a wife to refuse the conjugal *debitum*. There was also, however, a movement towards stabilization of moral theology under the influence of St. Alphonsus, a stabilization which was needed and most useful. It might even have prepared the way for a period of yet more fruitful development, and certainly was by no means hostile to such development. Unfortunately, immediately after Alphonsus, the Church began to fall upon hard times, with at first the corrupting influences of the abused rationalism of the Enlightenment, followed by the political upheavals of the late 18th and much of the 19th century. As a result there was a generally recognized cutting back on theological speculation. Discussions of the morality of avoiding pregnancy from complete acts of copulation were confined to the case raised by Sanchez more than 200 years before: rape outside of marriage. Theologians, on the one hand, were occupied with defending the *physical* integrity of the conjugal act, a defense absolutely necessary if the Church were to remain faithful to herself, the Revelation given her and its implications for the truly human life. The Magisterium, on the other hand, concerned itself with this same problem, and, like the theologians, did not enter into the question of self-defense from pregnancy for the wife victimized by sexual oppression within her own marriage. It was, quite arguably, *presumed*, by many if not most, that any attempt at complete copulation between husband and wife was morally exempt from any action which would render it sterile. An examination of the writings of the period, however, shows that this latter issue was simply lying quite dormant for the time. When it resurfaced in the 20th century, as we shall see in Chapters IV and V, it would meet with a tolerance of discussion on the part of the Magisterium which escaped the attention of almost all the laity and even of many theologians, and which confounded many presuppositions both of those seeking the lead of the Magisterium and those dissenting from it.

CHAPTER IV
1880-1960: PROGRESS AMIDST GREAT PROBLEMS

A Second Spring for the Church: this was the hope cherished in the hearts of Catholics throughout the difficulties we have described at the opening of our previous chapter, and the hope realized largely through the pontificate of Leo XIII and of the popes succeeding him on the throne of Peter. Indeed, after the years of suspicion which initially greeted his efforts to see this Second Spring realized, the addition of John Henry Newman to the Sacred College was truly a harbinger of a new era of fruitfulness and beauty for the Church and for the world she is called to serve and save.[1]

It would be foolish, of course, to pretend that it was or could have been an era of progress without problems; the shortness of this introduction to the present chapter is not in any way intended to underestimate the pain, the disappointments, the setbacks which marked the Second Spring, difficulties which were indeed part of the price to be paid for the progress to be realized. In the political context in which the Church had to work, in Germany, for example, even the genius of Leo XIII was not able to overcome all the suppression of true freedom for Catholic universities and seminaries which Bismarck had tried to control for the sake of his *Kulturkampf* policy. In Germany, of course, and with Bismarck, Leo XIII did have some noteable success, at least by 1890, and much of the re-vitalization of the universal Church found its source in the German Catholics of the period.[2] Not so, however, in France, where the persistently anti-clerical policies of the governments constantly oppressed the Church and eventually brought her to the loss of her financial resources, of much of her properties, and even of the presence of the religious orders. To make matters worse, Leo had to contend with an isolationist attitude among many of the more devout Catholics of France, - - a refusal to even begin to engage the political and intellectual milieu of the day.[3] In Italy, similar problems held back the Church's renewal. The blatant anti-ecclesial mood of the political powers showed itself from the day of Leo's election when a memorandum was circulated among government officials forbidding their participation in the coronation celebrations. Furthermore, intellectually talented Catholics were holding the line against any participation in the government which had taken over the Papal States in 1870. The ridicule and harassment which the government heaped upon the Church created practical problems which took time and energy which was badly needed to grapple with this newly emerging society. As a result, a certain stagnation in theology as well as in other areas showed itself.[4]

On top of this, Pius X was forced to issue strong directives against what purported to be efforts to represent the Catholic Faith to this bellicose though promising new culture; the strongly condemnatory decrees of *Lamentabili* and *Pascendi*

---

[1] Hughes, p., *op. cit.*, p. 280

[2] *ibid.* pp. 270-723

[3] *ibid.* pp. 273-276

[4] *ibid.* pp. 276-278

came as thunderbolts to Catholic theological circles in 1907, and, necessary as they were, had nonetheless a dampening effect on any theological adventuresomeness for several decades. Theology, and perhaps especially moral theology, came to be more and more a positivist listing of magisterial documents of various degrees of weightiness, often with little effort or at least little success at getting to the fundaments of the tradition; a theology and attitudes too often extremely cautious were the watchwords of the day.[5] World War I took up almost all the attention of Benedict XV[6]; and the coming of World War II, the attention of Pius XI at the end of his reign.[7] Pius XII succeeded in re-stimulating the theological enterprise, especially in the area of morality, as we shall see below, but only after the agony of spending the first seven years of his reign initially trying to head off, and, when that effort failed, then trying to mitigate and to bring to an end the worst war the world has yet seen.[8] It was not a period in which there could be much development of theology in a way which would bring a great amount of light to topics such as the subject of this study.

These difficulties notwithstanding, it is the almost unanimous opinion of Church historians and of theologians that the period beginning with the accession of Leo XIII and continuing into the reign of Pius XII represented some of the greatest progress which the Church has ever known in her efforts to meet a world needing to be evangelized. It is during this period that the great encyclicals began to appear in numbers and length which were unknown in the history of previous papal teaching.[9] These provided an overall encouragement and guidance for theologians, as in the case of *Aeterni Patris* (1879), *Providentissimus Deus* (1893), and *Deus Scientiarum Dominus* (1930).[10] Others provided guidance specifically in the area of moral, as in the case of *Arcanum Divinae Sapientiae* (1880), *Casti Conubii* (1930), *Quadregesimo Anno* (1931), and *Divini Redemptoris* (1937). Especially important for theology were the great encyclicals of Pius XII: *Mystici Corporis* (1943), *Divino Afflante* (1943), and *Humani Generis* (1950), as well as his allocutions after the war as he attempted to bring the impact of the Christian moral tradition to the problems of a world beginning to explode with the new possibilities offered by technologies then developing, both in medical as well as in other fields.

Throughout this same period after 1880, the pastoral authority of the Church, but especially that of the Popes, gave encouragement (vigilant, it is true; too much so, some would say, - - but still encouragement) to Catholics to pursue studies in history and Scripture with a rigor and thoroughness demanded by the state of those studies outside the Catholic Church. New institutions which enabled the bishop-pastors of the Church to confront and evaluate findings and theories in these fields

---

[5]*ibid.* pp. 281-283

[6]*ibid.* pp. 284-286

[7]*ibid.* pp. 290-292

[8]*ibid.* pp. 292-294

[9]Malone, G. K., "Encyclical", *N.C.E., op. cit.,* Vol. 5, p. 332

[10]Hughes, P., op. cit. pp. 279-280, 289, 293-294.

were established: the Pontifical Biblical Commission, the Pontifical Biblical Institute, the Institute of Thomistic Philosophy, as well as at least five new Catholic universities.[11]

At a lower, but nonetheless important level, official responses were forthcoming from such agencies of the Holy See as the Holy Office: in 1940, on sterilization and on the killing of the physically or mentally unfit;[12] in 1944 on the ends of marriage;[13] in 1952 on *amplexus reservatus;*[14] and in 1956 on situation ethics.[15] These responses, in some ways cautious and in other ways daring, reflected sometimes provisional and at other times permanent teachings of the Magisterium. In spite of occasional reverses, then, and indeed sometimes quite serious ones, coming from the secular as wells as the ecclesial sphere, and in spite of mistakes and perhaps at times overly cautious reactions from the teaching agencies of the Church, the period 1880-1960 represents an overall period of immense progress. It did indeed prepare the way for the era of the Second Vatican Council, which we shall treat in the next chapter. From such a period we can expect to find perhaps some sound considerations for our thesis; and, as we shall see, such is indeed the case.

A. AUTHORS, 1880-1960

Within the ecclesial context described above, we find a first move since the time of John Bossius in the 17th century towards a positive treatment of the thesis that there is indeed possible within marriage a sexual oppression of a wife by husband that may rightly be considered analogous to extra-marital rape, and may accordingly justify the wife thus oppressed in using even artificial means to avoid any ensuing pregnancy. As might be expected, we shall find such consideration given, not in an author of the more rigid school which rejected Sanchez' original doctrine allowing some artificial intervention by a woman to prevent pregnancy after an extra-marital rape attack, but in one author (and *only* one) of the growing number who accepted his doctrine on this point.

1. A Single Author Moves To Develop Our Thesis During The Period 1880-1960

Among authors who accepted Sanchez' doctrine, only one of them moves to apply that doctrine to the case of the wife sexually abused by her own husband. A. Schmitt, in his 1940 revision of Jerome Noldin's *De Sexto Praecepto et de Usu Matrimonii*[16] does not, it is true, accept the thesis of this present study in its totality. We hold that *any* non-abortifacient and medically safe means of preventing pregnancy in itself (and aside from considerations of a required proportionality of good to evil in its effects) is licit both for the rape victim outside of marriage and for the

---

[11]*ibid.,* pp. 279, 283, 288

[12]*E.S., op. cit.,* 3788 and 3790

[13]ibid. 3838

[14]*ibid.* 3907

[15]*ibid.,* 3918 ss.

[16]Oeniponte, ed. 31, 1940

wife seriously abused by her own husband's unjustly forcing her to copulation. Schmitt, however, admits only that a wife abused in this way may use *one* means of avoiding pregnancy, namely, *the expulsion of her oppressive husband's semen.* Indeed, Schmitt clearly implies that there is at least an analogy between sexual oppression outside of marriage and that inside of marriage a) by treating the two cases together and under the subject of "rape", b) by using the same terms *("vi oppressa . . . opprimitur"),* and c) by giving the same justification for the expulsion of the semen *("aggressionem externam ... agressor iniustus").* That this is, at least for the present century and the two centuries immediately preceeding it, a new development is evidenced by the fact that Schmitt cites no one else who holds this position. (He does not seem to know about Bossius.) In contrast to this silence, he does cite Lehmkuhl, Genicot, Vermeersch, and others in support of his position on *extra-*marital rape. It is interesting to note also that Godfrid Heinzel, in his later (1958) revision of Noldin-Schmitt removes (without explanation) this section entirely, thus indicating that he was not prepared to accept Schmitt's position on rape, either inside or outside marriage. In his 1940 edition, however, Schmitt writes:

> An unmarried woman oppressed by force (or a wife who is oppressed by a man not her own husband) is bound to fight off this external oppression in so far as she can, even though in the process the man spills the seed. But if she cannot offer this kind of resistance, it will be licit for her to expel the semen with a douche.
>
> The same, it seems, must be said of a woman who is oppressed by her own husband in those cases where the husband has lost his right to intercourse (a drunkard, a man who is not taking care of his family, or an insane man); for his action is considered an unjust aggression. I would not, however, allow for her to put a diaphragm in place before such a feared aggression takes place, for in this way she would be making the act be against nature from the very beginning.[17]

It should be noted how tentative Noldin makes his position ("The same it *seems,* must be said of a woman oppressed by her own husband. . . "), and how *limited* his application is to the means which he considers licit for the *extra-*marital rape victim (". . .to *expel* the semen by *douche. . .*").

Regarding this latter limitation, in Schmitt's mind the diaphragm is simply illicit, inside or outside marriage. What, in Schmitt's mind, makes copulation with a diaphragm under these circumstances a *"malum contra naturam ab initio?"* We can only speculate, for Schmitt gives us no further explanation; nor need we think necessarily he had a coherent explanation of this in his own mind, the whole question having been raised by him for the first time in several centuries. It certainly *seems* that he was still contending in his own mind with the standard wisdom accep-

---

[17]*ibid.* n. 69, d: "Mulier *innupta* (vel uxor ab alieno viro) *vi oppressa,* tenetur aggressionem externam repellere quantum potest, etsi exinde semen effundatur. Si vero hoc non potuit, licebit semen lotione expellere.

Idem dicendum videtur de muliere, quae a proprio viro vi opprimitur in iis casibus, ubi vir ius copulae amisit (ebrius, curam non habens familiae, amens); habetur enim aggressio iniusta; pessarium autem ponere, antequam talis aggressio timetur, non permitterem uxori, quia faceret actum ab initio contra naturam."

ted by theologians for centuries, namely, that there was something absolutely sacrosanct to the *physiological* act of copulation, regardless of whether or not it was a reasonable act freely consented to by both parties. (Although he does not cite Sanchez' argument that this act of copulation does not really begin as the sacrosanct "generative process" until several minutes after the deposit of semen, he does not repudiate this standard defense of expulsion of the semen after rape.)

Also, Schmitt seems to make no provision for even an *un*married woman who is in circumstances where she has good reason to fear being raped to forearm herself with a diaphragm already put in place so as to avoid a pregnancy should she be attacked. He does not speak specifically, it is true, either for or against the use of a diaphragm as a licit possibility for the woman who sees a clear threat of rape ouside marriage. Indeed, he does not mention the possibility of such a case. It must, however, be admitted that his statement of *principle* regarding such a device does seem to preclude its liceity.

> All action by which a woman seeks to impede the ascent of the semen into the uterus labors under the same basic malice, and can never be allowed. To this end the whole use of an occlussive pessary at the mouth of the uterus is directed, as is also the use of a sponge or anything else filled with a substance which will kill the sperm.[18]

Noldin-Schmitt then does make a distinct step towards accepting our thesis; yet at the same time his brief treatment of this problem at least *seems* to be lacking in coherence. He breaks with the concept of the absolute moral inviolability of any complete copulation between husband and wife by allowing for expulsion of the semen from the female generative tract;[19] yet he holds on to this same kind of inviolability by not allowing the copulation to be frustrated in its reproductive capacity *beforehand.* A writer in the next generation of theologians will speak to these limitations of Schmitt's doctrine, as we shall see, and quite effectively;[20] but for now we simply note that, whatever the limitations, Schmitt has moved us a step forward.

---

[18]*ibid:* "Omnis actio, qua mulier ascensum seminis in uterum impedire conatur, eadem malitia intrinseca laborat, nec ullo modo permitti potest. Huc refertur usus pessarii occludentis os uteri, vel spongiae, etc. cum substantiis semen necantibus."

[19]Noldin himself, prior to the editions of his work by Schmitt, made no provision for expulsion of the semen ever by a wife. In this earlier treatment, however, we run up against the problem we shall see again and again in other contemporary writers: he states his objections seemingly in the case of *agreement* between husband and wife in the seeking of copulatory orgasm, and not clearly in case of one party (the wife) who would be willing to forgo the copulation, but is forced to it by her husband at grave personal injustice to herself. The latter case, which is germane to our thesis, he does not treat, for instance, in his 1923 edition: "Omnis actio qua mulier semen receptum expellere conatur ad impediendam generationem ut irrigatione vaginam eluere, grave peccatum est. Neque molestiae quantum magnae, quas forte mulieres experiantur nisi semen vaginam eluentes eiciant, neque aegrotum quam pati solent, hanc agendi rationem excusat; *si enim* receptum semen servare nolint, a copula abstineant. (emph. add.)"

[20] Peeters, Hermes, OFM, *Manuale Theologiae Moralis,* Torino-Roma, 1963 Vol. II, p. 267, n. 344-2

2. Two Writers Specifically Reject Our Thesis

Schmitt moved a step forward towards our thesis, though accepting only expulsion of the semen for the wife victimized by her own husband. Like Schmitt, two other writers of this period also help, even if only by breaking the long silence on the issue. Unlike Schmitt, however, they reject outright and absolutely the liceity of any artificial intervention by a wife to prevent pregnancy, no matter in what act of oppression the husband has forced his semen upon her.

Marcellino Zalba, SJ, in his *Theologiae Moralis Compendium*[21] in 1958 is unmistakeably clear on this point. Like all who have considered this issue specifically, Zalba treats it as an *obiter dictum* of his treatment of remedies available to the woman oppressed by rape outside of marriage.

> The expelling of the man's semen: a) is not licit for a woman who has *consented* to the carnal act; b) *nor is such an expelling licit for a wife who has had that semen deposited in her by her husband, although she was with good reason opposed to this;* c) is licit, at least more probably, for a woman oppressed in rape by force or by deceit.
>
> The reason for the first point is that in any such expelling (of the semen by a woman who had consented to the carnal act) we have the evil of onanism; and for the second point, *that the husband has and retains his basic right (jus radicale) to copulation;* and as to the third point, cf: n. 1395; Dz 1184.[22]

It is interesting to note that, as with other writers previous to Zalba, *consent* to a *particular* carnal act is *essential* for that carnal act to become morally inviolable in an extra-marital situation, whereas within marriage the carnal act is *automatically* inviolable. It is presumed also that no withdrawal of consent by the wife, however justified that withdrawal might be, in any way affects the moral inviolability of the copulation. It *seems* that Zalba sees the essential consent as perduring and irretractible from the moment when the woman in the vows gives the *"jus radicale";* but since he gives not further explanation, we can do nothing but speculate on the possible basis of his opinion. It is important to note here also that, as we shall see in Chapter V, Zalba will entirely change his opinion on this matter ten years later, and basically espouse the thesis we are favoring.[23]

A second author is quite important for his indirect but nonetheless clear denial of our thesis. Godfrid Heinzel, SJ, edited the thirty-sixth edition of Noldin-Schmitt

---

[21] Romae, 1958

[22] *ibid.*, Vol. I, p. 888, n. 1614; "Seminis virilis expulsio: a) non licet mulieri quae in actum carnalem consenserit; b) *neque uxori quae illud susceperit a marito etsi rationabiliter invita;* c) licit probabilius mulieri quae vi vel dolo oppressa est. Ratio est quoad primum, quia in eo esset malitia onanismi; quoad alterum, quia maritus retinebat ius radicale: quoad tertium, cf. n. 1395; D 1184." (emph. add.) The references in the last line are to a treatment of extra-marital rape in another part of his volume and to Innocent XI's condemnation of abortion of the inanimate fetus in order to save a pregnant woman from disgrace or even murder.

[23] Zalba, M., SJ, "La portata del principio di totalità nella doctrina di Pio XI e Pio XII e la sua applicazione nei casi di violenze sessuali, "(hereafter "La portata. . . ") in *Rassegna di teologia,* Luglio-Agosto 1968, n. 4, pp. 231-232

in 1958. His rejection of our thesis is particularly striking because: a) he rejects, at least by clear implication, Sanchez' doctrine regarding extra-marital rape, and aligns himself with the opposition to that doctrine as that opposition was represented in our century by Benedict Merkelbach; b) he rejects our thesis that a wife basically abused sexually by her husband may use artificial means to prevent pregnancy; and c) he must go out of his way to make both of these points, since, as editor of Noldin-Schmitt, he must and does delete the paragraph which we quoted above from Noldin-Schmitt favoring both Sanchez' position and our own thesis.

> A woman who has given the right to her body may not deliberately impede its intrinsic purpose. Therefore any action by which a woman, in order to impede generation, seeks to expel the semen she has received is evil in itself *(in se mala)* and a grave sin. No difficulties can excuse it. Such difficulties may indeed excuse her from rendering the debt, but they cannot render licit something which is in itself evil *(in se malum)*.[24]

Nonetheless, in spite of this negative opinion of Heinzel, he indicates to us at least that the issue of oppression in marriage is again being seriously considered.

3. Writers Who Do Not Treat Our Thesis Specifically

This surfacing of interest in the question on the part of three authors nothwithstanding, we find in all other writers of the period 1880-1960 no specific position, - - indeed not even a mention of the issue. Where we might most expect to find the issue at least mentioned is, of course, in the writers who favored Sanchez' position regarding extra-marital rape. Indeed, this doctrine of Sanchez continued to be the center of lively debate throughout the period 1880-1960, a debate which was studied by Charles Curran in his doctoral thesis at the Gregorian University in 1960.[25] We will examine the connected issue of sexual oppression within marriage by reviewing briefly what we have found in the writers who formed the two camps, for and against Sanchez' doctrine.

a. Writers Who Accept Sanchez' Position

The following writers are representative of those who accept Sanchez' position, yet remain silent on our thesis during the period 1880-1960: Anthony Ballerini,[26]

---

[24]Heinzel, G., *De Castitate et de Sexto Praecepto,* Oeniponte, 1958, p. 63, n. 69-a. "Qui jus ad corpus tradidit, non potest data opera impedire finem ejus intrinsicum. . . Ergo, omnis actio qua mulier semen receptum expellere conatur ad impediendam generationem in se mala et grave peccatum est, nec ullis incommodis excusari potest. Talia incommoda possunt excusare a reddendo debito, sed actum in se malum non reddunt licitum." The complete n. 69 is reproduced in Heinzel, with the exception of the two paragraphs which we quoted in footnote 17, *supra.* Thus he intentionally abandons Schmitt's support of expulsion of the semen both for the rape victim and for the abused wife.

[25]Curran, *op. cit.,* p. 3.

[26]Ballerini, Anthony, *Opus Theologicum Morale in Busenbaum Medullam* edited by and with Volume 17 authored by Domenico Palmieri, 1889-1894, Practi, Vol. II, Tr. VI, Sect. VI, Dub. IV, n. 120

Domenico Palmieri,[27] Arthur Vermeersch,[28] J. Salsmans,[29] Joseph Ubach,[30] Augustine Lehmkuhl,[31] Charles Damen,[32] John Ferreres,[33] Bernard Häring,[34] Joseph Fuchs,[35] and Thomas Iorio.[36]

These writers and others[37] do not mention any analogous application of Sanchez' doctrine to the benefit of the wife abused within her own marriage. They do, however, generally maintain and even expand upon (cautiously) the received doctrine that: 1) a woman does indeed in certain instances have a right to refuse carnal relations altogether to her husband, and 2) it would be a grave injustice for him to force himself upon her in such circumstances. But on the issue of what she may

[27] *ibid.* It is difficult at times to tell whether Palmieri is simply recording the opinions of Balerini, or whether he is giving his own. There is no indication here that Palmieri is departing from Ballerini, as indeed he seldom does.

[28] Vermeersch, Arthur, *De Castitate et de Vitiis Oppositis,* Romae, ed. 2, 1923, n. 71

[29] Salsmans, Joseph, editor of Genicot, Edward, *Theologiae Moralis Institutiones,* Bruxelles, 1951, Vol. I, Tr. II, Sect. V, Cap, IV, n. 378 bis. Salsmans emphasizes here that expulsion of the semen is justified *only* after rape.

[30] Ubach, Joseph, *Theologia Moralis,* Friburg Bisgroviae, 1926, Volume I, Part V, n. 3. Ubach tantalizes us with the kind of unclarity we have noted above in Noldin-Schmitt (footnote 19, *supra*) by holding that expulsion of the semen is illicit "si copula fuit *legitima* vel *voluntarie admissa.*" He seems to *imply* that such is always the case in copula between husband and wife, but he does not *say* so. It is too much to presume that he had considered the possibility of such a category as intra-marital rape, but, as happens in a number of authors, his *formulation* does not exclude such a category.

[31] Lehmkuhl, Augustine, *Theologia Moralis,* Friburg Brisgoviae, 1914 Vol. I, Theologia Specialis, Pars, I, Lib. II, Div. III, nu. 1013. Lehmkuhl, like Salsmans and others, emphasizes that expulsion of the semen is justified only after *rape.*

[32] Damen, Charles, redactor of Joseph Aertnys, *Theologia Moralis,* 9th ed., Galopiae, 1918, Tom I, Lib. III, Tr. VI, Cap. III, Art. II, n. 605.

[33] Ferreres, John, and editor Mondria, Alfredus, *Compendium Theologiae Moralis,* 17th ed., Barcinone, 1949, Vol. I, p. 351, N. 502, N.B. Ferreres-Mondria takes rather more rigid views throughout, for instance in excluding Vermeersch's toleration of a husband's having relations with his wife who, *ipso nolenti,* is using a pessary. However, although Ferreres-Mondra *seem* to consider rape or anything analogous to it as possible only outside of marriage, their *formulation* does not exclude the possibility of a wife might *not* be "*sciens volens*", which is in their mind a necessary consideration for a woman (presumeably unmarried) to be justified in using a douche after an oppression. Logically therefore and without further restricting "*sciens volens*" to apply only to *extra*-marital oppression, the whole paragraph treating of expulsion after "oppression" could apply to the oppression of a wife by her husband.

[34] Häring, Bernard, CSSR, *La Legge di Cristo,* Brescia, 1957-1959, Vol. III, p. 310. Like previous authors we have treated immediately above, Haring's formulation, combined with the very strong position he takes of the necessity of respecting the needs of one's partner, would seem to point in the direction of our thesis. He does not, however, specifically mention the thesis we are proposing. As we shall see, however, by 1966 he does accept specifically the position of Noldin allowing for *douches* by a wife "raped" by her drunken husband. Cf. his English edition, *The Law of Christ,* Westminster (USA), 1966, Vol. III, p. 360.

[35] Fuchs, Joseph, SJ, *De Castitate et De Ordine Sexuali,* ed. 2, Roma, 1959, p. 64. Fuchs not only accepts Sanchez' position, but approves of an unmarried woman (and presumeably a married woman) imminently threatened by *extra*-marital rape placing a pessary or other pregnancy prevention device before an attack and in view of its threat. *(ibid.)*

[36] Iorio, Thomas, *Theologia Moralis,* Neapoli, 1954, Vol. II, p. 147, n. 226. Iorio allows only that Sanchez' position is *probable;* he is silent on our thesis, and allows no expulsion of semen for the woman involved willingly in fornication or adultery, unless she first retracts her consent out of repentance.

[37] cf. Curran, *op. cit.,* pp. 5-20 for extensive quotations from English-speaking authors who in the early 20th century and up until 1960 (the last year Curran studied) had accepted Sanchez' position regarding the rape victim: A. Bonnar, Stanislaus La Rochelle, Frederick Good, Otis Kelly, Charles McFadden, Edwin Healy, and Thomas O'Donnell. Yet none of these attempted to make an application, even an analogous one, to the wife oppressed by her own husband. Indeed, several could be interpreted as possibly opposing such an application, though such an interpretation is by no means certain. Cf. O'Donnell, *Morals In Medicine,* 2nd edition, Westminster, 1959, quoted in Curran, *op. cit.* p. 14, note 14, Cf. also Charles McFadden, *Medical Ethics,* p. 8, note 7. The present writer would hold that the whole problem treated in our present study never was intended by these authors to enter into their treatment.

do to remedy such an injustice should it be forced upon her, they are silent; indeed they do not mention that there could be such an issue.

At times, however, their treatment of oppression within marriage seems to fairly dance around the subject. Palmieri, for example, in his revision and completion of Ballerini's work after Ballerini had died, quotes his mentor, who had in turn reported the teaching of Busenbaum:

> A wife is not bound to render the debt. . . if the partner who is asking it is insane, because such a person is not capable of use of ownership, nor does he ask with reason and in a human mode. The same is true regarding a drunken husband.[38]

> . . . the duty of rendering the debt ceases in a wife when she fears rightly some grave harm to herself or to a child she has conceived. It is certain, says St. Alphonsus n. 950, that a wife is not bound to render the debt when there is grave danger to life or health. He proves this with the argument and authority of St. Thomas Supp. q.64 s.1: A man is bound to render the debt to his wife in those matters which pertain to the generation of children, *but only within the limits of his own personal wellbeing*. . . It is common teaching, says St. Alphonsus n. 953 that a woman is not bound to render the debt if she knows by experience that she cannot possibly give birth without probable danger to her very life.[39]

> (Where there is danger of death and a resultant freeing of a wife from the obligation of rendering the debt) not even the danger of incontinency for the husband who is making the request brings any obligation upon the wife; and the reasoning of St. Thomas is valid also in this hypothetical case. Besides, there are other means for a man to keep continent, and his use of them depends on his own free choice.[40]

All of the writers of this "Sanchez camp" treat of the limits of a wife's obligations, some with slightly more permissive views than others; but like Palmieri-Ballerini, they stop short of entering into the question of what a wife may do who, in a great injustice, is physically or morally overcome by lustful husband.

---

[38]*op. cit., Vol.* VI, Tr. X, Sect. VIII "De Matr.", Cap. II, Dub. II, n. 406 (LIX), p. 324: "Non tenetur reddere. . .si petens sit amens; quia talis non est capax usus dominii, nec petit cum ratione et humano modo. Quod valet etiam de ebrio."

[39]"(Etiam si alter, quantum in ipso est, integro fruatur jure petendi) cessare in altero debitum reddendi, cum grave damnum seu gravis periculum damni coniux merito timeat sibi vel proli iam conceptae. Certum est, ait S. Alp. n. 950, non teneri coniugem reddere debitum cum gravi periculo vitae aut sanitatis. Quod auctoritate et argumento probat S. Thomae Supp. q. 64 a. 1. Vir tenetur uxori debitum reddere in iis, quae ad generationem prolis spectant, salva tamen prius personae incolumnitate. . . Commune est, ait S. Alph n. 953, non teneri uxorem reddere debitum, si experta sit, non posse parere sine probabili periculo mortis."

[40]*ibid.* n. 411 "idcirco nec periculum incontinentiae in petente infert obligationem reddendi: ratio enim S. Thomae et in hac hypothesi valet et ceteroquin praesto sunt alia media incontinentiae vitandae, quia ex libera pendet voluntate."

It must be admitted, though, that when these writers do speak of any interruption of the physiologically complete copulation, they speak in terms which would *seem* to preclude the liceity of any measures a wife might take *prior* to oppression from her husband. For instance, Ballerini, again, shows the kind of formulation typical even of this more "permissive" school of Sanchez' followers:

Voluntary onanism is never licit.[41]

Palmieri then goes on to indicate what Ballerini (and Busenbaum before him) mean by "voluntary onanism":

> As our author indicates sometimes generation is impeded by taking a sterility drug; but more commonly by the abuse of marriage itself in the practice of Onan, of which Genesis speaks.[42]

This kind of description of "onanism" is typical of the formulations of theologians of this period, and indeed beyond it.[43] It is a formulation which, we hold, is basically correct. Unfortunately, in our judgment, it can also lead to false impressions, as we shall see now as we examine briefly the general characteristics of this pro-Sanchez school when it speaks of the morality of the use of marriage.

It is important that we see some of these general characteristics of this school in this matter because it is the school which came to prevail in the historical debate over the expulsion of the semen after a rape attack. This victory of Sanchez' view represented a dramatic, if subtle, spur to the development of our understanding of sexual morality in general and of marriage morality in particular. Inevitably, for example, it would - - and did - - affect the approach to the question of the oppressed wife. Yet, as we have seen, the overwhelming majority of the writers of this pro-Sanchez school remain silent on our question, and one of them (Zalba) even specifically rejects the liceity of any effort of a wife to prevent pregnancy from an act forced on her by her husband. Why this hesitancy and, in the case of Zalba, even explicit negativism regarding such an intervention from a group willing to defend the development championed by Sanchez? (Indeed, why the refusal of Sanchez himself and of most of his earlier followers to accept such an intervention by an oppressed wife as licit?) What are the characteristics of this school which would help explain their reluctance, or neglect, or even hostility towards such an intervention? We would note two characteristics especially.

First, these writers seem to regard the right to the conjugal act as a form of *material ownership,* - - ownership over something purely physical. They had cast off, it is true, the purely physicalist concept of *copulation* as being an act, in itself, immune from any licit human intervention to prevent it from resulting in a pregnancy . They thus parted company with the school represented by Merkelbach in

---

[41]*op. cit.*, Vol. II, p. 815, n. 922: "Onanismus voluntarius in nullo casu . . . licitus."

[42]op. cit. Vol. VI, p. 208: "Quod, ut auctor infra innuit aliquando fit sumendo. . . pharmacum sterilitatis; sed communius per abusum matrimonii ad instar Onan, de quo Gen."

[43]Among other authors whom we have mentioned above as supporters of Sanchez' school who use this same basically physiological definition of "Onanism": Vermeersch, *De Castitate*, Roma, 1921, nn. 257, 264, 268; Genicot-Salsmans, *Institutiones Theologiae Moralis,* 1964, n. 1080; Iorio, *op. cit.,* n. 1203.

our century and by other opponents of Sanchez in previous centuries, the school denying to a rape victim the right of expulsion of the semen. But in breaking away from this latter school, the followers of Sanchez used a *purely* material concept, not of rape, to be sure, but of the *conjugal act.* It was a material concept which indeed had much in common with the concept of the school opposed to Sanchez. Palmieri, for example, as we quoted him above, speaks of the insane husband as having no right to the conjugal act because

> ... he is not capable of the use of *ownership (dominium).* [44]

This is the same kind of formulation which, as we have seen, Lopez de Texeda used in the 17th century in denying that a husband physically forcing himself on his wife during the *bimestre* period was doing her any injustice.

> He is simply taking what is his.[45]

This typical expression no doubt was thought to be rooted in St. Paul's teaching that the body of the husband belongs not to him but to his wife, and the body of the wife in the same way to her husband.[46] It is, of course, an admittedly literalistic interpretation of Paul's words. (We are not here making the point that such a literalistic interpretation is erroneous, but simply that it is literalistic.) Indeed, the authors generally make use of the very words of St. Paul in expounding on the marital debt; and rightly so. But the interpretation is given of Paul that in some true sense (though within the limits of the marriage "contract") the genital parts of the body and the actions specific to them as genital organs, become the *property* of one's partner in marriage. The whole defense of the Sanchez school for the expulsion of the semen in the case of rape is, not only that no sacrosanct generative process begins in the first few moments after the rape attack, but also that the rapist had not entered into the contract for the conjugal exchange of the "use of marriage." Moreover the justification for *refusing* the marital debt in the case of danger of death or of grave illness is that neither partner could licitly have agreed in the marriage contract to rendering the debt under such grave *incommoda.* In spite of the debt's being refused and not honored at some point in time, copulation *remains a right* in justice. Danger of death or of grave illness are simply more than was "bargained for" in "the contract". Like a debt of money to be paid, so also the conjugal debt need not be rendered if doing so would put the debtor in extreme need. The same principles which apply to returning something loaned apply to the marriage debt.

This then is the first characteristic of the Sanchez school in these matters: the conjugal act is basically nothing but a physically *material* act. And we wish to make it perfectly clear that we do not find these reflections totally without merit. As we shall state in the theological considerations of our final chapter, there is indeed a dimension of justice in the morality of the conjugal act, and this dimension of justice does indeed involve the physical genitality of the couple and its procreational

---

[44] Ballerini, *op. cit.* n. 406, introduced with "LIX. 6": "... talis non est capax usus dominii..."

[45] Cf. *supra,* Chapter II, p. 19, notes 17 and 18.

[46] I Corinthians 7:4.

character. The question will have to be examined more profoundly, however, as to whether genital acts between husband and wife have any moral integrity if at the same time as being *genital* they are not also *relational,* i.e., expressive of mutual respect, and in that sense, at least inchoatively, of love. Does a husband, for instance, have a right in justice to a genital act which is *merely* and *exclusively* procreational? Does he not rather have a right to express in the genital act (and to have expressed to him in the same act) the mutual *esteem* which husband and wife owe to each other by virtue of both love and justice?

A second characteristic of this Sanchez school is the use of the term "human mode" to express a requisite for the moral use of marriage in the conjugal act. What the authors mean by "human mode", however, is not clear. It might refer to such things a emotiveness, gentleness, patience, tenderness, etc. Yet not necessarily so. For, as in Ballerini-Palmieri whom we quoted above, the context for speaking of a "human mode" of approaching the conjugal act is usually that of the case of the mentally ill husband, the *amens,* who, indeed, might be quite tender and not at all violent, inspite of being mentally out of contact with basic realities. Rather than apply to a merely emotive approach, then, the term *amens* seems, in these authors, to apply to the more fundamental human (i.e., rational) qualities of being *mentally* in contact with reality and basically *free* to govern one's life within that reality. In other words *"humano modo"* seems to refer to the basic power to exercise one's *intellect* and *will.*

Basic free consent is, in their thought, deemed a necessary prerequisite for any *right* to the conjugal act here-and-now. The basically insane husband has no right to the conjugal act because he cannot ask for it *humano modo,* i.e., *freely.*

Yet these authors give no indication that this consent is somehow *intrinsic* to the conjugal act, anymore than an act of consent is intrinsic to the physical act of eating. No hint is given that the conjugal act might be, by its very nature, a *free expression* of one's own self and of one's relationship of conjugal love towards one's marriage partner. One eats, whether or not he intends to eat; and one likewise has the conjugal act, whether or not he intends to express the conjugal relationship of love.

The *consent* to the conjugal act, then remains *extrinsic,* though necessary, to the conjugal act, whereas the elements *intrinsic* to the conjugal act are entirely *physiological.* As we shall have occasion to point out in the final chapter, the *expressive* character of the conjugal act has come to be upheld more and more by both theologians faithful to the Magisterium in the wake of *Humanae Vitae,* as well as by the Magisterium itself, especially in the Apostolic Exhortation *Familiaris Consortio* by which Pope John Paul II followed up the consultations of the 1980 Sixth Synod of Bishops.[47]

---

[47]Pope John Paul II, *Familiaris Consortio,* n. 32. Typis Polyglottis Vaticanis, 1981.

A third characteristic of the Sanchez school is that often their *formulations* leave room for a further development of the distinction between pregnancy-prevention steps which, on the one hand, are decided only by *only one* partner and those which, on the other hand, are the result of *collusion* between two consenting partners. The authors do not seem to be consciously aware of it, but repeatedly what seems at first a condemnation of *any* "onanistic" practice, "natural" or "unnatural", that is, *any* human intervention to prevent a complete copulation (or, in the case of condomistic copula, a facsimile of complete copulation) between husband and wife from resulting in pregnancy is couched in terms of *both* spouses' *willing* such an orgasmic act, and being *unwilling* to do without it for the sake of respecting their human integrity as sexual beings. For instance, Ballerini-Palmieri write:

> Wherefore the confessor must keep in mind the difficult case . . . of a married couple *(coniugum)* who because of poverty cannot take care of more children, or who, in another type of case, are rich and do not want to have a large family because the law would require equal distribution of their estate (which would break up the family fortune and cause the family, as such, to fall from the prominence enjoyed by the *parents*). Since, however, such couples do not wish *(nolint)* to live chastely in the sense of abstaining *(ut abstineant)* from the act, *they* resort to the sin of preventing conception . . .[48]

It is important not to make too much of this type of formulation found generally throughout the theologians whom we have been considering. It would be too much, for instance, to hypothesize that they had any conscious way a premonition of the possibility that the whole moral question would be different if one partner (the wife) were willing to "live chastely in the sense of abstaining from the act," but were forced, at great injustice, to submit to copulation against her will. (Indeed one cannot be entirely sure in the case of each theologian who speaks in terms of *coniuges* that this term always refers to two married persons who are married to each *other* and are *colluding* in their use of onanistic practices. The authors may be speaking of married *persons,* though the element of *willfully* indulging in contraceptive practices would be present even without collusion.) Indeed, if the authors had been conscious of *such a distinction* between one partner's willingness to do the right thing on the one hand, and the collusion of both partners on the other hand, and if the authors had been conscious of any *importance* in this distinction, then we would expect that they would have gone on to treat precisely the subject of this present study. This, as we have seen, they do not do, with the exception of Noldin-Schmitt, Zalba, and Heinzel.

Our point here, however, is that, whatever be the consciousness or lack of it in these authors regarding this distinction, their *formulation* of principles for dealing

---

[48] Ballerini-Palmieri, op. cit., p. 244: "Quare confessarius prae oculis habere debet casum difficilem, qui subinde occurrit, *coniugum* nempe, qui sive ob paupertatem non *possunt* alere numeriosiorem prolem, sive etiam divitiis *pollentes nolunt* habere prolem multiplicem, quae ob legum dispositionem, in partitione bonorum e statu *parentum* discederet. Cum autem ita caste vivere alioquin *nolint* ut ab opere *abstineant;* hinc crimen, de quo Auctor, impediendi generationem. . ." (emph. add.)

with the problem of "onanism" does not *exclude* the possibility that when we are dealing with *collusion* between man and wife in this matter we are not dealing with the same problem as that of the *wife* who is *willing* to abstain from conjugal actions but, nonetheless, has these actions forced upon her.

b. Writers Who Reject Sanchez' Position.

We have had to treat at length writers who favor Sanchez' position, since without accepting the possibility of a licit intervention to prevent a complete act of copulation from resulting in pregnancy outside of marriage in the case of rape, there is no logical way that such an intervention could be accepted for a wife sexually oppressed by her own husband. For the same reason, it will not be necessary to spend a great deal of time analyzing those writers who oppose Sanchez. We can expect support neither in principle nor in any specific application for our thesis from this latter group. It is sufficient simply to list some of the more prominent names and cite the places where they totally reject Sanchez' position. Their opposition, as Curran demonstrates clearly, was itself eventually universally rejected by moral theologians and, at least tacitly, by the Magisterium.[49]

Among those who are representative of this opposition to Sanchez' position are: Clement Marc,[50] Gennaro Bucceroni,[51] Joseph Aertnys,[52] and Benedict Merkelbach.[53]

c. Writers Who Are Silent On Sanchez' Position.

A number of writers simply do not enter into the question of expulsion of the semen either after rape outside marriage or *a fortiori,* after sexual oppression inside marriage. Among those who are silent on both issues are C. Capellmann,[54] P. Debreyne,[55] Raphael Tummolo,[56] Charles Coppens,[57] Austin O'Mally,[58] Felix

---

[49]Curran, *op. cit.*, p. 39.

[50]Marc, Clement, *Institutiones Morales Alphonsianae,* Romae, 1906 13th ed., Vol. I, Pars, II, Tr. V, n. 742. Marc cites Alphonsus' as his own opinion, although he seems to recognize at least some extrinsic probability for the Sanchez position.

[51]Bucceroni, Januarius, *Institutiones Theologiae Moralis,* 6th ed., Romae, 1914-1915, De Sexto Praecepto, Sect. II, n. 790

[52]Aertnys, Joseph, *Theologia Moralis,* ed. 8, Tornaci, 1913, Vol. I, Lib. II, Tr. V, Cap. IV, n. 192

[53]Merkelbach, Benedict, *Quaestiones de Castitate et Luxuria,* 3rd ed., Liege, 1929, Quaest. III Art. II, p. 44-45

[54]Capellmann, C., *Medicina Pastoralis,* 9th 3d., Aquisgrani, 1892, "De Abortu", p. 13, and "De Matrimonio", pp. 139-140

[55]Debreyne, P. - - Ferrand, A., *La Theologia Morale et les Sciences Medicales, 6th ed., Paris, 1884.*

[56]Tummolo, Raphael, editor of Gury, Joannes, *Compendium Theologiae Moralis,* 4th ed., Neapoli, 1928, Vol. I, n. 428

[57]Coppens, Charles, *Moral Principles and Medical Practice,* New York, 1887

[58]O'Mally, Austin, *The Ethics of Medical Homicide and Mutilation,* New York, 1910, p. 674-689

Cappello,[59] Joseph Antonelli,[60] Francis Hurth,[61] and Gustave Ermecke.[62]

4. Summary of Theological Writers 1880-1960

During this period, one main obstacle to our thesis is overcome: the concept of a generative process absolutely sacrosanct and morally untouchable simply because it is physiologically begun by the deposit of semen in the vagina. By the early 1900's, the right of a woman to defend herself by expelling a rapist's semen was taught by most theologians without any objection from the Magisterial authorities of the Church. Moreover, one theologian, Joseph Fuchs, in 1959 allows for a woman to put a "sterilet" in place if she has reason to fear extra-marital rape. And, most important, another writer, A. Schmitt, moves towards our thesis by admitting the right of a wife to expel the semen of a husband who has forced himself upon her with serious injustice. The same writer, however, explicitly rules out the placing of a "sterilet" or taking of other such steps *ahead of time* by a wife constantly threatened by such an injustice. Further and quite notable progress comes only, as we shall see, in the writers of the 1960's.

B. The Teaching Of The Magisterium 1880-1960.

The context of the teaching of the theologians whom we have examined thus far in this Chapter is the teaching promulgated, with various degrees of weightiness, by the Magisterium of this period. We will now examine: 1) the concrete teaching of the Magisterium as it refers to our subject; 2) the tacit acceptance by the Magisterium of some points of teaching commonly put forth by most theologians, as well as other points put forth in a tentative and pioneering way by a few; 3) the principles which are implicit both in teachings positively promoted and in teachings tacitly accepted by the Magisterium; 4) other principles which would be needed in order for our thesis to be defensible.

---

[59]Cappello, Felix, *De Matrimonio,"* Taurini, 1950, V "de matrimonio, n. 797.

[60]Antonelli, Joseph, *Medicina Pastoralis, 5th ed., Romae, 1932, n. 343-c, q. 2*

[61]Hurth, Francis, *De Statibus,* Romae, 1946, n. 701

[62]Ermecke, Gustave, editor of Mausbach, J., *Teologia Morale,* Münster-Westfallen, 1953-1961, Vol. III, pp. 151-152, no. 23. Fuchs *(De Castitate et De Ordine Sexuali* Romae, 1963, p. 93, note 42) mistakenly interprets Ermecke to be one of the first advocates of our present thesis, which Fuchs himself adopts for the first time in his own writings here in 1963. Fuchs believes that Ermecke is defending the right of the wife to use contraceptives ("Preservativi tecnici"), whereas actually the context is the question of a wife's being forced by her husband to cooperation in *his* contraceptive practices. In discussing the problem of the wife confronted with the demand of a husband who intends to *withdraw* in an *atto onanistico* and in allowing the classical doctrine that she may go along with this for grave reasons, Ermecke turns to the problem of dealing with the husband who will use a *condom* from the beginning of the act, and says: "In casi extremi, trovandosi di fronte ad una violenza fisica irresistibile, le è lecito *ammettere* anche l' uso di preservativi tecnici." "In extreme cases, finding herself faced with a physical violence which she cannot handle, it is licit for her *to put up even with* the use of contraceptives." (emph. add.) The German original bears this out: "Im aussersten Fall, bei physisch unüberwindlicher Zwangslage durfte auch die Anwendung technischer Verhütungsmittel *geduldet* werden." *(Katholische Moral-Theoligie,* Vol. III, p. 116 (emph. add.) Ermecke is thus simply giving the standard moral doctrine for cooperation in contraceptive acts. Indeed, he does not even treat of Sanchez' doctrine on rape outside of marriage, and thus can hardly be expected to treat of our thesis.

1. Specific Points Of Papal Teaching Pertinent To Our Thesis.

The teaching of the Magisterium during this period covers the following points concerning conjugal life:

(1) A woman must govern her life by the exercise of her own free will in refusing cooperation with a husband who intends to abuse the sexual act by withdrawal ("natural onanism"). This refusal is mandatory only if it is physically and morally possible, and will not result in more harm than good. One must refuse totally, however, cooperation with an act of *condomistic* abuse or with an act of extra-marital *rape*.[63]

(2) One may *tolerate* being abused sexually though condomistic copulation or rape where significantly more harm than good would result from total resistance.[64]

(3) One may not mutilate the body or choose physiologically mutilated sexual acts in order to avoid evils which can be avoided through the governance of one's life by one's own free will. Thus problems of deteriorating health (e.g., because of heart or kidney conditions) and of socio-economic problems may *not* be met by a couple's (or one partner's) decision to resort to sterilization or to sexual acts broken physiologically through the man's use of condoms or withdrawal, or through the woman's rejection of the sperm through diaphragms, douches, etc.[65]

(4) One may mutilate the body (e.g., by sterilization) by removing a seriously diseased part or even a healthy part whose presence or functioning is a serious threat which cannot be otherwise avoided.[66]

(5) It is not contrary to Catholic doctrine that the State may mutilate a person's body as a punishment of a person guilty of a serious crime in order to avoid having that crime repeated in the future.[67]

(6) A genuine decision to love one's spouse, especially by respecting and cultivating the most interior and human dimension of one's spouse, is a primary cause and element of marriage con-

---

[63] S. Poenitentiary, *E.S.* 3185, 1643, and 3718. These and the references following in notes 71-75 will be treated more in detail as this section on the Magisterium proceeds in the present chapter.

[64] *ibid.*

[65] *Casti Conubii,* Dz 3722.

[66] Pius XII To hematologists, in p. 705-706, *Discorsi*

[67] *Casti Conubii, op. cit.,* 3723

[68] *ibid.* 3722

sidered in its more comprehensive nature, and not simply under only one of its essential aspects, that of an institution for the procreation and education of children.[69]

These specific points of the teaching of the Magisterium will show themselves as we now consider the more relevant documents of the period. Among these, the most important and weighty, of course, are the Encyclicals, which, with the advent of Leo XIII, become the most obvious teaching instruments of the universal Church.[70]

LEO XIII

Arcanum Divinae Sapientiae,[71] Leo XIII's encyclical on Christian marriage, is concerned primarily with new problems of 1) the rising acceptance of divorce and 2) the efforts of anti-Christian and anti-ecclesial governments to make the spousal relationship a purely secular institution. It does not touch directly upon issues of the morality of sexual life. It does, however, speak briefly of one essential of Christian marriage: that the couple sacramentally mirror in their own relationship the love which exists between Christ and the Church. This kind of love, of course, is unbreakable and cannot be mirrored in divorce from a marriage *ratum et consummatum*. Leo also makes the point that this supernatural configuration of conjugal love to the mystical union between the Lord and His people is in harmony with the requirements of *human nature itself* for marriage.

> (In marriage) which is conformed to the exemplar of the mystical marriage of (Christ the Lord) and His Church, Christ brings to perfection that love which is consonant with human nature...[72]

Leo thus touched upon an element of marriage which, since then has invited distortions which would see this conjugal love as an end which, for serious reasons, one might pursue in such a way as to completely suppress the procreational character of the couple and of their physical union. Nonetheless this element of conjugal love was eventually to find its way into a more developed doctrine on marriage which would come later in the Church's life. For, despite the inevitability of its being distorted (as any truth can be), conjugal love is obviously an essential element of the Gospel which the Church is charged to bring to married couples.

PIUS XI

Indeed this element of conjugal love is considered quite seriously in Pius XI's *Casti Conubii,*[73] and with implications which the Church would appreciate more

---

[69]*Arcanum Divinae Sapientiae, E.S.,* 3142, and *Casti Conubii, E.S.* 3703.

[70]Malone, *loc. cit.*

[71]*loc. cit.*

[72]*ibid.*

[73]*op. cit., E.S.,* 3700-3724, especially *E.S.,* 3703

fully only years after its author's death. In this encyclical of 1930, Pius XI speaks of a true kind of primacy of love in marriage, especially Christian marriage. This is not to be interpreted, as the Pope makes quite clear, as in any way justifying the elimination of the procreational character from its unitive character in the conjugal act. Nonetheless, despite the abiding danger of such an unjustifiable conclusion, the doctrine of genuine primacy of love in marriage is, as it must be, upheld by Pius XI.

> (This unity in marriage excludes sexual relations with anyone but one's spouse.) This kind of unity is made much easier and happier and more ennobling, and will flourish from another source which is most outstanding, namely, *conjugal love,* which *pervades all* the obligations of conjugal life and in Christian marriage holds, indeed, a *kind of primacy.* The love of which we speak is not indeed one which depends on some merely fleshly inclination, which can so quickly vanish, nor upon mere flattering words. It rather depends on the making of a *deep decision of the soul.* This decision, according to the adage, "Love is proven by the deeds one performs", is proven out by what one does visibly. This *doing* in the society of the family does not include only helping out one another. It also must include - - and indeed this more than anything else is the meaning of this love - - that spouses should help one another to be formed and perfected internally more and more each day as human beings, so that by their life together they may grow more and more in *virtue* and especially in that *true love for God and neighbor* on which "the whole Law and Prophets depend".[74]

That Pius XI did not in any way intend this re-iteration of the doctrine of a genuine primacy of love to be an argument to make contraceptive actions a ligitimate substitute for the physiologically natural conjugal act is well known and is evident from the following passage:

> But as a matter of fact there is no reason, not even a most serious one, which can bring it about that what is intrinsically against nature can become consonant with nature and a good act. Since, however, by its very nature the conjugal act is destined for the begetting of children, those who, in making use of it, by their own intervention deprive it of this natural force and power act against nature and do something impure and intrinsically immoral. (Against doctrines defending contraceptive practices) the Catholic Church raises her voice and through our lips once again proclaims: Any use of marriage whatsoever in

---

[74]*E.S.* 3707: "Haec autem castitatis fides, et facilior et multo etiam iucundior ac nobilior efflorescet ex altero capite praestantissimo: ex *coniugali* scilicet *amore,* qui *omnia* coniugalis vitae officia *pervadit* atque *quemdam* tenet in christiano coniugio *principatum* nobilitatis. Caritatem igitur dicimus non carnali tantum citiusque evanescente inclinatione innixam, neque in blandis solum verbis, set etiam *in intimo animi affectu* positam atque, -- siquidem probatio dilectionis exhibitio est operis -- opere externo comprobatam. Hoc autem *opus* in domestica socetate non modo mutuum auxilium complectitur, verum etiam ad hoc extendatur oportet, immo hoc in primis intendat, ut coniuges inter se iuventur ad interiorem hominem plenius in dies conformandum perficiendumque; ita ut per mutuam vitae consortionem in *virtutibus* magis magisque in dies proficiant, et praecipue *in vera erga Deum proximosque caritate* crescant, in qua denique 'universa Lex pendet et Prophetae.'" (emph. add.)

which the act, by human intervention, is deprived of its natural power to create life is a breaking of the law of God and of nature, and those who commit such an act stain themselves with a sin which greatly imperils them.[75]

Thus Pius XI rules out a conjugal act substantially broken in its physiological structure, which is, of course, essentially a procreational structure.

At the same time he recognizes that it can easily happen that a person be forced into involvement in a contraceptive action which he/she does not approve, but must tolerate:

> Not rarely one of the spouses (in a marriage) *suffers rather than sins* in this matter, since for a reason which is altogether serious they put up with a perversion of right living, a perversion which he/she does not want. Such a person is therefore *without sin* providing only that he/she keep in mind the law of charity and do his/her best to dissuade and move his/her spouse away from sin.[76]

Before proceeding on to other pertinent doctrine found in *Casti Conubii*, we should note that what Pope Pius XI is defending against contraceptive corruptions is the *conjugal act;* it is not simply *any* complete physiological act of copulation. We do not claim to be able to prove what the Pope *might* have taught, given the degree of theological and doctrinal development of the time, had he spoken to the question: Is every complete act of copulation between husband and wife necessarily "the conjugal act"? The point is that *de facto* he neither raises this question nor responds to it. What he does, on the one hand, is to defend against contraceptive interventions that sacrosanct act to which a couple is rightly called by reason of their marriage bond: the conjugal act. There is, on the other hand, not the slightest bit of evidence in *Casti Conubii* that every possible act of complete copulation between husband and wife is *de facto* this sacrosanct act. There is nothing, for instance, which says that an act of copulation forced on a wife by her husband with grave injustice is the conjugal act. We would make here the point which we have made previously regarding the hermeneutics of Magisterial documents: they say what they say, nothing more. We conclude, therefore, that Pius XI did not intend to condemn the use of artificial means of preventing pregnancy where that *act to which a married couple is called* by reason of the marriage contract is *absent*. This "right-ful" act of conjugal love is obviously not present where a wife has a *right* to refuse, and yet has copulation forced on her by her husband.

We would contend moreover that if the teaching of Pius XI did not in 1930 make our point explicit, then it at least incited not merely theological, but doctrinal development in that direction. Such development will be seen only when theologians

---

[75]*ibid.* 3716

[76]*ibid.* 3718

have had the time and the occasion to note in the teachings of the Magisterium this opening to such development, and when Magisterial documents will themselves begin to indicate it.[77]

One doctrine was especially needed for such a development to emerge, namely, that the conjugal act is by its very nature an *expression* or *sign* of the conjugal bond with its essential love. *Casti Conubii*, as we have seen, speaks clearly of genuine *love* as being a part of *marriage* itself, and indeed as having a definite type of primacy among other elements. But *Casti Conubii* does not speak of the *conjugal act* as being itself a *sign* of that *love* by reason of the *very physiological structure* of the act. Indeed, it does not speak of the conjugal act as being a sign of *anything*, not even of procreation. The conjugal act is spoken of only as *effecting* procreation, not as *signifying* procreation. *Casti Conubii* does not, indeed, deny that the conjugal act is a sign of a conjugal love which is inseparably procreational. The encyclical, however, and indeed theologians in general in this period 1880-1960, speak of the conjugal act, not as an act which *says* something (basically what the marriage vows say, including their procreational implications), but only as an act which *produces* or *can produce* something, - - a child. A theology of the conjugal act as *sign* is eventually to show itself especially after 1960, however, and is to clarify considerably, even in papal Magisterium,[78] what Pius XI was defending.

Pius XI's treatment of this issue of contraception is of greatest importance among classic Magisterial *loci* on the nature of marriage and its sexual expression. We must, however, also note at least briefly what Pius XI said here regarding one particular form of contraception, namely, sterilization. For as we have indicated in our opening chapter, we would defend in our thesis the liceity, at least in very extreme cases, of a wife's resorting even to surgical sterilization in order to defend herself agains a pregnancy which might be forced upon her unjustly.[79]

The false impression is often found among Catholics, even among those who study Catholicism academically, that the Church has branded the very physiological act of removing a healthy reproductive system or one of its essential components as an intrinsically evil act.[80] As we shall see, one later Magisterial document[81] will correct such a misunderstanding. We should call attention here, however, to the clarity with which the Church's doctrine on this point is already expressed by Pius XI himself in *Casti Conubii*.

---

[77]*Humanae Vitae*, n. 13 in *E.V.*, Vol. 3, n. 599; and *Quaecumque Sterilizatio* n. 1, in *E.V.* Vol. 5, n. 1200

[78]*Familiaris Consortio*, n. 32: "Sic naturali verbo, quod reciprocam plenamque coniugum donationem declarat, conceptuum impeditio verbum opponit obiectivae contradictionis, videlicet nullius plenae sui donationis alteri factae: hinc procedit non sola recusatio certa ac definita mentis ad vitam apertae, verum simulatio etiam interioris veritatis ipsius amoris coniugalis, quo secundum totam personam dirigitur ad sese donandum."

[79]As we shall see, M. Zalba came to hold this by 1968; cf. Zalba, "La portata", *op. cit.*, note 23, p. 227, and p. 232-237.

[80]McCormick, R. and Bayley, Corine, *America*, Nov. 29, 1980, p. 337 in a letter defending their original article arguing for an end to the bann on sterilization in Catholic hospitals. "It does not help much to say that sterilization for self-defense can be justified. . .; for the official teaching does not say this, though it has apparently tolerated it being said."

[81]cf. *Quaecumque sterilizatio*, the above mentioned 1975 letter to the American Bishops *(Supra*, note 77)

It is to be noted first the thrust of Church teaching under Pius XI is directed against *eugenic* sterilization, especially as a policy enforced by the newly rising totalitarian governments of the time, as well as other governments overly impressed by the need for a planned society. Secondly, the Pope also re-iterates the teaching, much more pertinent to our thesis, that the individual may not destroy any part of the body, even for the benefit of the body as a whole, *unless there is no other way to provide for the overall survival of life or health.*

> Private persons cannot (licitly) destroy or mutilate or in any other way render their natural functions powerless, *except when the good of the whole body cannot otherwise be provided for.*[82]

This is a far cry from the impression often given, even by some Catholic theologians, that the Church has absolutized as evil any surgical removal of a healthy part of the body, the reproductive system included. There is not even any mention in the document of any limitation as to causes which would justify a mutilation. For instance, disease is not mentioned here; and the encyclical leaves open the possibility that some threat entirely extrinsic to the present physical condition of a person could justify such an intervention. The only requisites stated are that: 1) the overall health of the body be at stake *(bono totius corporis)* and 2) that the problem cannot be solved in another way *(aliter provideri nequeat)*. "Another way" could include, among other options, a less drastic operation or the exercise of the individual's free will. One could decide, for instance, to refrain from sexual intercourse where refraining is required, or even to escape from the power of a sexually abusive husband by leaving him, if that is possible.

Moreover, the overall health of the body, mentioned here by Pius XI as a goal which can legitimize such surgical intervention, is not to be interpreted as the *only* possible such justification. It is true, of course, that Pius XI does not mention any other goal, and that at first his formulation might seem to exclude any other goal as justification *("nec* possint... mutilare... *nisi* bono totius corporis aliter provideri nequeat"). This apparently exclusivist interpretation, it must be admitted, was certainly the cause of much of the rigid opposition to certain elements of our thesis in the early 1960's as we shall see.[83] Such an exclusivist interpretation also furnished some fuel to the arguments of critics of the tradition and of the Magisterial teaching found, e.g., in *Humanae Vitae*. Those critics claimed that Church doctrine was bogged down in some kind of "physicalism" or "biologism". Lest it be open to caricature by an exclusivist interpretation, the doctrine, as stated in *Casti Conubii* at this point, in our opinion, definitely needed development.

As we shall see, this kind of Magisterially guided development will take place under Pius XII. This development will repudiate the exclusivist interpretation mentioned above, i.e., that an organ could licitly be removed *exclusively* in order to save

---

[82]*Casti Conubii, E.S.* 3723; "(Ceterum, quod ipsi privati homines in sui corporis membra dominatum alium non habeant, quam qui ad eorum naturales fines pertineat,) nec possint ea destruere aut mutilare aut alia via ad naturales functiones se ineptos reddere, *nisi quando bono totius corporis aliter provideri nequeat."* (emph. add.)

[83]Zalba, "La portata" *op. cit.,* p. 226. Zalba was himself part of this opposition in 1961.

the *physical* health of the whole organism, but not in order to further a person's *spiritual* dignity or his *right to guide his life by free decisions* in accord with objective morality.

Not only did Pius XII repudiate, at least implicitly, any exclusivist interpretations of Pius XI's doctrine, but, as we shall note, under Pius XII theologians, without any Magisterial corrective action, were freely defending positions totally incompatible with such exclusivist interpretations. Among such positions was the liceity of the donation of the organs from living persons in the transplant of such basic organs as the kidney.[84] This was a development simply incompatible with an exclusivist interpretation of Pius XI's doctrine; such donations certainly did not contribute to the overall physical health of the mutilated person, i.e., the donor. Many theologians from 1960 to 1980 were also allowing for the use of at least temporary sterilization in the famous case of the religious Sisters and other women caught in the Belgian Congo uprisings of the early 1960's.[85] We shall see also the growing acceptance among some theologians of our own thesis, that a sexually oppressed wife may resort even to sterilization to avoid an unjust impregnation from her husband. Such developments went unopposed by the teaching authority of the Church.

Regarding Pius XI's teaching, then, we would in summary make the following points: 1) There is nothing in the encyclical text to indicate that Pius XI was treating here anything but sterilization for *eugenic* reasons, be it by State authority or private authority; 2) This is not to deny that, in some very real and inevitable sense, the doctrine against sterilization presented by the Pope here has application also to sterilization for "therapeutic" or other purposes. (To the contrary, we affirm that application, as we shall point out in our concluding chapter.); 3) Nor is it to resort to a consequentialist methodology or principle which would simply see the "ontic" evil of certain "regrettable" means as absorbed somehow by the proportionate good of one's chosen goal. We would indeed be following such a consequentialist methodology or principle if it were clear from Pius XI that the physiological act of sterilizing an otherwise healthy reproductive system is indeed intrinsically evil. Such is not the doctrine, however, as is shown from internal anaysis of *Casti Conubii,* from later authoritative interpretations of this doctrine, and from later theological development. To see the teaching in *Casti Conubii* as a somewhat limited step in the development of a fuller ecclesial doctrine on sterilization is simply to say that, at this point and in this encyclical, we need not necessarily look for anything more than that.

PIUS XII

Pius XII, unlike his predecessors, did not address the problems of married life in an encyclical, but, for this area of human and Christian life, rather made use of

---

[84]O'Donnell, Thomas, *loc. cit.;* Connery, John R., *Theological Studies,* Vol. 17, n. 4, (Dec. 1956) pp. 559-561; Lynch, John, *ibid.,* Vol. 18, n. 2, (Jan. 1957); Kelly, Gerald, *ibid.,* n. 3; For concessions from opponents, cf. Zalba, *Compedium,* Vol. I, n. 1577, ad. b., p. 862.

[85]Zalba, "La portata" *op. cit.* p. 225 gives a brief account of the controversy over the "Belgian Congo Solution".

the numerous discourses addressed to various professional groups to whom he gave audiences after World War II. He continued and developed somewhat the moral tradition of the Church in the area of marriage, especially as that tradition had been articulated by Pius XI in *Casti Conubii*. In the discourses of Pius XII we shall examine three themes which affect our thesis: contraception, sterilization, and the principle of totality.

a) Pius XII on Contraception

On the issue of contraception, Pius spoke quite clearly in the famous discourse to midwives in 1951. Referring to the condemnation of contraception (Onanism) by Pius XI in *Casti Conubii*, Pius XII stated:

> (This rejection of Onanism) continues in its full vigor today as yesterday, and indeed tomorrow and forever because it is not a simple precept of human law, but the expression of a law which is natural and divine.[86]

The teaching is clear and strong.

There are, however, in this discourse several teachings related to that on contraception which directly point towards our thesis and prepare the way for its eventual unfolding among theologians. One such teaching is that there is not only a right, but an *obligation* in certain circumstances to avoid a new conception.

> You do find yourselves sometimes faced with cases which are quite delicate, namely cases in which a woman cannot be asked to run the risk of pregnancy. Indeed pregnancy must be avoided. If. . . the conditions absolutely require a 'no', that is, an exclusion of a pregnancy, then it would be wrong to give a 'yes'.[87]

The unavoidable implication of this clear teaching is that, if a woman has an *obligation* to avoid a pregnancy, then she has a concomitant *right* to do so, and that any act forced on her, even by her husband, which would or could result in her becoming pregnant would be an act of grave injustice. The possibility of such grave injustice's being perpetrated within marriage itself is thus clearly implied by Pius XII, and thus one of the essential elements for an act at least truly analogous to rape, but within marriage, is established.

The second teaching is that the obligation to respect the physiological structure of the marital act is operative *because* that act is done *consciously* and *freely*. Pius

---

[86]To Midwives, DISCORSI, p. 162, "Questa prescrizione è in pieno vigore oggi come ieri, e tale sarà anche domani e sempre, perche non è un simplice precetto di diritto umano, ma l'espressione di una legge naturale e divina."

[87]*ibid.*, p. 165: ". . . Vi trovate talvolta dinanzi a casi assai delicati, in cui, cioè, non si può esiger di correre il rischio della maternità, la quale anzi deve essere assolutamente evitata . . . Se, a vostra sicuro e spermientato giudizio, le condizioni richiedono assolutamente un 'no', cioè l'esclusione della maternità, sarebbe un errore e un torto d'imporre o di consigliare un 'si'."

XII writes that every attempt to deprive the conjugal act of its life-giving power is immoral for a married couple.

    in their *carrying out* of the act[88]

There is implied here an *active intention* on the part of *both* man *and* wife to carry out the act; what merits repudiation by the Church is the effort to prevent conception while intentionally *carrying out* the conjugal act. This understanding of what Pius XII says here is consistent with a previous statement of his almost immediately after World War II, when he spoke to the Italian Medical-Biological Union of St. Luke:

> The sexual union is a natural power of which the very Creator Himself has determined the structure and the essential forms of activity with a precise purpose and with corresponding duties to which man is obligated *in every conscious use* of this faculty... The primary goal... willed by nature itself *in this use* is the propagation of life... The Creator Himself, for the good of the human race, has joined the *voluntary use* of that natural energy (of sexuality) to the goal which is inherent in it.[89]

The act which Pius XII, developing the teaching of his predecessor, is here discussing, then, is an *act* which is *conscious,* i.e., one in which man's *will* and *intellect* are involved. We must conclude, then, that not only are we free to hold that Pius XII did not mean to condemn the use of artificial means to avoid pregnancy from acts *unjustly forced* upon a wife by her husband, but that indeed his teaching clearly points precisely in the direction of the liceity of such self-defense.

b) Pius XII On Sterilization

We now pass to the issue of *sterilization* as it is treated in the discourses of Pius XII. In 1953, he spoke to the Twenty-Sixth Congress on Urology, and touched on the issue of female sterilization. The Pope rejected the argument from totality as a way of justifying such sterilization, even for the sake of avoiding a truly dangerous pregnancy. He pointed out that the danger to the mother's life which would justify sterilization must be a danger coming from some organs of the body itself, and not from a free act of her own will. If her own imprudent but *free* decision to have sexual relations is going to be the source of a serious health problem for her, then the moral solution is, not mutilation, but the free rejection of that imprudent decision.

> To justify the removal of the ovaries the principle of totality is brought in, and it said that it is morally permitted to intervene in healthy organs when the good of the whole body requires it. But here one is appealing erroneously to this principle. For in

---

[88]*ibid.,* p. 162: "... nel compimento dell' atto conigale..."

[89]To the Catholic Medical-Biologists, DISCORSI, p. 52-53: "È una potenza naturale, di cui lo stesso Creatore ha determinato la struttura e le forme essenziali di attività con fine preciso e con corrispondenti doveri, ai quali l'uomo è sottoposto *in ogni consciente uso* di quella facultá... Lo scopo primario... voluto dalla natura *in questo uso*, è la propagazione... Il Creatore stesso, per il bene del genere umano, ha legato *l'uso voluntario* di quella energia naturale al loro scopo immanente." (emph. add.)

> this case, the danger which the mother experiences is not coming directly or indirectly from the presence or the normal functioning of the fallopian tubes... The danger does not show up *unless freely chosen sexual activity* causes a pregnancy which would be menacing...[90]

Thus we can see that the sterilization which Pius XII rejected was a sterilization which was *not necessary* because the woman's health could be provided for not by violating the wholeness of the body, but by exercising her *free will* in an act of rational decision. Such as exercise of the free will is, of course, the highest expression of one's personal dignity. That dignity Pius XII was not willing to see submerged in an avalanche of technological "solutions" such as sterilization. The *implication* of this reasoning is, of course, that where an act of free will on the part of a woman, inside or outside of marriage, to *abstain* from sexual actions *will not and cannot* avoid the serious problems which Pius XII's talk envisages then she *may* indeed resort to sterilization. In a given case, of course, such could be precisely the dilemma of a wife forced unjustly to copulation by her husband. Whether the danger she seeks to ward off *must* be a *physical* danger such as Pius is here discussing, or whether it *might* also be an affront to her profoundly personal *rights* is an issue we will discuss when we treat Pius XII's teaching on totality. For now it suffices for us to see that he does indeed leave open the possibility for a woman to opt specifically for sterilization *if* there is no other less drastic remedy available for her *free choosing*.

In 1958, in his talk to hematologists, Pius XII once again pointed to this same opening for development. Here he concedes the liceity of taking anovulant pills to control exaggerated sensitivity and reactions of the ovaries or uterus. He condemns, however, the use of such drugs in order to prevent a pregnancy which the uterus or the entire organism of a woman is not able to carry to term. It is to be noted, however, that in making both the concession and the condemnation, he speaks in the context of the woman's *wanting* to continue sexual relations with her husband.

> Is it allowable for a married woman (to prevent ovulation) when, in spite of the temporary sterility, she *desires to have relations* with her husband?[91]

Though this formulation does not speak of the wife who desires for good reason *not* to have relations, it nonetheless clearly points toward a wife's right under certain circumstances of grave injustice to use even sterilization to protect her own personal dignity and rights which that dignity implies.

---

[90] To Urologists, DISCORSI, 291: "Pour justifier l'ablation des oviductes on allègue le principe cité tantôt, et l'on dit qu'il est moralement permis d'intervenir sur des organes sains, quand le bien du tout l'exige.
Ici cependant on en appelle à tort à ce principe. Car en ce cas, le péril que court la mère ne provient pas, directement ou indirectement, de la presence ou du fonctionnement normal des oviductes ni de leur influence sur les organes malades, reins, poumons, coeur. Le danger n'apparaît que si l'activité sexuelle libre entraîne une grossesse qui pourrait menàcer les organes susdits trop faibles ou malades."

[91] To Hematologists, DISCOURSI, p. 706: "È ciò permesso alla donna maritata la quale, malgrado questa sterilità temporanea, *desideri avere rapporti* col proprio marito?" (emph. add.)

The same must be said of the point which Pius XII then treats immediately in this same 1958 discourse: the need at times to "space" i.e., to postpone a pregnancy for several years after a delivery, be it for health, financial, or other sound reasons. Here once again, the Pope condemns the taking of "the pill" also for this purpose. He condemns it, however, in the *original context* expressed at the beginning of the paragraph, namely, that of the wife who *desires* to have sexual relations.

In this context, then, of a wife's desire for relations, sterilization is categorized as "direct" and is condemned. This leaves open entirely the question of the woman who must avoid a pregnancy for serious reasons, but who cannot obtain the willing cooperation of her husband regarding, e.g., the use of Natural Family Planning, and indeed, has sexual actions forced upon her physically or psychologically. We would maintain further that the formulation used by the Pope here not only raises this question, but indicates what the anwer should be.

Several paragraphs later, after encouraging the moral use of the "Ogino-Knaus" method, the Pope capsulizes his teaching both on contraception and on sterilization. Here once again, he clearly indicates the limits of his condemnation of the abuse of these practices:

> We have made it clear in our allocution of 1951 that married people *who make use* of their conjugal rights have the positive obligation, in virtue of the natural law as it is proper to their state of life, not to exclude procreation.[92]

It is obvious, we maintain, that a wife who is having sexual actions unjustly forced upon her can, in no basically *human* sense of the phrase, be said to "make use" of her conjugal right.[93] Nor can her husband be said to do so, a point we shall explore below.

c) Pius XII On Totality.

We have now seen what Pius XII says about *contraception* and about *sterilization*, as it relates to our thesis. But a third theme in his discourses influences our thesis: the *principle* of *totality*. The principle is treated by him from the very beginning of his discourses, and is referred to over and over again in the years of his pontificate.

Although there is considerable clarification which comes by repetition over those years, the essential elements of the principle are present even as early as his discourse to the Italian Medical-Biological Union of St. Luke in 1944. Among these essential elements are the following:

1) Man has a limited, but *direct* power over the parts of his body and their functions, as regards his cultivating them or suppres-

---

[92]*ibid.* p. 709; "Abbiamo precisato che gli sposi *che usano* dei loro diritti coniugali, hanno l'obbligo positivo, in virtù della legge naturale propria del loro stato, di non escludere la procreazione." (emph. add.)

[93]The revised Code of Canon Law of 1983 specifies that valid consummation must be *"humano modo"*. Cf. Canon 1061.

sing them. The power is *direct,* that is, a person may, for instance, suppress a part or function of his body as a means *directly* chosen and *directly* implemented for achieving the overall health of the body. There must be, of course, a reasonable proportion between the harm suffered by this *direct* suppression and the good achieved.[94] Man is *not* limited, however, to an *indirect* power, that is, to simply *permitting* or *tolerating* the suppression of certain organs or functions as a by-product of some good or indifferent action which he might undertake for serious reasons. In other words, the principle of totality is not the same as the principle of double-effect.[95]

2) Man has this power over the *parts* of his body and over their functions because he has, more basically, a direct though limited power over *the body itself* as a totality.[96] The power he has over the parts flows from his power over the totality, and *not vice-versa.* Thus, on the one hand, a man may destroy one part of his body for the sake of keeping the whole body alive, *if there is no other way to keep the whole body alive.*[97] He may for instance allow himself to be surgically castrated if the testicles are diseased. But he may also permit this even if they are *not diseased* and their continued *normal* functioning is feeding cancer growth elsewhere in his body. On the other hand, he may not destroy his *whole body* in the process of keeping *one part* alive, however desirable that otherwise might be in some situations. Thus, he cannot give his heart for transplant into the nation's president or into some great scientist who will die without this transplant, if the would-be donor needs the heart to stay alive himself. Nor could one take a heart thus needed from a mental retardate. In these instances, the ultimate natural purpose of the heart would be frustrated, namely, to serve the bodily well-being of the individual to whom it *belongs.*

3) Just as *truly* (though *not* in the *same way*) as the *parts* are subordinated to the good of the *whole* body, so also the body is subordinated to the good of the *person* as a *totality.* This implies that the whole body is to be used to achieve highly *personalistic* goals. By "personalistc goals" we mean goals which can be reached only by the exercise of those powers specifically characteristic of a *person,* i.e., the intellect and the will. These are powers given to persons by God in order that they may

---

[94] Cf. Zalba, *Compendium...*, Vol. I, n. 1580.

[95] Cf. O'Donnell, Thomas, *op. cit.,* p. 66. "It is to be noted that in such cases (of removing a part of the body which is diseased) there is no need of involving the principle of double-effect." Cf. also Zalba, *Compenium...*, *op. cit.,* n. 1574, under "Etiam tamquam..."

[96] To Urologists, DISCORSI, p. 198

[97] Cf. Zalba, *loc. cit.* supra in note 94.

attain necessary *knowledge* and make *decisions* expressive of love for neighbor, self, and God. This subordination of the whole body to these personalistic goals is *different* from the subordination of the *parts* of the body to the good of the *whole body*, in that man has the right to *destroy* parts of the body for the sake of the whole body. He does *not,* however, have a right to destroy the *body* as a whole for the sake of achieving personalistic goals.[98] Thus, in addition to the examples of heart transplant we gave in 2) *(supra),* we might note also that it would be wrong for a man to commit suicide in order not to reveal military secrets to his captors. The personalistic goal (loyalty), excellent in itself, cannot ever justify the actual destruction of the whole body.

4) Neither the individual himself nor anyone else may licitly aim to destroy the bodily life of an innocent person either as a means or as an end. One may, of course, perform surgery for the overall good of the innocent person himself (as in 1) supra), provided that he give his consent, insofar as that is possible.[99]

5) Because the *body as a totality* is thus truly, but limitedly, subordinated to achievements possible only to a *person,* so also the *parts* of the body and their *functions* may, for proportionately serious reasons, be used for the sake of achieving *highly important personalistic* goals. *Unlike* the life of the *body as a totality,* however, and *only* in cases where there is *no other way* to achieve these highly personalistic goals, these *parts* may be *suppressed* or *totally destroyed* if this is a *necessary* step to achieving proportionately worthwhile personalistic goals. In these cases, however, there need not necessarily be any direct physical benefit to the *body itself as a whole.* (As we said in 3) above, however, its life as a whole may not licitly be destroyed in the process of achieving the desired personalistic goals.) Thus, a healthy person may undergo medical experiments which in no way are meant to benefit *his own* total bodily health. Such experiments may indeed in some degree supress some function or damage some organ. But this is *licit* if proportionately worthwhile *personalist* achievements of increased knowledge and, above all, greater *help* for *the desperately sick* would result. For similar reasons, persons who have two healthy kidneys may give a kidney to other persons who have lost both of theirs.[100]

---

[98] To Plastic Surgeon, DISCORSI, p. 722

[99] To Pharmacologists, DISCORSI, pp. 695-696

[100] *ibid.;* We shall examine this passage more at length below. The important point is that Pius XII here, without raising any objection, discusses the voluntary experimentation on one's own body for the sake of advancing scientific knowledge which is truly needed for the relief of suffering. Although as far as we can discover, Pius XII did not approve the donation of living organs for transplant, neither did he reject it; and the principles he gives in this allocution for experimentation clearly allow at least a limited disposition of one's body for the physical welfare, *not of one's self, but of another.*

These elements, in principle, show themselves in the 1944 discourse we mentioned above, where Pius XII says:

> Man is in fact not the owner of his *body*; he is not absolute lord of his *body*. To the contrary, he has nothing but the use of *(è... l'usufruttuario)* of his *body*. From *this* fact there derives a whole series of principles and norms which regulate the use and the *right* to *stewardship (disporre)* over *organs* and *members* of the body. Limited though it is, this power of stewardship is a *direct power,* because these are constitutive *parts* of his physical being.[101]

Thus it is clear: 1) that man's power of stewardship over his whole body is *direct*, and not merely *indirect*; 2) that this power over the whole body is the source of his power over the *parts* of his body, and not vice-versa; and 3) that this power, though real, is limited.

In 1955 Pius returns to this theme of totality in his discourse to the Twenty-Sixth Congress of Urologists. Here he makes it clear that not only diseased organs may be removed, but also healthy ones, because *man's whole body* is subject to *direct*, even though limited *powers* given to *him as a human being* by his Creator.

> Three things condition the moral liceity of a surgical intervention which involves an anatomic or surgical mutilation: 1) that the keeping or functioning of the particular organ within the totality of the organism is provoking in the organism serious damage or is constituting a menace; 2) that this damage cannot be avoided or at least notably diminished except by the mutilation in question, and that the effectiveness of the mutilation is reasonably assured; and finally 3) that one can reasonably assess that the negative effect, that is the mutilation and its consequences, will be compensated for by the positive effect: suppression of the danger to the whole organism, mitigation of pains, etc.
>
> The decisive point here is *not* that the organ amputated or rendered incapable of functioning be *itself diseased,* but that to maintain it or its functioning involves directly or indirectly a serious menace for the whole body . . . *If there is no other means available,* then surgical intervention on the healthy organ is permitted.
>
> *This conclusion which we want to draw is deduced from the right of making decisions which man has received from his*

---

[101] To Catholic Medical-Biologists Union of St. Luke, DISCORSI, p. 46 "L'uomo invero non è il proprietario, il signore assoluto del suo corpo, ma soltanto l'usufruttuario. Da qui deriva tutta una serie di principi e di norme che regolano l'uso e il diritto di disporre degli organi e delle membra del corpo. . . Per quanto limitato, il potere dell'uomo sulle sue membre e sui suoi *organi* è un potere *diretto,* perche essi sono *parti* constitutive del *suo essere fisico.*" (emph. add.)

Creator in regard to his own body in accord with the principle of totality...[102]

The Pope then goes on to reject the removal or deactivating of healthy genital organs (e.g., the fallopian tubes) in order to solve medical problems being caused by other parts of the body. His rejection of such sterilization, however, is confined to cases where these problems can also be solved by the *free exercise of a woman's will* in avoiding or limiting sexual relations. Although only *medical* disaster to the whole person is the subject of this and most other allocutions, there is, however, no reason to rule out the licit possibility of warding off *other* disasters even more offensive to the *human as a person* because they are a violation of his dignity. An obvious example of such a violation would be the commencement of pregnancy from a sexual oppression, be it inside or outside marriage. If such an oppression can be warded off by the exercise of one's free will, then that is, by reason of our human and Christian calling to be *free* and to act *freely,* the first line of defense. Where, however, the oppression is not subject to avoidance by an act of a woman's free will, - - where it is oppression in the full sense: rape or "quasi-rape" - - a woman with very good reasons intervenes in the functioning or, if necessary, even in the very existence of the organs of her reproductive system.

That the body as a totality is subordinated to the personalistic life of the individual is evidenced in a particularly striking way by Pius XII in his talk to the International College of Neuro-Psychic Pharmacology in 1958. After re-iterating briefly the doctrine that the parts of the body are at the service of the whole *body,* and that one part may be sacrificed for the good of the whole *body;* the Pope goes on to say that the whole body is itself subordinated to the *spiritual* purposes of the *person:*

> To this subordination of the particular organs to the *organism* and to *its* own purpose, there is joined also the subordination of the organism itself to the *spiritual purposes* of the *very person.*[103]

The Pope then proceeds to discuss how these spiritual purposes might be realized by healthy persons submitting to medical experiments along with sick persons. Such experiments, on the part of the healthy persons, are not, of course, to their benefit *physically;* as the Pope notes, they may even cause, not only a suppression of certain normal functions, but even some damage to the organs of the volun-

---

[102]DISCORSI, p. 289-290 "Trois choses conditionnent la licéité morale d'une intervention chirurgicale qui comporte une multilation anatomique ou fonctionnelle: d'abord que le maintien ou le fonctionnement d'un organe particulier dans l'ensemble de l'organisme provoque en celui-ci un dommage sérieux ou constitue une menace; ensuite que ce dommage ne puisse etre evité, ou du moins notablement diminué que par la mutilation en question et que l'efficacité de celleci soit bien assureé: finalement, qu'on puisse raisonnablement escompter que l'effet négatif, c'est-a-dire la mutilation et ses consequences, sera compensé par l'effet postif: suppression du danger pour l'organisme entier, adoucissement des douleurs etc.
La point décisif ici n'est pas que l'organe amputé ou paralysé soit malade lui-meme; mais que son maintein ou son fonctionnement entrâine directement ou indirectement pour tout le corps une menace serieuse...
Si l'on ne dispose d'auqun autre moyen, l'intervention chirurgicale sur l'organe sain est permise dans les deux cas. La conclusion, que Nous venons de tirer, se deduit du droit de disposition que l'homme a reçu du Createur à l'egard de son propre corps, d'accord avec le principe de totatité..." (emph. add.)

[103]To Pharmacologists, DISCORSI, p. 696; "Mais à la subordination des organes particuliers envers *l'organisme* et *sa* finalité propre, s'ajoûte encore celle de l'organisme à *la finalité spirituelle* de la *personne elle-meme.*" (emph. add.)

teers.[104] In spite of this, they may be perfectly licit because they conform to the good of the person in *another* way, which, evidently, is *not* a *physical* one.

> Medical experiments (physical ones and psychological ones) can, on the one hand, involve certain damages to the organs or the functions; but, on the other hand, it can indeed be that they are perfectly licit, because they conform to the *good* of the *person* and do not transgress the limits imposed by the Creator on the right of man to govern himself.[105]

The Pope then goes on to describe one such experiment which had been brought to his attention:

> These principles evidently apply to experiments in pharmacology. Thus we have been able to read in the documents sent to us the account of an experiment in artificial delirium to which 30 healthy persons and 24 mentally sick persons were submitted. These 54 persons, did they give their consent to this experiment, and in a manner adequate and valid according to natural law? Here as in other cases this question of fact must be submitted to serious examination.[106]

It is evident that the Pope is here concerned as to whether the 24 sick persons had given a true consent. But what are his moral objections to the 30 healthy persons who had submitted themselves to the experiment *freely* for *personalist* reasons, namely to add important knowledge to the science of the human mind for the sake of healing the sick? *The Pope indicates no objection whatsoever!* Evidently he saw the volunteers in this experiment as subordinating their bodily organism to the *spiritual* purposes characteristic of a *person*. This is in accordance with the very principle with which he began this consideration.

> To this subordination of the particular organs to the *organism* and to *its* own purpose, there is joined also the subordination of the organism itself to the *spiritual purposes* of the *very person*.

This is the reason why Pius could say: "Medical experiments . . . can be . . . perfectly licit because they conform to the good of . . . the person . . ."

Thus we see how Elements 3), 4), and 5) which were formulated above[107a] are realized in papal Magisterium: a) Man may subject parts of his body, not only to

---

[104]*ibid.*

[105]*ibid.* "Des expériences medicales physiques ou psychiques peuvent, d'une part, entraîner certains dommages pour des organes ou des fonctions, mais, d'autre part, il se peut qu'elles soient parfaitement licites, parce qu'elles sont conformes au *bien* de la *personne* et ne transgressent pas les limites posées par la Créateur au droit de l'homme à disposer de lui-meme."

[106]*ibid.* "Ces principes s'appliquent evidemment aux expériences de psychopharmacologie. Ainsi Nous avons pu lire dans les documents, qui Nous onte été transmis, le compte-rendu d'une experience de délire artificiel, a laquelle trente personnes saines et vingt-quatre malades mentaux onte été soumis. Ces cinquante quatre personnes ont-elles donné leur assentiment a cette expérience, et cela d'une manière suffisante et valable au regard du droit naturel? Ici comme dans les autres cas, la question de fait doit être soumise à un examen serieux."

[107]*Supra cit.* note 103

[107a]*Supra.* p. 58.

purposes of his own overall *physiological* good, but also to a morally good expression of himself as a *person,* capable of growing in *knowledge* and of making *decisions* worthy of a human being; b) Under certain circumstances, it may be a morally good expression of one's self as a person to actually *eliminate* a member or function of the body for the sake of a highly valuable personalist goal which cannot be obtained by the exercise of one's free will or in any less drastic way; c) The one absolute *limit* of this kind of stewardship is that one *may not take one's life* literally or equivalently.

There are also a number of other places where Pius XII makes clear that the body and its parts are ordered to the good of the *total* person, and not simply to his *physical* good. In this 1952 allocution to histologists, he writes:

> (Man may exercise stewardship over his body) when and in the measure required for the good of the existence of his totality. We have already explained at what point the personal right of the patient to make decisions about his own self, about his spirit, about his body, and about his faculties, organs, and their functions, comes up against very definite limits...
>
> The master and user of such an organism . . . can intervene, with that frequency and in that measure required for the *good of the entire totality,* to paralyze, destroy, mutilate, or separate the members . . . (The principle of totality) affirms that the parts exists for the whole, and that, as a consequence, the good of the part remains subordinate to the good of the whole; the whole makes determinations for the part and can make use of the part in its own interest.[108]

Finally, in 1958, he stated to the Tenth Congress on Plastic Surgery:

> Christian morality responds that (physical beauty) is a good, though a corporal one, ordered to the *total* human being...[109]

It is true that Pius XII makes most of these statements in order to make the point that these parts are ordered to the good of the total *somatic* dimension of man. But, in Pius' mind, the *reason* the total somatic aspect of man is to be thus served by a proper stewardship of the parts of the body is that this *somatic* dimension is a constitutive part of "the *total human being."* The *totality* of the *human being* is the *ultimate grounding* of man's right to use the parts of his body for the good of his somatic dimension. The question naturally arises, then: Does not *that same* grounding give him a right to make disposition of parts of his body to serve the even higher

---

[108] To Histologists, DISCORSI, p. 198: "Il peut disposer des parties individuelles pour les détruire ou les mutiler, lorsque et dans le mesure òu c'est nécessaire pour le bien de l'être dans son ensemble. . ."; p. 200: "Nous avons expliqué en quel point le droit personnel du patient à disposer de lui-meme, de son esprit, de son corps, de ses facultés, organes et functions, rencontre une limite morale"; p. 205: "Le maitre et usufrutier de cet organisme. . . peut intervenir . . . aussi souvent et dans la mesure òu le bien de l'ensemble le demande, pour en paralyser, détruire, mutiler, separer les membres". . . p.206: "Le principe de totalité . . . affirme que la partie existe pour le tout, et que par conséquent le bien de la partie reste subordenné au bien de l'ensemble, que le tout est determinant pour la partie et peut en disposer dans son interêt."

[109] To Plastic Surgeons, DISCORSI, p. 722: "La morale cristiana risponde che essa è un bene, ma corporale ordinato a tutto l'uomo . . ." (emph. add.)

good of his *spiritual* and *personal* dimension, namely his dignity, his obligations and his rights?

In the last quotation we have given (Pius' remarks on plastic surgery) the answer is obvious. Even more so it is obvious in his approval of limited experimentation in neuro-psychic drugs in 1958. What is obvious then is that a proper stewardship of parts of the body *need not be limited* to man's *physical* health, but may serve also his desire for acceptance in society through reasonable physical beauty *via* plastic surgery, and his desire to come to the aid of those who cannot be helped without a certain amount of experimentation to which healthy persons must willingly submit.

2. Teaching of the Roman Congregations, 1880-1960

We must now examine briefly a number of Magisterial documents of authoritative, if less weighty importance than the papal writings we have just seen, namely various decrees and responses of the Roman Congregations. These official acts of the Holy See, like so many theologians of the period, appear to some to touch in a negative way on elements essential to our thesis. As we shall see, however, careful analysis will show that this is not the case. We shall consider 1) some Responses of the Sacred Penitentiary and 2) some documents of the Holy Office.

THE SACRED PENITENTIARY

The Responses of the Sacred Penitentiary during this period touch on only the following points:

1) the legitimacy of periodic abstinence and the cautious steps a priest-confessor might take to encourage a couple to use this method to solve problems of family size (1880);[110]

2) the obligation of a priest-confessor to instruct persons as to the evil of onanism, and not to leave them "in good faith," where he has very good reason to be sure that they are practicing this vice (1880);[111]

3) the difference between a wife's cooperating with an onanistic husband (she *may* for *serious* reasons)[112] as contrasted with cooperating with a sodomitic husband (she *may not*, since her positive cooperation in an act perverted from the beginning is required.) (1916);[113]

---

[110] *E.S.* 3148
[111] *E.S.* 3185
[112] *ibid.*
[113] *E.S.* 3643

4) and the resistance a wife must put up against a husband who insists, not on onanism (withdrawal), but on condomistic copulation (she must resist as much as if she were being raped). (1916)[114]

These points do not treat of *forced* sexual acts at all, with the exception of the last Response which re-iterates a traditional comparison between forced condomistic copulation and rape. One 20th century manualist remarks that this comparison is not entirely irrelevant to our thesis.[115] We would agree: this comparison at least insinuates that there is at least one act within marriage which should be properly categorized "quasi-rape". The Response does not, of course raise the question of how a woman may morally avoid pregnancy from this act of "quasi-rape" since her husband's very purpose in forcing this condomistic act on her is to avoid pregnancy. The traditional doctrine expressed in the Response does, however, alert a woman to the ugly character of what her husband is demanding of her. One could hope pastorally that this blunt statement might even lead a condomist husband to wake up to what he is doing and repent of it.

The comparison comes as a shock, of course, to our societal prejudices and even to our civil law presumptions that "there is no such thing as rape within marriage." (The same thing could be said also, of course, of the remarks of Pope John Paul, which we have cited at the beginning of this study, regarding the possibility of a mans having an adulterous heart towards his own wife.) The fact, however, that there can be a clearly identifiable sexual violence within marriage, as this Response of the Sacred Penitentiary indicates, should alert us also to the possibility that there may be other forms of sexual violence within marriage. Our thesis maintains that there are indeed such, and that a wife has a right to defend herself against pregnancy from such acts just as truly as does a woman subject to rape outside of marriage.

THE HOLY OFFICE

Not only the Sacred Penitentiary, but also the Holy Office made a number of important points relevant to our thesis when, in a Response in 1936, it spoke out against Nazi sterilization laws. First, the Holy Office states that:

> The surgical operation by which sterilization is obtained is *not* indeed *'an action intrinsically evil as to its substance'*, and therefore can be licit if at times it is necessary in caring for a person's well-being or health.[116]

---

[114] *E.S.* 3638

[115] Zalba, "La portata..." p. 232: "Prescindendo dal *paragone* che fece più d'una volta la Santa Sede tra la *vergine che patisce violenza* e la *moglie* che si trova di fronte a un *marito* che ricorre *all' onanismo artificiale, il quale ci sembra attendibile anche per quanto riguarda al modo di premunirsi di fronte all' oppressione ingiusta,* vogliamo reflettere sulle espressioni della *Casti Conubii* e alcuni discorsi di Pio XII." (emph. add.)

[116] *E.S.* 3760

The Response is in line with what, as we have seen, Pius XII would say later[117] regarding man's *direct* power over his body and its parts. It makes clear that we need not deal with sterilization *always* as something which may only be tolerated as a regretted by-product of *some other licit* action which we are obliged to perform. In other words, the principle of totality is not the principle of double-effect. There are times when a sterilization operation falls under the principle of *totality* because it is a licit *means* which a person has a right to use in order to achieve an end within the scope of his own *human, but God-given authority*. There are other times when the sterilizing operations falls under the principle of *double-effect,* because this operation (*not* an intrinsic evil as to its physiological substance) *can become evil* when it is, equivalently, the exercise of *rights which one does not have.* Such would be the case where serious problems connected with any future pregnancy can be solved, not of necessity by mutilation, but by the *exercise of one's own free will* in abstaining from actions which can cause the problem pregnancy. It is *these* cases where mutilation is not within the rights of the patient or the doctor that sterilization may not licitly be *directly* intended, i.e., it does not fall under the principle of *totality.*

It must be admitted, however, that the Response quoted above could appear to present one problem for the thesis we defend. For the Response specifies only that *direct* power over an organ may be exercised by removing it for the sake of health *(sanitatem)* and welfare *(salutem),* but does not *further expand on the meaning of this.* "Health" certainly refers to *physical* health; but the meaning of "welfare" is not spelled out to include the exercise of one's higher (spiritual) powers or one's dignity as a person. It is obvious, however, that "welfare" *by no means excludes* one's spiritual welfare and personal dignity.

The common teaching of theologians that one might mutilate himself in order to escape from death which is *unjustly* threatened is, as an application of the principle of totality, left untouched here. That common teaching, however, is based not simply on saving one's *physical* life (for mutilation is not allowed to escape a sentence *justly* imposed, even if it is the death sentence), but on vindicating one's *rights* which are being violated by a death *unjustly* threatened.[118]

Surgical sterilization of a healthy reproductive system, then, "is not an action intrinsically evil as to its substance." This is the first note we draw from this 1936 Response.

Second, the Response states that:

> If the action is taken in order to impede the procreation of offspring, it is an action 'intrinsically evil *from a lack of right in the one who does it,*' since neither the private individual nor the

---

[117]Cf. *supra* pp. 71-72.

[118]Zalba, *Compendium...*, Vol. I, n. 1575

public authority has a direct lordship over the members of the body *which would extend that far.*[119]

At first, this might seem to rule out our thesis. But it is evident from what we have said immediately above that such is not the case. The Response does not deny that man has a "direct lordship" to mutilate a healthy member of the body, but that this lordship does not extend to *eugenic purposes.* If one would have any doubt about this, however, the passage immediately following removes the doubt:

> The doctrine proposed by the Sovereign Pontiff in explicit words is to be applied in its entirety to the *law of sterilization, which is what we are talking about.* The fact that by this law defective offspring are to be avoided for a *merely eugenic reason* (or rather for escaping economic problems or other evils of the kind) is not *ad rem,* nor does it make up for the *lack of right in a person who does such a thing.* Therefore this kind of prescribed sterilization operation must be said to be, and is, *intrinsically unjust.*[120]

> It is to be admitted, therefore, the purpose of this *law,* which is to achieve the *healthy state and strength of future generations* and *to avoid defective offspring* is not to be disapproved. Nonetheless the *object* of the law as a whole must be disapproved, i.e., the *means* which is prescribed to obtain this end.[121]

The remainder of the Response simply summarizes the above exposition, condemning both sterilization done outside of the *right* of the one who does it, and the existence and application of a *law* imposing it. There is no reference to the subject of our thesis: copulation unjustly forced on a wife by her husband. As a matter of fact, the Response leaves wide open and invites development of the question: If there is no other way to avoid a pregnancy unjustly forced upon her, may a wife go so far as to seek a sterilization?

The many and manifold dangers of self-deception and of other abuses in such a position are evident. These are serious pastoral and prudential questions which we cannot hope to settle here. But ours is primarily a question, not of prudence, but of principle; and the principle we advocate is in no way ruled out by the Response we have just examined.

Other documents of the Holy See must be treated in the same way as we have treated this Response of 1936. It is true that at first they may seem, in some of their

---

[119] E.S. 3760; "Si autem ideo peragitur, ut prolis procreatio, impediatur, est 'actio intrinsice mala *ex defectu iuris in agente*' cum neque homo privatus neque auctoritas publica directum in membra corporis dominium habeat *quod eo usque extendatur.*"

[120] *ibid.* "Haec a S. Pontifice explicitis verbis proposita doctrina ex integro *ad legem sterilizationis, de qua agitur, applicanda est.* Quod vero hac lege proles manca arcenda praescribatur ob finem mere eugenicum vel potius ad praecavenda damna oeconomica aut talia alterius generis mala, ad rem id non facit, neque supplet *defectum iuris in agente,* propterea *praescripta sterilizationis operatio* dici debet et est *intrinsece iniusta."* (emph. add.)

[121] *ibid.* "licet ergo finis *legis* qui est: *procurare valetudinem et robur futurae prolis,* et *arcere prolem mancam,* improbandus non est, reprobari debet ex integro legis *obiectum,* i.e., *medium* quod ad finem obtinendum praescribitur." (emph. add.)

phraseology, to completely rule out any physically direct sterilization; but on closer examination it is obvious that they rule out: 1) sterilization done by one who goes beyond the rights a person has to exercise stewardship over his own (or, derivatively, another's) body; and 2) (as one might expect in the Nazi era) sterilization done especially with a *eugenic* purpose in mind. Thus, the Holy Office answered again in a Decree of 1940:

> Is a direct sterilization, either permanent or temporary, licit, either for a man or a woman? No. It is prohibited by the law of nature, and in such a way as to include eugenic sterilization.[122]

Pius XII, in 1951, made it clear that this Decree referred to the sterilization of the *innocent*,[123] thus indicating once again how sometimes the formulation of an official reply can be misleading, since this Decree does not mention the context of "innocence". Indeed, for one reading these Decrees superficially, there is occasional evidence which could give the impression of that "physicalism" or "biologism" of which the Catholic moral tradition is often accused; but a more attentive study will simply not allow any such indictment.

One point of doctrine would, as we have indicated above in our treatment of Leo XIII's *Arcanum Divinum* but more especially Pius XI's *Casti Conubii*, favor our thesis: that conjugal love does in some sense have a primacy as a cause and element of married life. One decree of the Holy Office in 1944, however, touches this issue in what, again, might seem at first a position negative to our own.

> (In certain writings it is asserted) that the primary end of matrimony is not the begetting of children, or that the secondary ends are not subordinate to the primary end (of begetting children), but *are independent of it.* . .
>
> . . .Can the opinion of some recent writers be admitted who either deny that the primary end of matrimony is the begetting and raising of children, or else teach that the secondary ends are not subordinate to the primary end, but are equally primary *and independent?*
>
> No.[124]

In response to any interpretation here negative to our thesis, we would simply point out that this decree shows its true meaning by denying the *independence* of the two types of ends, procreative and unitive. It was only a primacy of the unitive over the procreational or an equality of these two *which allowed for their separation* (so

---

[122]*E. S. 3788:* "An licita sit directa sterilizatio sive perpetua sive temporanea, sive viri sive mulieris? Negative, et quidem prohiberi lege naturae, eamque quod sterilizationem eugenicam attinet. . ."

[123]To Midwives, DISCORSI, p. 163

[124]*E.S.* 3838; "(In nonnullis scriptis asseritur) finem primarium matrimonii non esse prolis generationem, vel fines secundarios non esse fini primario subordinatos, sed *ab eo independentes?*

"An admitti possit quorundam recentiorum sententia, qui vel negant finem primarium matrimonii esse prolis generationem et educationem, vel docent fines secundarios fini primario non esse essentialiter subordinatos, sed esse aeque principales *et independentes?:* Negative." (emph. add.)

that one could thereupon justify pursuing the one while suppressing the other) which the Church has condemned and which this Decree repudiates. This is indicated by the equation of the terms "equally primary" and "independent" *(". . . sed esse aeque principales et independentes.")* Moreover, as is well known, the terminology of "primary" and "secondary" ends was deliberately avoided by the Second Vatican Council, though the same Council insisted that the full sense of *both* mutual self-giving *and* human procreation be preserved within the context of true love.[125] Paul VI, in our judgement, made this formulation more precise by stating in *Humanae Vitae* that these two *meanings* must be maintained *inseparable* in the conjugal act.[126] Thus, the Decree which we are considering, both upon closer internal examination of its text, and upon appeal to subsequent authentic conciliar and papal interpretation of the tradition which the text represents, does not deny that some primacy in a true sense must be accorded to love within marriage. As we shall see in the next chapter, Pope John Paul II gives this same interpretation by describing the two meanings of marriage as joined to each other by "an inseparable connection" *(nexum indissolubilem).*[127]

The only other document of the Holy Office which might touch on the morality of sexual relations within marriage is a Monitum of 1952, which saw grave moral problems in the practice of *"amplexus reservatus".*[128] We would point out, once again, that the presupposition of this Monitum is that the husband and wife are of *one mind* in indulging in such a practice, and not that the wife is being forced to an act which she does not want and from which she is quite willing to abstain for the sake of respecting her (and her husband's) human sexual integrity. The Monitum, therefore, does not oppose our thesis.

We would close this section on the Magisterium's teaching during the period 1880-1960 by noting, once again, that there is simply no direct treatment of the subject of our thesis in the documents. Indeed, the documents leave gaps as to both the matters treated and principles cited - - gaps and principles which fairly beg for the development of our point. Moreover, the same Magisterium was particularly vigilant during this period as to the many new theories and techniques being offered as worthy of consideration and application in sexual life. The Church officially and forcefully rejected many of these theories and techniques as incompatible with human nature as the Church knows it in Jesus Christ. Yet the Church's teaching authority never moved to condemn the opinion of one of her most well known moralists, A. Schmitt, who for the first time in centuries proposed that a complete copulation was not morally untouchable simply by reason of the fact that it had taken place between husband and wife. She never rejected his teaching that there was possible, even within marriage, the kind of sexual oppression which would entitle a woman to use at least certain techniques in order to avoid a pregnancy. Any

---

[125] *Gaudium et Spes,* n. 51 in *E.V.,* Vol. 1, n. 1483.

[126] *Humanae Vitae,* n. 12, in *E.V.,* Vol. 3, n. 598

[127] *Familiaris Consortio,* n. 32, third paragraph.

[128] *E.S.* 3907

physicalist absolutism regarding copulation even *outside* of marriage had been demolished, of course, by the Magisterium's peaceful acceptance of Sanchez' position long before the 1950's. We hold then that, by explicitation or by implication, the principles which we maintained at the beginning of this section "B"[129] on the teaching of the Magisterium from 1880 to 1960 are elements truly acceptable within the Church's teaching, and have been shown to be so.

There was as yet, however, one other element of doctrine which needed to be expressed by the Church as her own doctrine: that God has made the conjugal act to be, in its very physiological nature, a unique *sign* or *expression* of conjugal love in all its unitive and procreative character. A truly ecclesial doctrine of the conjugal act as a *sign* will develop clearly, as we shall see, in the period 1960-1980. The development will show in the doctrine of Vatican II and of *Humanae Vitae*, and will reach perhaps its clearest statment in the teaching of Pope John Paul II after his consultation with the Bishops of the Sixth Synod in September, 1980.

C. Summary of the Period 1880-1960

Despite many and at times great obstacles, both within her own community and in the civil society of the world to which she is sent, the Church in this period made great progress both in her own self-understanding and in her *engagement* with the modern world. This progress was due in no small part to the Thomistic revival and the other theological enterprises promoted by Leo XIII, as well as to the efforts begun under Pius XII to meet the modern technological world in the midst of the contemporary problems in which it found itself.

In a clear and perhaps special way this progress touches our understanding of the nature of marriage and the meaning of sexual actions within marriage. Specifically, this progress prepares the way for the acceptance of the thesis we defend in the following ways:

1) The last traces of a merely "physicalist" vision of human copulation as a purely physiological action which is *ipso facto* absolutely morally inviolable disappear as Sanchez' position (developed somewhat beyond his views) is universally accepted.

2) The limitation of an oppressed woman to steps she may take only *after* a sexual assault outside of marriage is abandoned. (Fuchs).

3) The right and even the duty of a wife at times to refuse sexual actions is maintained and even developed in theology (Pius XII).

---

[129]Cf. *supra* pp. 57-58.

4) The right of a wife to use at least *one* method to avoid an unjust pregnancy is re-asserted after centuries of silence on the issue (A. Schmitt).

In all of this development, the Magisterium offers no resistance, and, indeed, contributes to it by the particular attention it gives, especially in the allocutions of Pius XII, to the principle of totality and its proper development and articulation.

Thus in the years 1960-1980, the stage is set for an acceptance, surprising to many, of the main point of our thesis. It was an acceptance which would be vocal on the part of a number of theologians who were unquestionably taking their inspiration from the teachings of the Magisterial statements of that period. It was also an acceptance tacitly encouraged by the Magisterium itself.

CHAPTER V:
SEXUAL OPPRESSION IN MARRIAGE AND A WIFE'S RIGHT TO DEFENSE AGAINST IMPREGNATION.

The thesis of this book is that a wife who is threatened by a pregnancy which may result from sexual actions unjustly forced upon her by her own husband may in some cases licitly resort to artificial means to avoid such pregnancy. Thus far we have seen in Chapter II that this thesis was considered from 1600 to 1750 by many theologians of that period as an *obiter dictum* to their treatment of *extra*-marital rape. Universally, with one exception (Bossius), the thesis was rejected, even among writers who accepted Sanchez' more lenient opinion regarding rape victims outside marriage. Moreover, throughout this and the later periods, no consideration was given to any intervention which even a rape victim might make except the expulsion of the semen. Thus no consideration was given explicitly to sterilization, barrier methods, etc.

After 1750, the issue altogether disappeared from discussion until, as we have seen, A. Schmitt in 1940 revived it by approving the expulsion of the semen for a wife who is sexually victimized by her husband. At the same time, however, he specifically rejected any steps she might take *beforehand* and *in view of* a sexual oppression which she sees as *likely* to occur from an abusive husband. Contemporarily with Schmitt, two authors (Zalba and Heinzel) rejected even this limitedly open position of Schmitt. Also during this same period, 1940-1960, other authors, who do not yet take up our issue, have already universally accepted the right of victims of extra-marital rape to expel the semen as best they can providing that there is no danger of actually aborting a fertilized ovum in the process; and at least one author (Fuchs) allowed for a woman who has good reason to fear the imminent danger of *extra*-marital rape to put a pessary in place prior to any actual attack in order to ward off any possible pregnancy.

From these developments up to 1960 comes the notable acceptance of our thesis among theologians, without any resistance on the part of the Magisterium, in the period 1960-1980, as we shall now chronicle it. Indeed, our study will show in this period not only no resistance from the Magisterium, but actually an ecclesial acceptance of a view of marriage which favors our thesis. This view is shared both by those charged with Magisterial responsibility within the Church as well as by theologians who work in obvious support of Magisterial positions.

One event of the early 1960's, sad as it was in itself, nonetheless furnished significant stimulus for a serious reconsideration of the essential meaning of the Church's teaching on contraception and sterilization: the plight of religious Sisters and other women caught up in the uprisings in the Belgian Congo. These women were given anovulant drugs by doctors on the missions in order to ward off pregnancy which might otherwise result from the rape which was a constant threat in that chaotic episode. Obviously the doctors who did this, and their moralist advisors, did not consider their action either contraception or sterilization in the sense in which the Church stood against such interventions for the prevention of pregnancy. Immediately, however, a debate arose among theologians on the issue.

The Magisterium, however, made no effort to intervene, it is to be noted, and, as we shall see, even quietly reviewed the case and tacitly accepted the actions of the mission doctors as being in harmony with the moral doctrine of the Church. Thus, to the surprise not only of many of the general public but also of many professional theologians, the case was made that, not only the use of pessaries and other similar devices whose liceity Fuchs defended for women threatened by rape, but also sterilization itself, at least of the temporary kind brought about by "the pill", is a licit line of defense against pregnancy from sexual oppression, at least outside of marriage. Of necessity this point had to be made regarding victims of sexual oppression outside of marriage before it could be applied to wives victimized within marriage. Indeed, the establishment of this point not only cleared the way for the acceptance of the thesis of this book, but even "by the very dynamic of logic", as one author expressed it,[1] *impelled* the acceptance of the thesis, at least in many theologians' minds. At the same time, authors who contributed to this development admitted that much misunderstanding and dispute in this matter was caused by inconsistency in the use of such terms as "direct sterilization", and called for a realignment of our terminology in this regard.[2]

A. Authors 1960-1980

A surprising number of authors in the 1960's accepted our thesis, both prior to and after the appearance of Pope Paul VI's Enclyclical Letter *Humanae Vitae* in 1968. While a large number of theologians who subsequently rejected the teaching of that encyclical on the point of contraception and of sterilization would today have no objection to an abused wife's using these artificial means to avoid pregnancy, we will not consider the opinions of these dissenting writers. For, in our judgement, their opinions are based on some form or dirivative of situationism. Not only does the present writer not accept this or any other approach which denies exceptionless moral prohibitions, but such an approach puts its proponents outside the scope of this study. There are, however, several theologians who, though they did eventually dissent from basic teachings of *Humanae Vitae*, yet favored our thesis at a time before *Humanae Vitae* when we cannot discover any trace of the dissent which was to show itself later (Fuchs and Häring). We shall therefore include them as proponents of our thesis within the limits we have stipulated for this study.

Well in advance of the publication of *Humanae Vitae* and up to the very year of its appearance, a number of authors explicitly accepted our thesis in substance. It should be obvious, then, that we are not somewhat belatedly attempting to soften what some might consider the "hard saying" of *Humanae Vitae*. For the substance of the point we here defend was taught at least eight years before the encyclical, and indeed by many who defended the doctrine of the encyclical before that encyclical even appeared, as well as afterwards. The point we are making, then, was a logical, if somewhat sudden, development of a line of thinking long in preparation among orthodox theologians.

---

[1]Zalba, "La portata...", p. 231

[2]Palazzini, "Si può e si deve proteggere l'equilibrio della persona", *Sutdi Cattolici*, 27 (1961) p. 64

In his 1963 edition of his *De Castitate et Ordine Sexuali,* Joseph Fuchs adds an important paragraph to previous editions:

> The arguments which we have presented for the rights of a woman rape victim lead some authors, not without reason, to attribute the same rights to a wife who -- in the case where she was not obliged to render the debitum -- has undergone a *true violence* (physical or moral) of her *husband* (v.g., a drunk one).[3]

The only difficulty one might note with this position of Fuchs is that, at first, he seems to be allowing this kind of defense only *after* the "true violence" has taken place, whereas our thesis is that an abused wife may take such measures even *beforehand,* if necessary.

Just two paragraphs above this statement, however, where Fuchs is presenting "the arguments for the rights of a woman rape victim", he includes the right of a woman in imminent danger of being raped to place a pessary in position or to take sterilizing pills *before* the attack:

> Thus in the same way (as a woman raped may seek to expel the semen after the attack) a woman in danger of being raped may licitly prevent fecundation by placing an occlusive pessary or by the use of pills which temporarily sterilize.[4]

What Fuchs says here about the unmarried woman, then, we must presume he intends also for the abused wife, namely, that she may take measures *prior to* and *in view of* a copulation which she forsees will be unjustly forced upon her.

Fuchs also reflects the growing theological consciousness of the importance of the conjugal act's being a genuine expression of *love*, at least in a substantial and virtual way:

> Without any personal love no motive by itself suffices (for the conjugal act); without it there is always sin, at least venial. Not even the intention of having a child suffices. For even then the act would be a "using" of another person as a means to the end of begetting a child. But the more the charity pervades the act the more the couple act humanly.[5]

Another author, Hermes Peeters, OFM, in his *Manuale Theologiae Moralis,* written in 1963 for, it seems, a primarily missionary application to problems in undeveloped countries, also espouses our thesis. He writes:

---

[3]Roma, 1963, p. 93: "Argumenta, quae pro iuribus mulieris oppressae attulimus, adducunt aliquos auctores, non sine ratione, ad attribuenda eadem iura uxori, quae – in casu quo non erat obligata ad debitum reddendum – *veram violentiam* (physican vel moralem) *mariti* (v.g., ebrii) subiit." (emph. add.)

[4]*ibid.:* "Similiter mulier in periculo ne opprimatur appositione pessarii occlusivi vel usu pillularum temporarie sterilizantium licite foecundationem praevenire potest."

[5]*ibid.* p. 119: "SINE ULLO AMORE PERSONALI nullum motivum solum sufficit; secus ibi semper est peccatum, saltem veniale. Neque sufficit sola intentio prolis; nam etiam tunc actus fieret "usus" alterius personae tamquam medii ad finem generationis. Atque quo magis caritas positionem actus pervadit, eo humanius coniuges agunt."

> What a woman violated in rape can (licitly) do . . . must be said also of a wife forcefully oppressed by a husband who has lost his right to copulation. The opinion of Noldin, however, does not seem correct. . . (when he says:) "I would not, however, allow for a wife to put into place a pessary *before* some feared aggression (from her husband) because it would make the act against nature from the beginning." But to put a pessary in place is not an act against nature. What is against nature is to put a pessary in place and *then to allow copulation.* But this is not what the woman is doing in the case we are discussing. Therefore, if it is licit for her to defend herself against the semen by a douche, it is not apparent why this would not be licit for her by using a pessary. You might perhaps object that there is some danger that she will afterwards consent, and that then the prevention of conception will become illicit; and that, if she does change her mind and consent, she can licitly do so by simply not using the douche, whereas once the pessary is in place an illicit act is unavoidable. To this I answer: If the danger of such a consent on the part of the woman is forseen, then the use of the pessary is illicit; if there is not such danger foreseen, then it is licit.[6]

Peeters mentions adultery, drunkenness, insanity, venereal disease, and legal or mutually agreed separation as reason why a man might lose his right to copulation. His treatment of these reasons is quite brief, however, and there is no cause to think that he would limit it strictly to these reasons.

Bernard Häring, who was silent on our question in his first edition of the *Law of Christ* in 1959, writes in his 1966 English edition, revised immediately after the end of Vatican Council II:

> Vaginal douches. . . are a frustration of the natural fruitfulness of intercourse. . . and hence considered as gravely culpable. But they would be lawful in instances when a woman is raped by a man not her husband and (according to many theologians) also if she is 'raped' by a drunken husband.[7]

The last line and a half was added by Häring to his 1959 treatment of postcoital douches. It must be admitted that Häring's treatment is a rather brief repetition of the usual justification for such douches, and does not enter into further application of the principles fundamental to the question. For example he does not

---

[6]Roma: "Quid possit mulier stupro violata, cf. supra, n. 325. Idem dicendum videtur de uxore vi oppressa a marito qui ius copulae perdidit (n. 352). Non tamen recta videtur sententia Noldin (IV, 69): "pessarium autem ponere antequam talis aggressio timetur, non permitterem uxori, quia faceret actum ab initio contra naturam". Pessarium ponere non est actus contra naturam, sed contra naturam est pessario posito copulam *admittere;* hoc autem mulier in casu non facit. Quodsi ei licet sese contra semen defendere lotionibus, non apparet cur hoc non similiter liceret pessario; nisi forsan dicas: est periculum ne postea consentiat et tunc impedire conceptionem fit illicitum, quod ommittendo lotiones vitari potest, sed posito pessario vitari non potest; ad hoc respondeo: si periculum talis consensus praevidetur usus pessarii esset illicitus, secus autem licitus."

[7]Philadelphia, Vol. 3, p. 360

treat the use of a pessary put into position beforehand or of any kind of sterilization (permanent or temporary) for a woman *threatened* by rape *outside* of marriage; *a fortiori*, as one might expect, he does not speak of such options for an abused *wife*.

Jan Visser, CSSR, edited the 1967 edition of the Aertnys-Damen classic manual, *Theologia Moralis*, and included, for the first time in any edition of that manual, the following:

> May a wife if she refuses the debt justly because of fear of evil for any offspring or even for herself should she conceive again, render herself sterile?
>
> The case is not treated *ex professo* by the authors, but rather as an *obiter dictum* on the occasion of disputing about the right of a woman who fears unjust aggression from a man *not* her husband to defend herself against an unjust imposition of an offspring who would be illegitimate. . . Those who deny such a right to women in general in regard to rape *a fortiori* hold that such defense is illicit for a wife towards her own husband. Among the others (who admit the right of the rape victim to defend herself from pregnancy), however, there is no consensus. Some (of the latter writers) are inclined to say *no,* (that she may not take steps to ward off a pregnancy from a carnal act unjustly imposed on her by her own husband). They reason that, although in this concrete instance the husband unjustly asks for the conjugal act, he preserves nonetheless his fundamental right to her body, a right which includes all that is necessary for the begetting of a child. Others, however, are inclined to say *it is licit*, because whatever there is of the man's fundamental right, certainly here-and-now he has no right to ask, and therefore the wife has the right (and perhaps the obligation) of refusing; and if he tries to extort the act from her, she has a right to consider herself as if she were a virgin being violated.
>
> This latter position seems to be quite probable, but *in practice* can be applied *only rarely*. For it is required: a) that a man ask for relations in a way which is *definitely unjust* because *procreation* would be *unreasonable*. But it is obvious from the answers which we have previously given that, if the necessity of abstaining brings with it the grave danger of incontinence or if it brings grave burden (which ordinarily is the case if it has to go on for a long time), then the obligation of abstaining does not bind, and therefore the man does not ask *unjustly*. (It is true that in thus asking for his *just* rights, the man may at the same time offend against *charity*. But an offense against *charity* does not of itself bring a loss of a *right*.) There could be a case, however, v.g., if a man is drunk, or if it is outside the sterile period of the month and periodic abstinence is quite possible for

the couple; b) that the wife absolutely does not want to engage in the sexual act and does not consent to its pleasure; c) that the wife resist the husband as would a virgin being violated, i.e., giving away to the act *only passively* (if because of an extremely grave burden which threatens her she cannot escape it) as is the case when a man uses a condom...

For when she places an obstacle to conception, at no point may she intend the conjugal act which is apt for procreation.[8]

Thus Visser in this most extended treatment of the issue up to that time in the 20th century takes a rather cautious approach, but in no way rules out our thesis either in principle or in practice. Quite to the contrary, he clearly accepts it. Even the emphasis he puts on the requirement that the man's request be "definitely unjust" refers to his own and the common teaching that a man has some kind of an obligation not to demand relations from a wife who is, e.g., chronically and seriously ill. Such teaching holds, however, that he may, without injustice, *ask* such relations, and the wife *may* (not must) licitly grant such relations despite some grave *but not fatal* burdens it might bring upon her. She especially may grant sexual relations under such burdensome circumstances if her sickness is causing *prolonged* abstinence, and thus creating a serious temptations for a husband who, no matter how good a man his is, is nonetheless weak in sexual self-control. Indeed she may in these cases where abstinence would become an almost perpetual thing be *obliged* out of charity or even out of justice to have sexual relations, though Visser does not expand on the charity-justice distinction enough to clarify the distinction in practice.

Cautious as Visser's approach is in the passage we have examined thus far, his conclusions, which follow immediately, make it clear that he has somewhat greater problems in accepting any kind of *sterilizing* action in such cases than he does in accepting the use of diaphragms, spermicides, and other "barrier" methods. Yet here once again he recognizes that in extreme cases such sterilizing (anovulatory) actions may indeed be the only possible recourse of a victimized woman:

---

[8]Roma, Vol. IV, pp. 289-290: "An uxor, si iuste debitum renuat propter timendum malum prolis, aut etiam proprium ex nova conceptione, possit se infoecundabilem reddere.

Casus non tractatur ex professo ab auctoribus, sed magis obiter tangitur occasione disputationis circa ius mulieris, timentis iniustam aggressionem ab *extraneo*, se defendendi contra iniquam impositionem prolis illegitimae (supra n. 309, Obic. 1). Qui hoc ius mulieri in genere abnegant relate ad talem aggressionem, a fortiori hoc illicitum tenent pro uxore erga maritum suum. Inter coeteros autem non est consensus. Quidam inclinant ad sententiam *negativam*, hac ratione quia, quamvis in casu concreto maritus iniuste petat actum coniugalem, conservat tamen ius radicale ad corpus uxoris ominbus requisitis praeditum ut possit prolem generare. Alii tamen inclinant *ad liceitatem*, quia quidquid sit de viri iure radicali, certo hic et nunc ipse ius non habet petendi, ideoque uxor ius (et forsan obligationem) habet renuendi; et si vir copulam vi extorquere vellet, ipsa se habere potest tamquam virgo violata.

Ultima sententia sufficienter probabilis videtur, attamen *in praxi raro* videtur applicari posse. Requiritur enim: a) ut vir *certo iniuste* petit *propter procreationem irrationabilem*. Ut tamen ex responsis ad praecedentes quaestiones patet, si necessitas abstinentiae grave periculum incontinentiae aut grave incommodum secum fert, quod ordinarie fit si per multum tempus perdurare deberet, obligatio abstinendi iam non urget, ideoque vir *non iniuste* petit. Laesio autem *charitatis* de se non causat amissionem *iuris*. Casus tamen haberi posset, v.g. si vir petit ebrius, aut aliquando extra tempus uxoris infoecundum, dum abstinentia periodica possibilis sit; b) ut uxor actum coniugalem omnino renuat et delectationi non consentiat; c) ut viro resistat tamquam virgo violata, i.e. actui cedens solummodo passive, si propter gravissimum incommodum minatum evadere nequit, eodem modo ac si vir uteretur condom (supra n. 322, II). Cum enim ipsa obstaculum conceptioni posuit, nullo momento intendere potest actum coniugalem aptum ad procreationem." (emph. add.)

From these principles it follows: 1) *Only in the rarest of cases* may a wife use *anovulatory* means for this purpose of self-defense. For in using such means she would intend to create a condition of infecundity which is *somewhat stable,* while at the same time the right of the husband to ask for relations *cannot be excluded* with such stability, especially in view of the danger of incontinency. Also the wife cannot be sure *with such stability* about *her own intention* of positively resisting and of maintaining a passive attitude; 2) Since in practice it is very difficult to deny to a husband his right of asking and even more difficult to dissent in the proper way from the act and from the pleasure, and to positively resist, it seems that *we should keep away from publicizing* a general type of right of this kind regarding a wife's self-defense.

It is to be noted also that certain other kinds of reasons (for justifying such self-defense) are excluded even though they are grave burdens for the wife, e.g., an excessive request for relations. Our argument here applies *only* to reasons for denying the act because of the *unreasonableness* of *begetting* a child (at this time.)[9]

We would note here that other authors and even one national conference of bishops will later observe the same kind of caution which Visser here evidences in presenting this kind of teaching, but not with the same intensity as does Visser.

Finally, in this period prior to *Humanae Vitae* we have the teaching of Marcellino Zalba, SJ, in an article which he published in August, 1968, almost on the eve of the encyclical.[10] We have followed the lead of Fr. Zalba in our previous chapter in which we analyzed Magisterial teachings, especially those of Pius XII, as those teachings could have reference to our thesis. We noted also in that chapter that Zalba had originally, in 1958, opposed the point we wish to make in our thesis. We shall here briefly review the 1968 article in which he made a substantial change in his thinking especially clear. We shall cite the passage in which, as a result of the kind of analysis of papal teaching which we have made in Chapter IV, he felt justified in revising his thought.

In his article, Zalba first reviews briefly the controversy which arose in 1961 over the giving of anovulant pills to nuns and other women during the uprisings in the Belgian Congo in 1960. He notes the surprise of many, even professional

---

[9]*ibid.:* "Ex hisce sequitur: 1) *rarissime* uxor in hunc finem defensionis uti posset mediis *anovulatoriis.* Per ista enim intenderet creare *aliquo modo stabilem* conditionem infoecunditatis, dum *non ita stabiliter excludi possit* ius petendi a parte mariti praesertim propter periculum incontinentiae; *nec ita stabiliter* certa erit de propria intentione positive resistendi aut passive se habendi.

2) Cum in praxi valde difficile sit in casibus concretis viro abnegare ius petendi ac difficilius adhuc debito modo actui et delectationi dissentire ac positive resistere, *abstinendum videtur a publica generica propositione* iuris talis defensionis quod uxorem spectaret.

Nota quod certo excludendae sunt aliae causae gravis incommodi, v.g., petitio immoderata, etc.; agitur de solis causis denegandi propter *irrationabilem* conceptionem prolis." (emph. add.)

[10]"La portata del principio di totalità nella dottrina di Pio XI e la sua applicazione nei casi di violenze sessuali", in *Rassagna di teologia,* Luglio-Agosto, 1968, n. 4, pp. 225-237.

theologians, at the willingness of many moralists to defend the action, and admits that he himself was among those who repudiated it in the controversy which followed the episode. Then he attempts to sum up the main point of his former opponents, a point to which he is now evidently converted:

> The direct sterilization condemned by the Magisterium as intrinsically evil is the direct sterilization ordered to the prevention of procreation in persons who *want* to exercise their sexual function, or who with perfect right are *obliged* to exercise it by reason of the marriage contract. The specific malice of a sterilizing action consists in *deliberately* positing actions between a husband and wife which are contrary to the dynamism of the sexual faculty. Where no such obligation of sexual activity exists, and where as a matter of fact there exists a contrary obligation to avoid sexual activity, and that obligation is upheld by a woman's decisive act of the will, may one not say that such a woman, under threat of being violated, acts morally in impeding a conception which she is determined will not take place, insofar as it depends on her?[11]

Zalba then examines some conclusions which A. Valsecchi attempted to draw from this same point, and rejects them as going "beyond the limits of logic" in trying to make a case for artificial contraception for a wife who *wishes* to be infertile for sexual relations which she *wishes* to have with her husband. Zalba immediately, however, continues on to admit that the arguments favoring artificial means of defending an *extra*-marital rape victim from a pregnancy's beginning as a result of the attack must, by logical necessity, apply also to the *wife* sexually victimized by her *own husband*.

> We think, nonetheless, that the conclusion which they wish to draw from the defense allowable to an *unmarried woman* in danger of violence, in favor also of the *wife unjustly violated* in her own marriage is logical and worthy of careful consideration.[12]

Zalba notes then that he and others had not been able, in 1961, to accept both the action taken by the doctors in the Belgian Congo case and a similar treatment of the plight of the abused wife. The obstacle, he now recognizes, was an incomplete understanding of the moral tradition of the Church as that tradition was expressed in the Magisterium of Pius XI and especially of Pius XII. He therefore undertakes a

---

[11] *ibid.*, p. 226: "La sterilizzazione diretta, condannata dal magistero come intrinsecamente cattiva, è quella ordinata a impedire la procreazione in soggetti che *vogliono* esercitare la funzione sessuale, o che a buon diritto potrebbero essere *obbligati* a esercitarla in forza del contratto matrimoniale; la malizia specifica dell 'azione sterilizzante consiste nel porre *deliberatamente* atti tra loro contrari nel dinamismo della facolta sessuale, cioè da una parte atti per loro natura - e, quindi, per divina disposizione - ordinati alla generazione, mentre dell'altra degli altri che ne impediscono gli effetti connaturali. Non esistendo nessun obbligo di attività sessuale, ma al contrario il dovere di evitarla, mantenuto da una volontà decisa, non si può dire che la donna in rischio di essere violentata ostacola moralmente una generazione che non può avvenire mai fisicamente per quanto dipende da essa."

[12] *ibid.*, p. 227: "Pensiamo, però, che la consequenza che si vuol dedurre dalla difesa concessa alla nubile in pericolo di violenza, in favore della moglie ingiustamente violentata nel matrimonio, sia logical e degna di accurata considerazione."

review which we have used in Chapter IV to guide us through the same pontifical teachings. He sums this pontifical teaching up under three headings:[13]

> 1) Man has a limited, though *direct* authority from the Creator over the members, the organs, and the functions of his body.
>
> 2) Man also has a limited, though *direct* authority over his *whole body.*
>
> 3) *Both of these powers,* i.e., that over the *parts* of the body and that over the *whole* body, are subject to the rightful needs of the *soul*[14] and above all the interests of the *person.*

Zalba recognizes that this third point is the one not well undertood by those (including himself) who objected to the procedures in the Belgian Congo case and to their application to the plight of the abused wife. He therefore proceeds to quote a number of papal texts where this third point is intimated, texts which we have already examined along with additional ones. He then concludes this review of papal teaching with the statement:

> We can assert with full conviction that pontifical doctrine does not exclude the putting of physical functions, even those which as functions are quite normal, at the service of the legitimate interests of the acting person *(soggetto).* This may be done in order to ward off from the *body itself* hardships which are being imposed upon the person contrary to the person's will. Or it may be done to deliver the *soul* and the *spirit* from calumny, rejection, societal difficulties, etc. Or it may be done so that the person may enjoy simply that *condition of liberty* which the person does not want to give up, either by a decision of his or her own, or by something done to the person without his or her decision by someone else's illicit conduct, the normal consequences of which (e.g., a pregnancy) the person would then have to accept.[14a]

It would seem that Zalba is here indicating an application of the principles of self-defense for the abused wife much wider than, as we have seen, Visser did. The latter author, it will be remembered, limited the use of this kind of self-defense entirely to the case where it would be *irrational to conceive another child,* and excluded other motives which might be used to justify a wife's resorting to artificial means to head off pregnancy. Visser seemed to exclude resort to such means where,

---

[13]*ibid.,* pp. 229-230

[14]Zalba seems here to be referring to the needs of the soul to have a balanced neurological system through which intellect and free will can function adequately. An organ which is disturbing such neurological balance could legitimately be removed or suppressed, if there is *no other way* to salvage basic integrity of psychic functioning. Frontal lobotomy would be one example of a possible case in point.

[14a]*ibid.* pp. 230-231: "Possiamo asserire con piena convinzione che la dottrina pontificia non esclude il servizio delle funzioni fisiche, anche in se normali, agli interessi legittimi del soggetto, sia a ragione di evitare all 'organismo corporale disagi che gli venissero imposti controvoglia, sia per liberare l'anima e lo spirito da diffamazione, disprezzi, difficoltà sociali e via dicendo, sia perche la persona possa godere semplicemente di quella situazione di libertà alla quale non vuole rinunziare, ne affettivamente ne effettivamente, con una condotta irregolare le cui consequenze normali dovesse accettare."

for instance, a husband is at the moment drunk, but, at this point of the marriage, there is no true reason why the couple could not reasonably accept another child. The repugnance the wife might feel in having relations with him in his drunken state, or her unwillingness to have a child conceived from *such* an act, would not, it would seem in Visser's thought, justify her resorting to artificial preventatives. The *begetting* itself of another child is *not*, in Visser's thought, at this moment in time an *irrational* act. As Visser put it:

> It is to be noted also that certain other kinds of reasons (justifying such self-defense) are excluded, even though they are grave burdens for the wife, v.g., an excessive request for relations. Our argument here applies *only* to reasons for denying the act because of the *unreasonableness of begetting a child (at this time)*.[15]

Zalba, to the contrary, outlines principles which seem to us to allow for a much wider, though always a properly discerned, application. Thus, Zalba speaks of a human being's having power to dispose of his various physical parts (including, obviously, his reproductive parts) not only for the sake of warding off physical evils to the whole organism, but also for the sake of delivering

> the soul and spirit from calumny, rejection, societal difficulties, etc.

or for the sake of safeguarding the person's right to

> enjoy simply that condition of liberty which the person does not want to give up either by a decision of his or her own or by something done to the person without his or her decision by someone else's illicit conduct the normal consequences of which (e.g., a pregnancy) the person would then have to accept.[16]

Is it an indignity for a woman to have to conceive a child from a husband who, in a state of drunkenness, forces himself on her? Or from a husband who, in a phase of moral regression, perhaps temporary, is insisting on sexual relations four or five times a day? In both of these, as well as in other similar instances, is the woman not faced with indignities of "soul and spirit" from which she may rightly defend herself by preventing the "normal consequences" which she would have to accept, i.e., a pregnancy begun under very sad circumstances? Visser, it would seem, definitely excluded such cases if (the here-and-now circumstances [drunkenness, lust] of the carnal act *not* being considered) it would *otherwise* not be unreasonable for this couple to conceive another child. Zalba, in contrast, at least incites the questions and seems to leave open the possibility of a positive answer.

Having established these basic principles from the teachings of Pius XI and Pius XII, Zalba then proceeds to their "logical application" to problems of sexual oppression. He makes four points:

---

[15]*supra cit.*, note 9. (emph. add.)

[16]*ibid., supra cit.*, note 14a.

1) That not only a douche or other effort *after* an attack of sexual oppression is justified, but also a *forearming* of the woman's organism is justified in order to ward off pregnancy, possible should a genuinely threatened attack actually take place.

2) That this forearming of the organism of a woman is justified not only for an unmarried woman threatened by rape, but *also for a wife threatened with sexual abuse within her own marriage.*

3) That a request for sexual relations which at a given moment of marriage are with certainty *unjust* is *in no way included* within the *marriage contract.*

4) That these three points above, of which Zalba is now persuaded contrary to his former views, are not only exempt from any previous papal condemnation, but are actually in *positive conformity* with papal teaching.

We shall briefly examine these points as Zalba makes them.

First of all, he makes the point that, in contrast to the opinion of A. Schmitt, who first re-opened this whole issue in 1940, and of others, who were involved in the "Belgian Congo controversy" which arose in 1961-1962, a woman threatened by rape may use means *beforehand* to render herself sterile, and thus to save herself from a pregnancy which might be unjustly forced upon her should the attack actually be realized.

> A consequence of this papal doctrine is, in our view, that opinion which we gave above on the liceity of *forearming,* within the organism, the *sexual faculty* against a damaging and unjust aggression or against its injurious consequences, whether these are by the submission of the *organism* to undue trials or risks, or by the submission of the *whole person* to such evils. These undue trials and risks a person *may impede (beforehand)* in the rightful stewardship of his or her natural functions with the same right which belongs to the person *(afterwards)* to *cast out* the unjust cause of these trials or risks. The supposition is that these trials and risks are a continuation of an injustice the person has undergone and that they do not injure any higher right of another person.[17]

---

[17]*ibid.* p. 231: "Consequenza, a nostro parere, di questa dottrina pontificia è quell'opinione suddetta, sulla liceità di *premunire* l'organismo, e in esso la *facolta sessuale,* contro un 'aggressione ingiusta e dannosa, o contro le sue consequenze nocive, sia per *l'organismo* sottomesso a travagli e rischi indebiti, che per *l'essere totale dell' individuo;* consequenze che la persona può *impedire* nella retta amministrazione della sue funzioni naturali con lo stesso diritto che gli compete per *scacciare* la causa ingiusta delle medesime, supposto che queste siano una continuazione d'una ingiustizia subita e non nuocciano a nessun superiore diritto altri." (emph. add.)

Here Zalba is clearly moving beyond a right *merely to expel the semen* ("cast out" - - *"scacciare"*) *after* an attack, to a right to *prevent beforehand* ("impede" - - *"impedire"*) the consequences of some future unjust presence of semen. He is also, in the last sentence, clearly excluding all actions, either prior to or consequent to an attack, which would be tantamount to an abortion. (These exercises of rightful stewardship must "not injure any higher good of another person.")

Not only does Zalba move beyond the previous position allowing only vaginal or uterine douche after a rape attack, but he maintains also that his *new position* is a *logical,* though indirect, *consequence* of the *previous* standard doctrine of theologians:

> The doctrine of very many prudent moralists who allow for a timely uterine douche to *expel* semen intruded by an act of violence provided such a douch includes no danger of an abortion) is an *indirect confirmation of this our opinion...* If it is not illicit to impede sperm introduced into the vagina violently from entering the ovum when the woman has undergone sexual violence, then we find no reason for not suspending ovulation for the same purpose and in the same circumstances of violent force. The nature of the act is the same, and the material means used are morally indifferent in themselves either by reason of the *object* (of the act) or by reason of the *circumstances*.[18]

Thus Zalba not only accepts the opinion that efforts to prevent pregnancy from a sexual aggression may be legitimately made before as well as after an attack, but also holds that such an opinion is in continuity with previous developments among moralists.

Zalba's second point is that efforts to prevent pregnancy by steps taken either before or after an act of sexual violence are open, not only to a woman attacked outside marriage, but *also to a wife* seriously abused within a marriage. He lists three requisites to justify this kind of defense: 1) that the wife *sincerely reprove* her husband for even attempting to force sexual actions upon her to her own or her children's grave detriment; 2) that she *at no moment approve* of the copulation or of the pleasure possibly experienced; and 3) that she have a *definite right* to refuse her husband, and *appeal* to that right on the basis of the injustice which he is inflicting upon her:

> Although one cannot insist enough on the absolute necessity that the woman *sincerely* reprove her partner for this evil action of his, without any *participation or taking pleasure* in the fact that it is happening, nonetheless we are of the opinion that it follows obviously, by the very dynamic of logic, that the case of

---

[18]*ibid.:* "La dottrina di moltissimi prudenti moralisti che permette di fare tempestivamente lavaggi uterini per *espellere* il seme intruso per violenza, è dunque, purche non vi sia pericolo di causare un aborto, *una conferma indiretta di questa opinione.* Se non è illecito impedire che la spermatozoo introdotto violentemente negli organi femminili investa l'ovulo, quando la donna ha subito violenza sessuale, non troviamo nessun motivo per sospendere l'ovulazione allo stesso fine e nelle stesse circostanze di violenta costrinzione fisca. L'indole dell' azione morale è la stessa, i mezzi materiali sono ugualmente indifferenti, perche nè l'uno nè l'altro hanno significato morale in sè stesso per l'*oggetto* che per le *circostanze.*" (emph. add.)

the unmarried woman who suffers sexual violence and the case of the wife who is living a married life are the *same.* Of course, this implies a decisive act of the will on her part, as well as a *right* which exists with *certainty* and is *invoked* by the wife with certainty and with all its logical consequences. (Note that we say that this right to refuse relations must exist with certainty;) and that, of course, it is a delicate point and one not easy to determine. It is the right to refuse a sexual relation which is being unjustly extorted by the husband.[19]

Working on this basis that there can indeed by times when the carnal act is unjustly demanded by the husband, Zalba then moves on to the third point in his "logical application" of the principles of papal teaching: that unjust demands of this kind are *not included in the marriage contract:*

> We insist: we are here dealing with a defense against an aggression which is with certitude *unjust* because the request *does not enter into the marriage contract.* (This unjust aggression) is not consented to internally. It is refused externally. It would be brought to nothing, were that possible (to the wife). At one time we were inclined to a contrary view, because it seemed to us that the husband had in such a case a basic right *(diritto radicale)* which he was violating only in the *mode* in which he was exercising it. Thinking better of it, however, it (now) does not seem to us rash or improbable to say that the husband has *no right whatsoever* to acts which are not the object of the conjugal contract. These acts (of unjust aggression) can therefore be compared to *extra-marital acts.*[20]

Zalba's fourth and final point in applying papal doctrine to our question is that his opinion is not only not excluded by papal statements, but is in *positive harmony* with them.

> This opinion of ours, howevermuch delicate and easily open to abuse and illusory thinking in actual practice, seems to us more in conformity with the doctrine of Pius XI and Pius XII (than our previous, more rigid opinion). We say "in conformity", not

---

[19]*ibid,:* "Pur avvertendo che mai si insisterà sufficientemente sull'assoluta necessità di *sincera* riprovazione della cattiva azione della comparte, senza *nessuna partecipazione* e senza *nessun compiacimento* nel fatto stesso, opiniamo per ovvia conseguenza che la dinamica della logica uguagli i casi della nubile che patisce violenza sessuale e della moglie che vive in matrimonio, però con la volontà decisa e col *diritto certamente esistente* e *certamente* da essa *invocato* con tutte le conseguenze (quando esiste questo diritto è di nuovo questione delicattisima e non da determinarsi facilmente) di rifiutarsi al rapporto sessuale, ingiustamente estortole dal marito." (emph. add.)

[20]*ibid.:* "Insistiamo: si tratta d'una difesa contro un'aggressione certamente ingiusta, perche la richiesta *non entra nel contratto matrimoniale;* che non si ammette internamente; che si rifiuta esternamente; che si annullerebbe se fosse possibile. Un tempo inclinavamo al parere contrario, perche ci pareva che il marito avesse in un tale caso un diritto radicale, che soltanto venisse violato in quanto al *modo:* pensandoci però meglio, non ci sembra ne temerario ne improbabile dire che il marito non ha *nessun diritto* agli atti che non sono oggetto del contratto coniugale; che può dunque, essere paragonato cogli *estranei al matrimonio."* (emph. add.)

> merely "not subject to rejection". Certainly we think that our opinion here expressed in no way departs from the natural law reasoning invoked by those popes to bring out the intrinsic malice of a true abuse of marriage, for this abuse consists, according to their very own explanation of it, in the fact of *deliberately using* the faculty and at the same time *frustrating* its natural purpose. This abuse, they argued, thus contradicts the divine plan, that is, the ontological orientation, the finality assigned to it by God in the actuation of our sexuality, the finality written right into the very way in which nature acts...[21]
>
> This argument of natural reason which is expounded by both pontiffs when they speak of the *use* of matrimony (when they are speaking, that is, of the *deliberate and free* actuation of the faculty) we think is expressly *limited* to this actuation precisely as *deliberate and free.* This limitation excludes, at least from their consideration, the case of the married woman who is undergoing an *unjust violence* on the part of her husband.[22]

We would close this consideration of Zalba's reversal of his previous opposition to our thesis by mentioning briefly his recognition of the realities of abuse to which this doctrine can be subjected.

> One cannot insist enough on the absolute necessity that the woman *sincerely* reprove her partner for this evil action of his, without any participation or taking pleasure in the fact that it is happening.[23]
>
> ... this right (to refuse intercourse) must exist with *certainty;* and, of course, that is a *delicate point,* and one not easy to determine.[24]
>
> This opinion of ours, however much *delicate* and *easily open to abuse* and *illusory thinking* in actual practice...[25]

---

[21]*ibid.*, p. 232: "E questa opinione, quanto mai delicata e facile ad abusi e illusioni nel suo pratico impiego, ci sembra in più conforme colla dottrina di Pio XI e di Pio XII; diciamo conforme, e non soltanto esente di riprovazione. Certamente pensiamo che non si stacca in nulla dall' argomento di ragione naturale da essi invocato per dimostrare la malizia intrinseca dell' abuso matrimoniale; perche questo abuso consiste, secondo la loro esposizione, nel fatto di usare *deliberatamente* la facolta e insieme frustrare il suo fine naturale, contraddicendo in questo modo il piano divino, cioè all' ordinamento ontologico, alla finalità da Dio assegnata all' attuazione della sessualità, quale iscritta nel modo d'agire della natura." (emph. add.)

[22]*ibid.:* "Questo argomento di ragione naturale che viene esposto comunemente dai pontefici quando parlano dell'uso del matrimonio (e quindi dell'attuazione *deliberata e libera* dells facoltà), pensiamo che ha avuto una *limitazione* espressa a questa attuazione proprio in quanto deliberata e libera, escludendo così almeno dalla loro considerazione il caso della donna sposata che subisce una violenza ingiusta da parte del marito." (emph. add.)

[23]*supra cit.* note 21.

[24]*supra cit.* note 19.

[25]*supra cit.* note 21.

25a

From these expressions, it is obvious that Zalba is aware of the dangers to which his teaching is open in actual pastoral practice. His emphasis, however, in contrast to that of Visser, is, in our judgement, one of positively promoting the peace of conscience and the defense of the dignity of wives, rather than of holding back information from the public out of concern for its possible misuse.

The authors we have treated thus far - - Fuchs, Peeters, Häring, Visser, and Zalba - - all write before the publication of *Humanae Vitae*, and their position favorable to our thesis continues after the encyclical appears.[25a] One might well surmise, of course, that Häring and Fuchs, after *Humanae Vitae*, would support it for reasons quite different from principles represented in the manual tradition. After the appearance of *Humanae Vitae*, however, three more authors adopt the position we are favoring: Christopher Derrick in 1969, Anselm Günthör, OSB, in 1974, and Bertrand de Margerie, SJ, in 1974 and 1978.

Christopher Derrick is a British Catholic layman and a former pupil of the great Anglican apologist for Christianity, C.S. Lewis. Although not a professional moralist, he brings to moral questions, and in an especially clear way, in the present writer's judgement, to the issues of marriage morality, a talent for expression which it would be foolish to ignore in a study such as this. His defense of *Humanae Vitae* appeared in 1969[26] and is based on the premise that two elements must be present for the conjugal act to be present: 1) a substantially integral love between the partners in a marriage; 2) the substantially integral physiological act which the Creator has designed to express this love. Where either of these elements is deliberately withheld, there is no conjugal act. We leave it to the reader to judge how well Derrick expresses the moral tradition of the Church.

> Rape, as defined by law, is a rare occurrence. But the male sex, in all its heat and power and arrogant greed, might do well to bear in mind the possibility that certain other acts of sexual intercourse, even within a marriage, might have that ugly character.
>
> The old fashioned legalistic books will tell you that marriage confers upon each partner a total right over the person, the sexuality of the other; and that this "conjugal right", when invoked reasonably, must never be refused. That word "reasonably" is a lawyer's word, and in the context a delicious one: the matter will hardly be referred to a jury of 12 good men and true. Nonetheless, the fact needs to be faced that a husband's demands can often be unreasonable, and indeed thoroughly cruel. His technical "right" could then be deemed irrelevant.
>
> Aware of the uglier social realities, various writers have invoked such situations in general defense of contraception. A correspondent to the *Tablet* asks: "What would be the Pope's attitude to the Catholic woman with already a family too large

---

[26]*Honest Love and Human Life*, New York, 1969.

for the cramped accommodation in which she is obliged to live, whose husband is in the lower wage sector and is of irresponsible temperament, caring nothing for 'safe periods' nor the practice of self-control, merely insisting on sexual satisfaction as often as he feels the need? How could it be wrong for this woman to avail herself of the pill?" Only great innocence will suppose that this is a rare kind of situation; only gross callousness will take it lightly.

In such a husband's "unreasonable" demands, enforced by physical or psychological pressure, it might be accurate to see something morally indistinguishable from rape. If a marriage is in that state, it has long ceased to be a community of love: on the male side at least, the sacralising gift of self has now become a distant memory, obscenely caricatured in this present greedy devouring. If the evil of contraception lies in the sin against love and honesty, it could be argued that in this kind of extreme case - - and, to varying degrees, in other cases less extreme - - circumstances might make the sin impossible. That wife, no less than the threatened virgin, could rightly defend herself. Love and honesty will not be affronted: long ago, they have been sent packing, and they aren't around at this sad time.[27]

Thus, in spite of the fact that Derrick is taking a "conservative" position in defending *Humanae Vitae,* this is a position which, as we have seen, many moralists down the centuries to the present day have considered quite unorthodox. His position is based on the conviction that the conjugal act is by its very physiological structure designed by the Creator to be a sign of mutual self-giving in married life, and that where the basic committment to love is internally refused or the physiological structure of the act is externally destroyed, then we are dealing with something which is no longer the conjugal act: "It might be accurate to see something morally indistinguishable from rape."[28]

This aspect of the conjugal act as a *language* for expressing the conjugal committment will be urged upon the Church by Pope John Paul II in his Apostolic Exhortation *Familiaris Consortio* in response to the Sixth Synod of Bishops held in 1980. Derrick is one of the first English-speaking exponents after *Humanae Vitae* to explore this analysis of the intrinsic nature of the conjugal act.[28a] It enables him to embrace the point of our thesis unhesitatingly.

Anselm Günthör, OSB, also adopts this position without hesitation in his three volume manual based on the teachings of the Second Vatican Council and published in 1979:

---

[27]*ibid.* pp. 146-147

[28]*ibid.*

[28a]For others who do so before and after *Humanae Vitae,* cf. *infra,* note 61.

> It can happen that one of the spouses - - in general, it will be the woman - - desires to observe right order in sexual life, while the other does not observe this order and uses contraceptive means or *even forces the woman to have a great number of children in an irresponsible manner and without any control, without any will or ability to then provide for these children in an adequate manner.*
>
> The spouse who is thus going down the wrong path can perhaps bring such pressure to bear on the well-intentioned one who would like to live their conjugal life in the right way as in effect to violate this spouse from the moral point of view. *Violence which is psychological can have its paralyzing effect just as well as can violence which is physical.* Let us think, for example, of the conduct of a man who with his hostility and his coarseness renders the life of his wife insupportable if she refuses to act in a wrong way; or take the example of the man who out and out denies her the financial means to take care of the needs of the household. This heavy and continuous moral pressure can unnerve a woman to the point of inducing her to go along with matrimonial acts in which her husband uses contraceptive means...[30]

And now a few words as to the opposite kind of *case in which a husband brings children into the world in an irresponsible manner* and *violates his wife physically or psychologically.* This woman *may licitly protect herself* against conception by use of the least injurious means available. The use of a sterilizing or contraceptive means on the part of a woman physically or morally violated is different from the conduct condemned by the encyclical *Humanae Vitae.* This encyclical condemns direct sterilization undertaken in view of the conjugal act which is then to be *freely chosen;* it condemns also the use of contraceptive means in the carrying out of a conjugal act which is, once, again, *freely chosen.* In this case the use of anticonceptional means represents an intrinsic contradiction to the totality of the *sign* and therefore of the *love itself.* In contrast to this, the wife who is physically or psychologically violated and who in her need has recourse to sterilizing or contraceptive procedures *does not, in fact, want the union* which is imposed upon her when

---

[30]Gunthor, Anselm, *Chiamata e Risposta*, Roma, 1979, vol. 3, p. 724-725, n. 631: "Può succedere che uno dei coniugi – in genere la donna – desideri osservare il giusto ordine nella vita sessuale coniugale, mentre l'altro non l'osservi e adoperi mezzi contraccettivi, *oppure constringa la donna ad avere un gran numero di figli in maniera irresponsabile e priva di controllo, senza volere e potere poi provvedere loro in misura sufficiente.* Il coniuge che percorre la via sbagliata puo forse esercitare una tale pressione sull'altro, che pur vorrebbe conservare l'ordine della vita coniugale, da violentarlo, praticamente, sul piano morale. *La violenza morale può consequire il suo effetto paralizzante quanto quella fisica.* Pensiamo per es. al comportamento di un uomo che con la sua ostilità e la sua grossolanta rende insopportabile la vita alla moglie che si rifiuta di agire in maniera sbagliata, o che le nega addirittura i mezzi finanziari per le esigenze della casa. Questa pressione morale pesante e continua può snervare la donna a un punto tale da indurla a collaborare agli atti matrimoniali in cui l'altro adopera mezzi contraccettivi..." (emph. add.)

the procreation of new life would be irresponsible. Therefore she can defend herself against a pregnancy imposed upon her against all justice and all love. She can defend herself against a pregnancy which would wound her deeply in her own personal dignity. In her case she is not going against the teaching of the Church, but is applying in a right way the principle of totality, according to which a person may defend himself against a threat of grave injury towards his own person. The case of this woman is similar to that of young girls and religious Sisters who fear being violated, e.g., during the disorders which arise under conditions of war. Just as they may licitly protect themselves from a pregnancy imposed upon them, so also a wife may do so who finds herself in a situation of the kind which we have described.[32]

The overall concurrence of Günthör with the thesis we are defending here is so obvious from the above quotation as to need no further explication from us now. We would note, however, the following points which we consider highly significant in Günthör's presentation:

1) The irresponsible conception of children is considered comparable in seriousness with the sinful use of artificial contraceptives.

2) Psychological pressure brought to bear against a woman is recognized as at times being as powerful as physical force in violating the free will of a person subjected to it.

3) The evil of contraceptive practices condemned by the Church is identified as the breaking of the character of the conjugal act as a *sign,* a *symbol,* or an *expression* of the complete self-giving of a couple in married love.

4) That where this self-giving in married love no longer exists, the physiological structure of the sexual act no longer has an absolutely sacrosanct character, and may be broken for the good of the woman upon whom it is forced against her will.

---

[32]*ibid.* pp. 725-726: "E ora due parole a proposito *del caso* opposto *in cui il marito mette al mondo figli in maniera irresponsabile e violenta fisicamente o moralmente la moglie.* Questa donna può lecitamente *proteggersi* contro il concepimento adoperando i mezzi meno nocivi. L'uso di un mezzo sterilizzante o contraccettivo da parte di una donna violentata fisicamente o moralmente è diverso dal comportamento condannato dall'enciclica. Questa condanna la sterilizzazione diretta compiuta in vista dell'atto coniugale *liberamente voluto,* nonchè l'uso di mezzi contraccettivi nel compimento di un atto coniugale altrettanto *liberamente voluto.* In questo caso l'uso dei mezzi anticoncezionali rappresenta un'intrinseca contraddizione alla totalità *del segno* dell'amore e quindi *all'amore stesso.* Invece la moglie fisicamente o moralmente violentata, che nel bisogno ricorre a un mezzo del genere, *non vuole affatto l'unione* impostale, nè può volerla, qualora la procreazione di una nuova vita fosse irresponsabile. Pertanto può difendersi contro una gravidanza impostale contro ogni giustizia e ogni amore e che la ferirebbe gravemente nella sua dignità personale. Nel suo caso ella non va contro la dottrina della Chiesa, ma applica nel modo giusto il principio di totalità, secondo il quale l'uomo può difendersi contro la minaccia di un grave danno per la propria persona. Il caso di questa donna è simile a quello delle ragazze e delle suore, che temono di esserve violentate per es. durante i disordini che si verificano in occasione di eventi bellici, Come esse possono tutelarsi contro una gravidanza loro imposta, così lo può fare anche una moglie, che si trova nella situazione di necessità da noi descritta." (emph. add.)

We should note that, in addition to these points of Günthör's doctrine which we think represent an authentic advance in the theology of marriage, there is one other relatively minor point which we would see as not being sufficiently refined: the categorization of *any* sexual act between husband and wife, no matter how distorted it may be, as the "conjugal act". We would question whether, e.g., a contraceptive act, willingly indulged in by both parties, should be dignified with the name "conjugal act", and we question this for both pastoral and theological reasons. Without going further into the point, however, we here note only that the next theologian whom we consider has the same reservations as do we.

Bertrand de Margerie, SJ, writes in 1974 in his book *The Sacraments and Social Progress:*[33]

> Equally, however - - and for the first time in the history of the Church's magisterium, - - Paul VI has emphasized the immorality of the conjugal act forced "on one's partner without regard to his or her condition or personal and reasonable wishes in the matter." This is "no true act of love," *nor does it even deserve to be called a conjugal act;* much rather should it be called *marital rape,* absolutely counter to the conjugal love which constitutes the right and the duty of husband and wife. In these conditions, the duty to accept procreation ceases to exist, for the matrimonial contract implies a mutual giving in love of free wills and not merely of bodies. Neither of the marriage partners, in placing his or her sexuality at the service of the other partner, intends to become the slave of passions uncontrolled by reason. The marriage contract is not one of slavery, but of mutual liberation. Because husband and wife are endowed with free will, they cannot serve one another except in respecting one another's inalienable dignity.[34]

It is to be noted that, whereas Christopher Derrick has suggested merely that "it *might* be accurate to see something morally indistinguishable from rape"[35] in an unjustly forced "conjugal act," de Margerie does not hesitate to state here categorically:

> This is no true act of love nor does it even deserve to be called a conjugal act; much rather should it be called marital rape, absolutely counter to the conjugal love which constitutes the right and the duty of husband and wife.[36]

Four years later, the same Father de Margerie writes:

> N. 13 of the Encyclical begins as follows "...a conjugal act imposed upon one's partner without regard to his or her condi-

---

[33]Chicago

[34]*ibid.,*

[35]*loc. cit. supra,* note 28 (emph. add.)

[36]de Margerie, *loc. cit.*

tion and lawful desires is not a true act of love, and therefore denies an exigency of right moral order in the relationship between husband and wife."

There is a great deal of talk today about the liberation of women. How could we fail to stress the liberating significance of the passage quoted for certain wives, victims of the sexual violence of husbands addicted to alcohol? Their passion drives them in the direction not of conjugal love but of a *real "intraconjugal rape"*, as we said elsewhere. . . The matrimonial contract is not an instrument of mutual slavery or of the subjection of one of the spouses to the other, but the loving alliance of two freedoms in view of their mutual and full liberation. We agree, therefore, with Fr. Zalba's opinion....: The duty of accepting procreation might cease to exist when the violence of one of the spouses has forced the sexual act upon the other in a way contrary to the inalienable dignity of his *(sic)*person.

Paul VI, let us note clearly, has continued on this point the magisterium of Pius XII, always assuming the *free* character, explicitly affirmed, of sexual activity, which involves responsibilities. . . The irresponsibility of one of the spouses, who, in passion and under its sway, wishes to inflict on the other his absence of love, might in certain rare cases and under certain conditions free the latter from the obligation of a motherhood which might be irresponsible parenthood which God did not want, though wanting and loving infinitely their *(sic)* fruits. True conjugal love exercises its rights in non-violence. The mutual donation to which spouses are committed has as its limit the inalienable dignity of each of their persons.[37]

This article of de Margerie has some special significance because it was one of a series of articles by various eminent theologians published as part of *Osservatore Romano's* observance of the tenth anniversary of encyclical *Humanae Vitae*. Of particular note also is de Margerie's continued use of such strong categorizations as "real intra-conjugal rape" to describe evaluatively a sexual act unjustly forced on a wife by an irresponsible husband; he is not content to speak merely of an "analogy to rape." Noteworthy, too, is de Margerie's insistence on the continuity of his position with the Magisterial doctrine of Pius XII. It is true that he seems to be cautious regarding the frequency with which "real intra-marital rape" might occur ("in certain rare cases and under certain conditions") and thus shows himself alert to possible distortions and abuses of his doctrine. This is, of course, a question of prudence.

Not a question of prudence, however, but one of principle is the distinction between, on the one hand, an act of irresponsible parenthood which God detests and,

---

[37]"Reflections on some aspects of *Humanae Vitae* to which less consideration has been given," in *L'Osservatore Romano* (English edition), May 25, 1978, part I (emph. add.). His reference numbers are to paragraphs of *Humanae Vitae*.

on the other hand, the destruction of a new human individual who might result from such an act, an individual we must reverence, love, and honor as a human person as truly as does God Himself. Here de Margerie makes it clear that his position is in no way to be considered an opening for any kind of abortifacient practice whatsoever on the part of an abused wife. "Irresponsible parenthood...God did not want, though wanting and loving infinitely their *(sic)* fruits."[38]

In summary, then, it is obvious that the doctrine of a number of theologians in the period 1960-1980 represented a dramatic contrast to the overwhelmingly dominant teaching of the theologians of the 17th century who first raised the question of sexual oppression within marriage. And, as we shall now see, the Magisterium throughout the period 1960-1980 did not intervene in any way to discourage this development towards accepting the concept of intra-marital sexual oppression and a wife's consequent right to defend herself against pregnancy, even by the use of artificial means. Indeed, in spite of its great vigilance in rejecting a number of theories and procedures for dealing with issues of sexual morality, the Magisterium actually began officially to espouse principles which would favor such development.

B. The Magisterium: 1960-1980

It would be too much to claim that the Magisterium throughout the period 1960-1980 explicitly taught our thesis: that there is possible a sexual oppression within marriage of such a nature as to justify an abused wife's use even of artificial means to avoid the onset of a pregnancy. Throughout the Magisterial teaching, however, principles which, in the judgement of the present writer, could lead only to the acceptance of such a thesis are found. Moreover, the silence of the Magisterium in the face of precisely the application which we advocate for those principles leaves unquestionable the Church's acceptance of our thesis as *at least compatible* with present doctrinal development, if not actually demanded by it. These principles and the Church's benign attitude towards the way in which writers such as Schmitt, Visser, Peeters, Zalba, Derrick, Günthor, and de Margerie were applying them we find scattered throughout the pontificates of John XXIII, Paul VI, and John Paul II.

JOHN XXIII

John XXIII, in his short but highly significant service as Pope, spoke only once, in 1961, on the morality of conjugal relations.[38a] He did, however, speak to three issues which are unquestionably fundamental to our subject: 1) the basic rights and dignity of women; 2) a wife's co-equal share with her husband in being morally responsible for the welfare of the family; and 3) the obligation of any person, male or female, to defend his/her own rights and dignity.

---

[38]*ibid.*

[38a]Regarding "population control", however, he wrote: "... in this matter no one is permitted to use methods and procedures which may indeed be permissible to check the life of animals and plants." cf *Mater et Magistra*, n. 193.

Regarding the basic rights and dignity of women, in his encyclical letter *Pacem In Terris,* Pope John wrote:

> The part that women are now playing in political life is everywhere evident. This is a development that is perhaps of swifter growth among Christian nations, but it is also happening extensively, if more slowly, among nations that are heirs to different traditions and imbued with a different culture. Women are gaining an increasing awareness of their natural dignity. Far from being content with a purely passive role or allowing themselves to be regarded as a kind of instrument, they are demanding both in domestic and in public life the rights and duties which belong to them as human persons.[39]

Pope John is here speaking directly, of course, of the phenomenon of women's entrance into the political arena. His teaching, however, has some significance for our topic.

First, he recognizes that there has been a gradual but authentic development of consciousness throughout the world regarding the rights and dignity of woman. This would partially explain how it could have happened that theologians in the 17th century treated the subject of sexual oppression within marriage with scant attention to the possibility that a wife's personal *right* might indeed radically limit the conjugal *debt.* Only time and the Spirit-guided assimilation of woman's unique dignity in the order of nature and of grace would make possible the more clearly focused vision which the Church has today of woman.

Second, Pope John rejects the vision of woman as a mere instrument to be used in a non-personal way for the purposes of men or of society. He specifies domestic life itself as one ambient in which her dignity as a person rules out her being used as a mere instrument. This doctrine of John XXIII, we maintain, is incompatible with certain *mores* of previous centuries of Christians who saw the *"marriage debt"* of a wife as her obligation to accept being used as a merely material instrument for purposes of producing a child.

In another passage, Pope John speaks also of the wife's responsibility regarding the welfare of the family as being *co-equal* with that of her husband. Pope John writes:

> Human beings have also the right to choose for themselves the kind of life which appeals to them: whether it is to found a family - - in the founding of which both the man and the woman

---

[39]*E.V.,* Vol. 2, n. 19, par. 3: "Quod deinde mulieres in re publica intersunt, nemo projecto est, cui non pateat; quod fortasse celerius apud populos fit christianam fidem profitentes, et tardius quidem, sed late apud gentes aliarum memoriarum heredes alioque vitae cultu imbutas. Mulieres enim, cum cotidie magis sint suae humanae dignitatis consciae, tantum abest ut patiantur se vel pro re quadam inanima vel pro instrumento quodam haberi, ut potius sive intra domesticos parietes, sive in civitate iura et officia humana persona digna postulent."

> enjoy equal rights and duties - - or to embrace the priesthood or
> the religious life.[40]

Such teaching leaves no room for any paternalistic view of family authority which would exempt a wife from or deprive her of responsibility for decisions regarding family size, maintenance of her own health, etc. The teaching does not mention the husband even as a kind of supreme court by whom, after the wife's views had been dutifully listened to, the final decision would be made (though the Pope does not reject this concept of a husband's authority). The wording is clear:

> In . . . founding (a family) . . . both the man and the woman
> enjoy *equal rights and duties.* . . .[41]

In still another passage, regarding the obligation of every person, male or female, to defend his or her own basic rights and dignity as a person, Pope John writes:

> Man's awareness of his rights must inevitably lead him to the
> recognition of his duties. The possession of rights involves the
> duty of implementing those rights, for they are the expression of
> a man's personal dignity. And the possession of rights also
> involves their recognition and respect by other people.[42]

This particular doctrine, while strengthening our argument, would perhaps go even beyond the point we wish to make. For we are here defending only the *right* of a wife to prevent a pregnancy's being forced on her unjustly by her own husband. The teaching of Pope John, however, would here seem to indicate that, all other things being equal, a wife would have also an *obligation* to take such measures.

In summary, then, Pope John XXIII: 1) recognizes as legitimate a developing appreciation of the rights and duties of woman as a person over and above the valid but considerably more limited vision of her dignity in previous centuries, even among Christians; 2) teaches that in matters of the welfare of the family, the wife cannot abdicate her obligation to take responsibility by her personal thought and decision; and 3) explicitates what may have been only implicit in the minds of many: that neither man nor woman has a right to acquiesce in the violation of his or her own dignity or rights, including the right to carry out one's responsibilities.

PAUL VI

Pope Paul VI, at the very beginning of his reign, expressed his intention of continuing the development of the Church's self-understanding and life as that work had

---

[40]*E.V.*, Vol. 2, n. 7: "Insuper hominibus iure integrum est vitae genus eligere, quod praeoptent: adeoque aut sibi condere familiam, in qua condenda vir et mulier paribus fruantur iuribus et officiis, aut sacerdotium vel religiosae vitae disciplinam capessere."

[41]*ibid.* (emph. add.)

[42]*E.V.*, Vol. 2, n. 19, p. 38, par. 3: "Quod si in homine aliquo conscienta nascitur suorum iurium in eo etiam conconscientia officiorum suorum necesse est nascatur: ita ut qui iuria quaedam habeat, in eo pariter officium insit sua iuria, tamquam suae dignitatis significationes, reposcendi; in reliquiis vero officium insit iura eadem agnoscendi et colendi."

been begun by his predecessor.⁴³ This intention showed itself, of course, in Vatican Council II's documents, which now, under Paul VI, began to move towards their final form and publication.

Among the Council documents, none affects our thesis more than *Gaudium et Spes*. The history of this pastoral consitution "On the Church in the Modern World" is a complicated one. It would, then, in our judgement, be a mistake to seek in *Gaudium et Spes* any kind of highly elaborated, formulatedly coherent theology of marriage. We here treat the document rather as a *partially* elaborated theology of marriage, along with many elements whose interrelation remains largely yet to be assimilated and explicitated by theologians and eventually by the Magisterium itself.⁴⁴

This imperfectly systematic approach of *Gaudium et Spes* notwithstanding, it is possible to see in the document certain principles so clearly taught that they will have to be included in any more articulated post-Conciliar synthesis on marriage. One such principle is that the conjugal act is of its nature a *sign*. The conjugal act, then, is a way, not only of *effecting* something, namely the beginning of a new human life, but also of *saying* something, namely, that this man and woman give themselves to one another in that unique species of friendship which we call marriage.

That a marriage is a form of friendship is not, of course, a belief foreign to Catholic teaching. What is a new emphasis, however, for a Magisterial document is the teaching that, for this marital *friendship*, that is, *love*, the conjugal act is uniquely a - - indeed *the - - sign, expression, symbol.*

> Married love is an eminently human love because it is an affection between two persons rooted in the will and it embraces the good of the whole person; it can enrich the sentiments of the spirit and *their physical expression* with a unique dignity and ennoble them as the *special* elements and *signs* of the *friendship* proper to marriage.⁴⁵
>
> *Married love is uniquely expressed* and perfected *by* the exercise of the *acts proper to marriage.* Hence the *acts* in marriage by which the intimate and chaste union of the spouses takes

---

⁴³*Ecclesiam Suam, E.V.*, Vol. 2, n. 184

⁴⁴Cf. Ratzinger, Joseph, *Theological Highlights of the Second Vatican Council*, 1966, New York, pp. 154-167; Haring, Bernard, in Vorgrimmiler, *Commentary on the Documents of the Second Vatican Council*, New York, 1969, Vol. V, pp. 225; Wiltgen, Ralph, *The Rhine Flows Into the Tiber*, New York, 1967, pp. 205-211, 252-254, 267-271.

⁴⁵*Gaudium et Spes*, n. 49, in *E.V.* n. 1475: "*Ille autem amor,* utpote eminenter humanus, cum a persona in personam voluntatis affectu dirigatur, totius personae bonum complectitur ideoque *corporis* animique *expressiones* peculiari dignitate ditare easque tamquam elementa ac *signa specialia* coniugalis amicitiae nobilitare valet." (emph. add). Our English translation of *Gaudium et Spes* here in this chapter is taken from Flannery, *Vatican II, The Conciliar* and *Post-Conciliar Documents*, New York, 1975. We note also that what the Council documents offer here is a new *emphasis* on the sign-nature of the the conjugal act as designed in its very physiological structure to express marital love. The sign-nature of the act was mentioned, at least obliquely, by Pius XII on one occasion (To Midwives, DISCORSI, p. 168-169).

place are noble and honorable; the truly human performance of *these acts* fosters the self-giving they *signify* and enriches the spouses in joy and gratitude.[46]

Thus the Council explicitly and directly teaches that the conjugal act is a *sign* uniquely and singularly structured in its material dimension to express its spiritual dimension, namely, the life-long friendship which is the marriage commitment.

The Council teaches the same thing also indirectly when it portrays the conjugal act as having a *meaning*, i.e., as conveying a *message* of personal commitment. This committment includes an intellectually understandable content *(sensum)*.

> Objective criteria must be used, criteria drawn from the nature of the human person and human action, criteria which respect the total *meaning (sensum)* of mutual self-giving and human procreation in the context of true love; all this is possible only if the virtue of married chastity is seriously practiced.[47]

In another place, the Council *implies* that the conjugal act is a *sign* by noting that:

> Man's sexuality and the faculty of reproduction wondrously surpass the endowments of lower forms of life...[48]

But how, one must ask, does the human conjugal act transcend that of the lower animals? In that the conjugal act is capable of reproducing a new individual of the same species as its parents? Certainly not, for that is obviously a capacity inherent in copulation even in the lower animals. What then, is the difference? As we have seen above, the Council emphasizes one aspect of the conjugal act which would indeed differentiate it from the mere copulation of the lower animals: its nature as a *sign,* i.e., as a *medium* of communicating one's *self* and the *sense* of one's marital committment. There is nothing else obvious in the Council documents which would indicate why the conjugal act "wonderfully transcends the endowments of the lower forms of life."

A second principle which stands out in *Gaudium et Spes* is that married love which, as we have seen above, is expressed with singular fitingness in the conjugal act, is of the *same pattern* as the *love of Christ for the Church.* It is, indeed, more than of the same pattern of the love between Christ and the Church; it is actually caught up in this love and becomes, in a sacramental way, part of the love between Christ and the Church.[49] This love is, therefore, a far cry from a mere erotic attraction

---

[46]*ibid.*, in *E.V.* n. 1476: *"Haec dilectio proprio matrimonii opere singulariter exprimitur* et perficitur. Actus proinde, quibus coniuges intime et caste inter se uniuntur, honesti ac digni sunt et, modo vere humano exerciti, donationem mutuam *significant* et fovent qua sese invicem laeto gratoque animo locupletant." (emph. add.)

[47]*ibid.* n. 51, in *E.V.* n. 1483: "... obiectivis criteriis, ex personae eiusdemque actuum natura desumptis, determinari debet, quae integrum *sensum* mutuae donationis ac humanae procreationis in contextu veri amoris observant; quod fieri nequit nisi virtutem castitatis coniugalis sincero animo colatur." (emph. add.)

[48]*ibid.* "Indoles vero sexualis hominis necnon humana generandi facultas mirabiliter exsuperant ea quae in inferioribus vitae gradibus habentur..."

[49]*ibid.*, n. 48

which is pursued in selfishness and soon fades away in wretchedness.[50]

The love which is entered into by the marriage commitment and *which, therefore, is to be expressed in the conjugal act* is a love which,

"embraces the good of the whole person."[51]

One, and a final point we will note in *Gaudium et Spes* is the *basic equality of husband and wife.*

> The unity of marriage, distinctly recognized by our Lord, is made clear in the *equal personal dignity* which must be *accorded to man and wife* in mutual and unreserved affection.[52]

In summary then, *Gaudium et Spes* teaches (explicitly for the first time in a Magisterial document)

1) that the conjugal act in its physiological dimension is designed by God precisely as a sign to express the love to which a married couple commit themselves;

2) that the love which the conjugal act is physiologically designed to express is patterned on and is a participation in the love between Christ and the Church; and

3) that the husband and wife have an equal right to be honored at all times in their personal dignity.

From these teachings of the Council we would argue then that, if a couple by entering into the marriage bond have a right to the conjugal act, each of them has a right to that act only in its *integrity*. This integrity of the act, for certain, includes a *physiological* integrity, but also *more* than that. For part of the integrity of the conjugal act is that it be a *sign* expressing a *basic* and *genuine love* (however imperfect and in need of further maturity) for one's self and one's spouse. In fact, this love must be at least substantially in conformity with the love between Christ and the Church, which love includes full respect for our human dignity as well as for both the divine and the human dignity of Jesus Christ. This basic and genuine love of necessity includes a respect for the fundamental rights and dignity of one's spouse. It is of the nature of the conjugal act in its very physiological structure to *speak* of this respect. A man or woman has no right to engage in this physiological dimension of the conjugal act while simultaneously and deliberately withholding the respect for one's partner which is fundamental to any true love. They would have no more right to do this than they would to mouth physiologically the marriage vows while withholding internally something fundamental to the marriage commitment. Our canonical jurisprudence rightly refers to such mere mouthing of the marriage vows as "simulation" *(contra bonum prolis, contra bonum sacramenti, contra bonum*

---

[50]*ibid.,* n. 49 in *E.V.,* Vol. 3, 1475: "Longe igitur exsuperat meram eroticam inclinationem, quae, egoistice exculta, citius et misere evanescit."

[51]*ibid.*

[52]*ibid.,* in *E.V.,* Vol. 3, n. 1476: *"Aequali* etiam *dignitate personali cum mulieris tum viri* agnoscenda in mutua atque plena dilectione, unitas matrimonii a Domino confirmata luculenter apparet." (emph. add.)

fidei) and pronounces *invalid* a marriage "entered into" in this way. There *is no marriage* in such cases precisely because there *are no vows* - - merely physiological actions which *could* have been constitutive dimensions of the vows, had the internal disposition not been withheld. We maintain that the teaching of Vatican Council II implies that the same "invalidity" must be predicated of any "conjugal act" which is used with the inner intention, and, even more, the obvious manifestation of such an intention, to dishonor the personal dignity, violate the fundamental rights, and frustrate the serious obligations of one's spouse.

The next important document we must look at is from the pontificate of Paul VI in his 1968 encyclical letter *Humanae vitae*.[53] The Pope makes three points which are particularly important to our considerations: 1) that the conjugal act is of its nature a *sign;* 2) that it is a sign of *love;* and 3) that it is an immoral violation of the conjugal act precisely as a *sign* of *love* for a husband to impose copulation on his wife against her true interests.

The first point Paul VI makes, then, is that the conjugal act by the very nature which God has given to it, is a *sign,* that is, an act which is capable, not merely of *effecting* something (the conception of a child), but also of *saying* something (basically, what the marriage vows themselves say.) Not only does Paul say that the conjugal act is a sign, but he is more insistent and clear on this point than even *Gaudium et Spes* was. Indeed, as we shall see, there is every evidence that his condemnation of artificial contraception in this encyclical is based precisely on the nature of the conjugal act as a *sign*.

It is impressive simply to list the places where Paul VI refers to the *sign*-nature of the conjugal act. In an introductory section, we see the *significance* of the conjugal act referred to for the first time in the encyclical:

> With living conditions as they are at present, and given the *significance* which marital relations possess for harmony and fidelity between man and wife, might it not be well to revise moral rules as they now stand?[54]

Later, in Section 9, he speaks of conjugal love as

> . . . before all else . . . fully human, a thing both of the *sense* and *spirit*.[55]

Tentative as such references to the sign-nature of the conjugal act may appear, the Pope then moves to a bold appeal to the concept in the central and crucial Sections 11, 12, and 13. In Section 11 he writes:

---

[53]*E.V.*, Vol. 3, pp. 280-319

[54]Section 3. The English translation here is taken from Durand, A.J., *Humanae Vitae*, 1978, Bethlehem, PA. Cf. the original in *E.V.*, Vol. 3, n. 589: "An ratione habita sive vitae condicionum, quae nunc sunt, sive *significationis*, quam maritales amplexus quoad concordiam mutuamque fidelitatem coniugum habent, normas morales, quae hodie obtinent, recognoscere non conveniat. . ."

[55]*ibid. E.V.*, n. 595: "Est ante omnia amor plene humanus, hoc est *sensibilis* et spiritualis."

> Nor do (these acts) cease to be right even if foreseen to be infertile for reasons beyond the control of the married pair, since they do not lose their function of *signifying* and strengthening the deep relationship between them.[56]

And again, the key Sections 12 and 13:

> This doctrine, often set forth by the authoritative teaching of the Church, is firmly based on the unbreakable bond established by God between the two *meanings* inherent in the act of marriage, namely, that of unity and that of procreation.[57]

> If each of these essential aspects, that of unity, and that of procreation, is safeguarded, the use of marriage fully retains the *significance* of true mutual love. . . [58]

> It follows that when this gift of God is used in such a way that the gift itself is deprived of its *meaning* and purpose, even partially, the result is hostile to the nature of man and wife and to their profound union.[59]

And finally at the end of Section 16:

> . . . they use marital relations to *bear witness* to their love for each other. . .[60]

The present author sees no way of escaping the conclusion of L. Ciccone in his ample commentary on and defense of *Humanae Vitae,* where he makes the point that this *sign*-nature of the conjugal act is one of the foundations of the encyclical's teachings throughout the key Sections 11, 12, and 13:

> The insistence with which (the encyclical) speaks of the "meanings" of the conjugal act indicates clearly that the conjugal act is being considered *above all (sopratutto)* as a kind of *signifying* thing, as a "sign".[60a]

> When (a couple) want to give to their love the fullest possible expression, the urge which is proper to love and pushes towards total communion (right up to and including a unity of the two persons) finds *its proper language* in the very psycho-physical

---

[56]*ibid.,* n. 597, Section 11: ". . . iidemque legitimi esse non desinunt etsi infecundi praevideantur propter causas a coniugum voluntate nequaquam manantes, cum non cesset eorum destinatio ad coniugum coniunctionem *significandam* roborandamque." (emph. add.)

[57]*ibid.,* n. 598: "Huiusmodi doctrina, quae ab Ecclesiae Magisterio saepe exposita est, in nexu indissolubili nititur, a Deo statuto, quem homini sua sponte infringere non licet, inter *significationem* unitatis et *significationem* procreationis, quae ambae in actu coniugali insunt." (emph. add.)

[58]*ibid.:* "Quodsi utraque eiusmodi essentialis ratio, unitatis videlicet et procreationis, servatur usus matrimonii *sensum* mutui verique amoris. . ." (emph. add.)

[59]*ibid.,* n. 599: "Quapropter cum quis dono Dei utitur, tollens, licet solum ex parte, *significationem* et finem doni ipsius, sive viri sive mulieris naturae repugnat eorumque initmae necessitudini. . ." (emph. add.)

[60]*ibid.* n. 602: ". . . ipsi utantur commercio ad mutuum *testandum* amorem. . ." (emph. add.)

being of man and woman, as they make use of their sexuality in its entirety.[61]

In realizing the absolutely central role which this concept of the conjugal act as a *sign* (as contrasted with *effective cause)* of procreation plays in establishing the doctrine of *Humanae Vitae,* it is helpful to note the sequence of the Sections 11 and 12, where the key re-affirmation of the Church's doctrine repudiating artifical contraception is found. Section 11 ends by re-iterating that doctrine:

> ... Any use of marriage must remain *per se* oriented towards the procreation of human life.[62]

Having given this teaching here at the end of Section 11, the encyclical then immediately opens Section 12 by giving the *basis* for the teaching.

> *This doctrine...* is firmly based on the unbreakable bond established by God between the *two meanings (significationem)* inherent in the act... [63]

Thus, the repudiation of contraception is based, not on the fact that the contraceptive act cannot *produce* something (a pregnancy), but on the fact that it cannot *speak of* something (the conjugal commitment -- which is, of course, inherently procreational). Indeed, the conjugal act used during the infertile periods, or after menopause, or after a justified hysterectomy cannot *produce* a pregnancy, but in all these situations it can *say* something: "We give ourselves to one another in the lifelong friendship of marriage, together with all the procreative capacity which we in this moment have."

The re-affirmation, at the end of Section 11, of the traditional teaching along with the basis given, at the beginning of Section 12, for that teaching we would see, along with L. Ciccone, as the heart of the encyclical:

> ... The central point towards which the rest (of the encyclical) converges either as preparation or as justification and development, seems to be this affirmation with which Section 11 ends, and with which Section 12 begins... This supreme governing principle of the morality of the conjugal act forms the premise for re-affirming the moral goodness of the conjugal act *both* when it will be (truly) unitive and (at the same time) productive of a pregnancy, *and* when it will be unitive, though *not* productive of a pregnancy, as the couple clearly see. From this also

---

[60]"L' Enciclica *'Humanae Vitae'.* Analisi e 'Commentario" in *Divus Thomas,* 1969, p. 301.

[61]*ibid.,* p. 302. Cf. also *ibid. passim,* pp. 302-304. Other writers prior to *Humanae Vitae* had focused on the nature of sexuality as *sign* or *language.* Cf. Davies, M.D., "Love and Contraception" in *The Irish Theological Quarterly* (1966), pp. 327-351. Janniere, A., "La Differenciation sexuelle" in *Sexualité Humaine,* Paris, 1966, p. 313; and Antoine, P., "Sens de la sexualité et recherche d'une etique" *ibid.,* pp. 335 ss; Martelet, G., *Amour Conjugal et renouveau conciliaire,* Lyon 1967. Ciccone, *loc. cit.,* cites all these. After *Humanae Vitae,* cf. especially, Kippley John, *Birth Control and the Marriage Covenant,* 2nd edition, Collegville, 1981, and James Mulligan, *The Pope and The Theologians,* Emmitsburg, Md., Mt. St. Mary's Press, 1968, p. 97.

[62]The present writer's own translation. As others (Ciccone, Martelet) have pointed out, many of our "official translations" do not render the sense of "per se." Some simply ignore the phrase. Cf. *E.V., ibid.,* n. 597: "Quilibet usus matrimonii ad vitam humanam procreandam *per se* destinatus permaneat." (emph. add.)

[63]Section 12, *op. cit.* (emph. add.)

there comes a deepening for the moral judgement we make of two fundamentally different ways in which the conjugal act can be carried out, i.e., without or with an intervention which artifically disassociates its two *meanings*.[64]

Thus we hold that *Humanae Vitae* clearly teaches the nature of the conjugal act as a *sign* which by the very structure given it by our Creator is meant to convey a *meaning*.

But what meaning? In answer to this question, the encyclical is once again clear: *the love* of the couple as both a unitive and a procreative love. This is evident throughout the passages which we cited above from the encyclical regarding the nature of the conjugal act as a *sign*. These passages make it obvious that it is a *unitive* sign, i.e., a sing of the love which the couple directs towards each other, and a *procreative* sign, i.e., a sign that they accept their union as a call to give life in collaboration with their Creator. Moreover, if there be any doubt that what is to be expressed in the conjugal act is this *love,* one need only point out that the four sections of the encyclical immediately preceeding the central ones 11 and 12, are entirely an analysis of conjugal *love*[65] It is only after this analysis of *love* that the encyclical re-iterates the human rightness and dignity of any conjugal act which remains with its natural orientation

> to *express* and consolidate their *union*.

By reason of this strong papal emphasis on the unifying and life-giving *love* of the couple, we would, once again, make our own the evaluation given by L. Ciccone:

> The principle on which the moral evaluation of the conjugal act is founded is *no longer* whether or not the act is *physically entire,* but whether or not it is a genuine, unaltered, and complete *expression of conjugal love,* which love is by its very nature fruitful, i.e., oriented towards and open to the communication of life.[66]

The third and final pertinent point of doctrine is found in *Humanae Vitae,* Section 13, and recognizes the basic illiceity of any sexual act, even a physiologically complete one, which is forced on a wife against her justified protests.

> If explanation be needed, it should suffice to point out that the use of marriage, forced upon a partner without regard for the other's condition or reasonable wishes, is no genuine act of love. Indeed, it is a rejection of the conditions which moral

---

[64]Ciccone, *op. cit.,* p. 271 (emph. add.)

[65]Sections 7-10 in *E.V. ibid.,* nn. 593-596.

[66]Ciccone, *op. cit.,* p. 285. It is to be noted that Ciccone insists that to be an expression of conjugal love, the act must be physiologically integral.

order rightly demands of the relationship between the married.⁶⁷

It is to be noted that sexual oppression within marriage is here condemned as immoral precisely because it is *not an act of love*. To the best of our knowledge and that of at least one outstanding defender of *Humanae Vitae*,⁶⁸ this is the first time in a Magisterial document that the illiceity of an unjustly forced sexual act within marriage is clearly indicated. The premises were, indeed, laid down in previous Magisterial teachings that love pervades all else in Christian marriage and holds there a true primacy (Pius XI),⁶⁹ and that the conjugal act is an expression of mutual self-giving (Pius XII).⁷⁰ *Gaudium et Spes,* as we have seen, moved this teaching onto the Conciliar level. It is only in *Humanae Vitae,* however, that the Church Magisterium, in the teaching of Paul VI, declares explicitly the moral illiceity of a "conjugal act" gone through without love as a normative principle of its morality.

In this regard, it seems to us that Paul VI was far ahead of most of the moralists of his day. We have, in this chapter, been able to gather only a handful of names of theologians who, in some genuine sense, favored our thesis. But, we might ask with the apostle Andrew, "What are these among so many?" With L. Ciccone, we must note:

> It is certainly peculiar that moralists have been so slow in accepting the contradiction which an act presents for the basic requirements of morality when it is not an act of true love. The splitting off of the exercise of sexuality from love was almost always recognized, even outside Christian morality, as one of the vilest degradations, one of the most serious moral disorders, which has its extreme expression in prostitution. This, of course, outside marriage. Faced, however, with the same splitting off of sexuality from love, but this time *between married people,* moralists seem to have remained prisoners of *an excessively juridical point of view* from which they had become accustomed to look upon matrimony and the conjugal act. Once they had settled the fact that the act was "apt for the generation of offspring", they had settled its liceity; and thus a whole casuistry grew up. What was licit or illicit for a married couple was decided on one point alone: Was the *"ejaculation of the semen into the vagina"* sufficiently safeguarded or not?
>
> A simple comparison between the conjugal morality proposed in *Humanae Vitae* and that which was habitually espoused in almost all the moral manuals would be enough to show how much headway we have made in one or two decades. Such a

---

⁶⁷*E.V.,* n. 599: "Homines enim merito animadvertunt, usum matrimonii alteri coniugi impositum, nulla ratione habita eius status eiusque iustorum optatorum, non esse verum actum amoris, atque adeo iis adversari rebus, quas circa necessitudines inter coniuges moralis recte postulat ordo."

⁶⁸Ciccone, *op. cit.,* p. 294

⁶⁹*E.S.,* n. 3707

⁷⁰To Midwives, DISCORSI, p. 168-169.

comparison would offer a typical example of an authentic but sane evolution of moral theology, not by repudiating principles or turning them absolutely upside-down, but by their development and integration into a wider and more complete prospective which allows for clarification of aspects previously ignored or insufficiently weighed.[71]

The doctrine of *Humanae Vitae* then, in the present writer's judgement, gives evidence that Paul VI himself was concerned to give official impetus to the mandate of the Vatican Council II that special care be given to the perfecting of moral theology,[72] a perfecting much needed.

Humanae Vitae, then, insists that 1) it is integral to the nature of the conjugal act, that it be a *sign;* 2) that the act is, in its very physiological structure, a sign of *love;* and 3) that an act of *sexual oppression* within marriage is as *immoral* as artificial contraception.

> These two forms of partially altering the conjugal act are thrown together under one condemnation of *moral illiceity.* Whether it is an act vitiated by contraception or one stripped of true love, they are both a "no" to God and His plan, an abuse of his gift, and a violence against man in his nature, which nature is the work of God.[73]

Paul VI, then, recognizes the category of sexual oppression within marriage. He does not, it is true, then proceed to recognize explicitly the right of a wife thus abused to use artificial means to avoid the inception of a pregnancy. Neither, we would point out, does he condemn such an option as it had been defended by theologians prior to *Humanae Vitae.* Neither, as we have seen early in this chapter, do theologian defenders of *Humanae Vitae,* subsequent to 1968, find anything in the encyclical which might threaten their defense of such a use of artificial anti-conceptives. Rather these theologians, closely aligned with the teaching of *Humanae Vitae,* find *there* in *its* principles a vindication for their position and that of this study.

One other document of the pontificate of Paul VI touches on our subject: the Response of the Sacred Congregation for the Doctrine of the Faith in 1975 to inquiries made by the National Conference of Catholic Bishops in the United States regarding surgical sterilization.[74] This Response illustrates some of the problems associated with the interpretation of Magisterial documents, but, in its own internal evolution, also confirms one central point essential to our thesis. For it makes clear that the Church is not repudiating absolutely the physiological act of sterilizing a perfectly healthy reproductive system, but such a sterilization *when it is done for "contraceptive purposes".* "Contraceptive purposes", moreover, is clearly intended

---

[71]Ciccone, *op. cit.,* pp. 295-296. (emph. add.)

[72]*Optatam Totius,* n. 16, in E.V., Vol. I, n. 808

[73]Ciccone, *op. cit.,* p. 298 (emph. add.)

[74]March 13, 1975, in *E.V.,* Vol. 5, n. 1199-1203

to refer to procedures enabling a person to avoid pregnancy from sexual actions *clearly foreseen* and *freely willed*. The Response makes it clear that sterilization to avoid pregnancy from sexual actions *not* clearly foreseen and freely willed is *outside* the scope of the document's condemnation.

> Sterilization intended in itself is not orientated towards the overall good of the person properly understood *if it injures the ethical good of the person*. It does not, that is, preserve the proper order of things and goods *if it injures the ethical good*, which is a person's highest good. Sterilization injures this ethical good when, by deliberate choice, it deprives of an essential component a sexual act which is *foreseen and freely chosen*.[75]

Later the Response re-iterates this mention of *freely* chosen sexual activity as a necessary element in any truly contraceptive intervention:

> Any cooperation of (Catholic hospitals) is absolutely forbidden which amounts to institutional permission or approval of actions which of themselves (that is by their nature and by their condition) are directed towards a *contraceptive end, namely*, that the connatural effect of sexual actions may be impeded when those *sexual actions are being deliberately allowed by the sterilized person*.[76]

It is necessary to note that the opening sentence (and some other parts) of the Response could *mislead* the casual reader into thinking that the Congregation intended to condemn *"any sterilization whatsoever"* of a healthy reproductive system:

> *Any sterilization whatsoever* which of its own self and by its own condition has immediately this one effect, namely that the generative faculty be rendered incapable of achieving pregnancy, is to be considered a direct sterilization, as that term is understood in the declarations of Papal Magisterium, especially of Pius XII. It remains, therefore, absolutely forbidden according to the teaching of the Church...[77]

It is only later, in the two passages which we first quoted from this 1975 Response, that the Congregation makes it clear that it is speaking out only against attempts to render infecund sexual actions which are *freely and deliberately chosen*. This later clarification would seem to be consistent with the Congregation's tacit

---

[75]*ibid., E.V.*, n. 1200: "Sterilitas enim in se intenta non dirigitur ad personae bonum integrale recte intentum 'rerum bonorumque ordine servato', *si quidem eius bono ethico, quod est supremum, nocet*, cum ex proposito privet esentiali elemento *praevisam libereque electam* activitatem sexualem." (emph. add.)

[76]*ibid.*, n. 1202: "Quaevis eorum cooperatio institutionaliter adprobata vel admissa ad actiones ex seipsis (hoc est, ex natura et conditione ipsarum) in finem contraceptivum ordinatas, nimirum, ut impediantur effectus connaturales *actuum sexualium a subiecto sterilizato deliberate admissorum*, est absolute interdicta."

[77]*ibid.* n. 1200: "Quaecumque sterilizatio quae ex seipsa, seu ex natura et conditione propria, immediate hoc solummodo efficit ut facultas generativa incapax reddatur ad consequendam procreationem, habenda est pro sterilizatione directa, prout haec intelligitur in declarationibus Magisterii Pontificii, speciatim Pii XII. Absolute, ergo, interdicta manet iuxta doctrinam Ecclesiae,...."

acceptance of the solution used in the case of the Belgian Congo Sisters, as well as the opinions of Zalba, Visser, Günthör and the other authors we have reviewed in this chapter.[78]

The "directness", then, of the *"direct* sterilization" condemned by Pius XII and, here, by the Congregation does not refer to the *physical* directness of the effect of any sterilizing operation whatsoever. Such physical "directness" is not absolutely ruled out; it can be justified under the principle of totality to save a woman (married or single) from being unjustly impregnated from a sexual act which she does not *will.* She has a right to take such a step for the sake of basic self-defense. The "directness' which is condemned refers to directly achieving a state of sterility to which a woman has *no right,* because she *freely wills and intends* the sexual actions which could produce a pregnancy.

One final document from the era of Paul VI comes, not from the Holy See, but from the American Bishops. *Human Life in Our Day* is their response to *Humanae Vitae* and gives evidence (though not as much as does the encyclical itself) of awareness of the new principles which must shape our theology of marriage. The Bishops first of all indicate that their own acceptance of *Humanae Vitae* is not rooted in any outdated over-reverence simply for the biological structures of human organs or actions:

> Christian sexual morality derives... *not* from the inviolability
> of *generative biology,* but ultimately from the sanctity of life
> itself and the nobility of human sexuality.[79]

Secondly, the Bishops, however briefly and inchoatively, pick up from *Humanae Vitae* the role of the conjugal act as God-given *sign* and *language.* The Bishops also indicate that this sign and language is *contradicted,* not only when contraceptive measures break the act in its physical structure, but also when a spouse's internal committment to love is withdrawn:

> Both conciliar and papal teaching emphasize that the interrelation between the unitive *meaning* and the procreative *meaning* of marriage is impaired, even *contradicted,* when acts expressive of marital union are performed *without love* on the one hand and without openness to life on the other.[80]

JOHN PAUL II

As we have seen in the opening paragraphs of this study, John Paul II caused a great deal of comment and even consternation in his teaching that a man can be

---

[78]This our interpretation of the Congregation's intent *not* to condemn sterilization as a means of self-defense against unjust impregnation was confirmed in a private conversation with Archbishop Hamer, Secretary of the Sacred Congregation, in November, 1980. This type of self-defense, according to the Archbishop, is now "classic doctrine in moral theology," and was carefully reviewed by the Congregation at the time the Belgian Congo case was receiving great notoriety. The 1975 Response to the American Bishops was phrased *precisely to avoid condemning* this doctrine of the moralists.

[79]*Human Life In Our Day",* A collective Letter of the American Hierarchy, November 15, 1968, Washington, D.C., p. 9. (emph. add.)

[80]*ibid.,* p. 11

guilty of "adultery in the heart" in regard even to his own wife. The same Holy Father does not, however, speak explicitly to another point which challenges our contemporary thought patterns, the point we are studying: sexual oppression, i.e., rape, within marriage. As we shall see, however, all the supporting principles which would justify both this categorization and an oppressed wife's consequent use of artificial means for self-defense against the beginning of a pregnancy are present in John Paul's teaching. Moreover the teaching of the theologians who hold this position remains untouched by the official teaching agencies of this Pope who is recognized as being particularly concerned to correct any distortions of authentic Catholic doctrine. Finally, it is in the reign of John Paul II that at least one national hierarchy – the Irish – officially, if somewhat *sotto voce*, adopts the very position of these theologians.

As to teachings issuing from Pope John Paul II himself, we shall confine ourselves to his Apostolic Exhortation *Familiaris Consortio*,[81] which is a synthesis, not only of the Pope's many Wednesday audience discourses on Christian marriage, but also of the teaching he wishes to uphold after the consultation offered by the 1980 Synod of Bishops in Rome. We shall give here a rather cursory consideration of three themes which, without explicitly adopting the thesis we propose, yet, like the Magisterial developments we have previously examined, clearly point to it: (1) the need, in moral questions, for a *personalist* analysis which is truly compatible with the Catholic Faith; (2) the increased and necessary consciousness of the *dignity of women*; (3) the centrality of personal and genuine *love* between spouses in our considerations of marriage morality. We shall also consider somewhat more extensively a fourth element of John Paul's teaching which in the judgement of the present writer is of decisive importance: the nature of the conjugal act as God-given *sign* or *language* for married couples to use.

John Paul does not hesitate to promote, first of all, a truly Christian Personalism, i.e., an appeal to dimensions which are uniquely proper to the *person* as a *person* in our ethical evaluations. Such a Christian personalism does not, of course, amount to an individualism which ignores all existence but one's own; nor does it allow for an arbitrary manipulation of the body and its functions, as if "the person" were constituted only by the spiritual faculties of man, and not at the same time by his bodily ones. Nor does this Christian Personalism of John Paul II allow for the disgarding of all negative moral absolutes, i.e., of the type to be respected universally and without exception. (Homosexual actions, masturbation, and pre-marital or artificial substitutes for the conjugal act "need not apply" for vindication – no matter what the "advantages"! – not to mention abortion and other direct attacks against the bodily life of the innocent).

This Christian Personalism does, however, involve an unwillingness to consider the conjugal act as something with *only* a *biological* dimension, as a *merely biological* "thing" which is "contracted for" by marriage, as a *merely biological* "means" to which a husband is entitled for the procreation of offspring. One passage of *Familiaris Consortio* makes this point particularly clear:

---

[81]MCMLXXXI, Typis Polyglottis Vaticanis for both the original Latin and the English translation.

> Consequently, sexuality, by means of which man and woman give themselves to one another through the acts which are proper and exclusive to spouses, is *by no means something purely biological,* but concerns the innermost being of the human *person* as such. It is realized in a truly human way only if it is an integral part of the love by which a man and a woman commit themselves totally to one another until death.[82]

This emphasis on "the human person" as such, and on the body-soul unity by which *alone* a person can claim to be expressing himself, is re-iterated throughout *Familiari Consortio.*[83] Thus, whatever the bad name some kinds of "personalism" may (rightly) have among some Catholic writers, Pope John Paul clearly recognizes a type quite sympathetic to the Catholic Faith. This Christian Personalism does not allow us to judge a biological action as morally good unless that action is expressing a morally good decision of the person.[84]

Indeed, in the case of the conjugal act, a person must be expressing that *one* moral decision for which the biological action *calls* by reason of God's own creative plan: the basic decision for conjugal love. Where a basic conjugal love is not being expressed, the biological dimension has no moral value whatsoever, and need not be maintained in its physiological wholeness. This would justify a wife's breaking the physiological dimension of the conjugal act where that *physiological* dimension is the *only* one present. This would be the case where the *mental* dimension of the act has been withdrawn by a deliberate decision (i.e. on the part of the husband) *not* to love, but to exploit her.

The second element in *Familiaris Consortio* relevant to our position is the contemporary awareness of the equal dignity woman has with man, the dignity and the right she has to make free, responsible choices. The Pope writes:

> Above all it is important to underline the equal dignity and responsibility of woman with man. This equality is realized in a unique manner in the reciprocal self-giving by each one to the other. . . . What human reason intuitively perceives and acknowledges is fully revealed by the word of God: the history of salvation is, in fact, a continuous and luminous testimony of the dignity of woman.[85]

---

[82]*ibid.,* n. 11 (emph. add.)

[83]*ibid.,* n. 8: "moral values. . . are the values of *the person as such."* (n. 11) "Sexuality is realized in a truly human way only if it is *an integral part of love. . .* (n. 11): "As an incarnate spirit, that is, a *soul which expresses itself in a body and a body informed by a soul, man is called to love in his unified totality."* Cf. also n. 31, par. 3 and 4. (emph. add.)

[84]Neither, of course, does this Christian Personalism allow for a purely proportionalist solution which would justify any external action as morally good simply because a person *intended* it to be an expression of love in spite of the fact that the external act is in basic conflict with the dignity of man's bodily life. John Paul II's Christian Personalism, as is obvious from his teaching on artificial contraception, homosexuality, and abortion, would never allow that such acts could be "converted" into "morally good acts" by reason of their proportionately good effects.

[85]n. 22

In other places, John Paul cites this respect for the personal freedom and dignity of woman as one of the more promising phenomena in contemporary life,[86] its foundational nature in conjugal love,[88] and its necessity for the development of proper family relationships.[89]

John Paul insists, then, on a woman's right to *consent freely* to what touches her personal dignity which is of *equal value* with her husband's. It is quite impossible to reconcile such a basic right of a woman with any alleged right of a husband to demand a sexual act from her when such an act would threaten her with a pregnancy which would violate her basic obligations to herself and/or her children.

The third element in *Familiaris Consortio* which supports our thesis is the teaching that a personal commitment to *love* is part of any *moral* use of the power of transmitting life, i.e., of the conjugal act. Indeed, Pope John Paul insists that the Church has an obligation to speak out on the morality of genital actions precisely because of the sacredness, not simply of a new human life which could be created, but of the *love* that must exist between husband and wife.

> Precisely because the *love* of husband and wife is a unique participation in the mystery of life and of the love of God himself, the Church knows that she has received the special mission of guarding and protecting the lofty dignity of marriage and the most serious responsibility of the transmission of human life.[89a]

The passage which we quoted above regarding the *personalist* analysis on which the Pope insists make this same point.[89b]

The Pope is clear then: (1) that moral questions cannot be judged on a *merely* biological basis which has been abstracted from its personalist dimension; (2) that woman is *equally* a person with man; (3) and that the personalist element of the commitment to mutual love is *central* to the moral integrity of the conjugal act. These three elements of Pope John Paul's teaching are the context of a fourth element which is a dramatic confirmation of much which had been written by certain theologians and even taught in the Magisterium, but which somehow, in the judgement of the present writer, has not yet penetrated the thinking of many, even professional moralists: the nature of the conjugal act as a *sign*, as a *language,* given to husband and wife by the Creator-Father in its very physiological structure (the release of the male fluids by the husband and the acceptance and harboring of them by his wife) to be their own exclusive *sign* and *language* for the love which is

---

[86]n. 6

[87]n. 24

[88]n. 25

[89]*ibid.*

[89a]"Idcirco omino quod coniugum *amor* participatio singularis est vitae mysterii atque ipsius Dei amoris, se scit Ecclesia peculiare recepisse officium custodiendae et tuendae excelsae dignitatis matrimonii necnon gravissimum munus vitae humanae tradendae." (emph. add.)

[89b]*Supra,* pp. 116-117.

uniquely between them. The conjugal act is, by its very nature, a physiological way, not only of *producing* something (a baby), but of *saying* something ("We love each other as only husband and wife can.").

To this theme of the conjugal act as a *sign* and *language* the Pope dedicates the entirety of number 32 of *Familiaris Consortio*. We simply quote most of that passage here, emphasizing in our quotation the elements which can be categorized only as elements of *communication: meaning (significatio), sense (sensus), language (verbum),* and *truth (veritas)* which the conjugal act *declares (declarat);* or their opposites: *contradiction (contradictio), simulation (simulatio), deceit (fallacia)*.

> In the context of a culture which seriously distorts or entirely misinterprets the true *meaning (significatione)* of human sexuality because it separates it from its essential reference to the person, the Church more urgently feels how irreplaceable is her mission of presenting sexuality as a value and task of the whole person, created male and female in the image of God.
>
> In this perspective the Second Vatican Council clearly affirmed that "when there is a question of harmonizing conjugal love with the responsible transmission of life, the moral aspect of any procedure does not depend solely on sincere intentions or on an evaluation of motives. It must be determined by objective standards. These, based on the nature of the human person and his or her *acts,* preserve the full *sense (sensum)* of mutual self-giving and human procreation in the context of true love. Such a goal cannot be achieved unless the virtue of conjugal chastity is sincerely practised." It is precisely by moving from "an integral vision of man and of his vocation, not only his natural and earthly, but also his supernatural and eternal vocation," that Paul VI affirmed that the teaching of the church "is founded upon the inseparable connection, willed by God and unable to be broken by man on his own initiative, between the two *(ambae)* meanings of the conjugal act: the unitive *meaning (significationem)* and the procreative *meaning (significationem.)*" And he concluded by re-emphasizing that there must be excluded as intrinsically immoral "every action which, either in anticipation of the conjugal act, or in its accomplishment, or in the development of its natural consequences, proposes, whether as an end or as a means, to render procreation impossible."
>
> When couples, by means of recourse to contraception, separate *these two meanings (ambas illas significationes)* that God the Creator has inscribed in the being of man and woman and in the dynamism of their sexual communion, they sit in judgement on the divine plan and "manipulate" and degrade human sexuality – and with it themselves and their married partner – even though

they do not change their intent to express a total self-giving. Thus the *innate language (naturali verbo)* that expresses the total reciprocal self-giving of husband and wife is overlaid, through contraception, by an *objectively contradictory language, (verbum . . . objectivae contradictionis)* namely, that of *not* giving oneself totally to the other. This leads *not only* to a positive refusal to be open to life *but also* to a *falsification of the inner truth (simulatio . . . interioris veritatis)* of conjugal love, which is called upon to give itself in personal totality.

When, instead, by means of recourse to periods of infertility, the couple respect the inseparable connection between the unitive and procreative *meanings (significationum)* of human sexuality they are acting as *ministers* of God's plan and they benefit from their sexuality according to the original dynamism of total self-giving, without *deceit (fallaciis)* or alteration.[89c]

That the conjugal act, then, is of its very nature *sign* and *language* is the clear teaching of Pope John Paul.

The teaching of Pope John Paul in *Familiaris Consortio* does not, then, deal explicitly with the issue of sexual oppression within marriage, or with an oppressed wife's use of artificial means to avoid the beginnings of a pregnancy. The Holy Father does, however, teach that:

1) A sexual act does not pass the test of morality purely on the basis of its physiological integrity, without any consideration

---

[89c]n. 32: "In adiunctis cultus humani, qui graviter deformat, quinimmo etiam aberrat a vera *significatione* sexualitatis humanae, quoniam eam ab essentiali coniunctione sua cum persona ipsa divellit, Ecclesia sentit magis urgere nec substitui posse officium suum exhibendi sexualitatem velut bonum opusque totius personae, quae ut mas ac femina ad imaginem creata est Dei."

"His de rebus Concilium Vaticanum Secundum manifesto edixit: Moralis. . . indoles rationis agendi, ubi de componendo amore coniugali cum responsabili vitae transmissione agitur, non a sola sincera intentione et aestimatione motivorum pendet, sed obiectivis criteriis, ex personae eiusdemque *actuum* natura desumptis, determinari debet, quae integrum *sensum* mutuae donationis ac humanae procreationis in contextu veri amoris observant; quod fieri nequit nisi virtus castitatis coniugalis sincero animo colatur."

"Admonens quidem Paulus VI, Pontifex Maximus, ut totum hominem totumque, ad quod is vocatus est, munus complectatur, quod non tantum ad naturalia et terrena sed etiam ad supernaturalia et aeterna pertinet, hoc affirmavit super Ecclesiae doctrina: in nexu indissolubili nititur, a Deo statuto, quem homini sua sponte infringere non licet, inter *significationem* unitatis et *significationem* procreationis, quae *ambae* in actu coniugali insunt. Et concludens id denique inculcavit: tamquam suapte natura inhonestus quivis respuendus est actus qui, cum coniugale commercium vel praevidetur vel efficitur vel ad suos naturales exitus ducit, id tamquam finem obtinendum aut viam adhibendam intendat, ut procreatio impediatur."

"Quotiens vero coniuges, methodis contra conceptionem utentes, disiungunt *ambas illas significationes,* quas Creator Deus in naturam ipsam inseruit viri ac mulieris atque in dynamicam actionem eorum communionis sexualis, sese gerunt tamquam arbitri divini consilii et detorquent deiciuntque sexualitatem humanam et cum ea propriam personam atque personam coniugis, immutato momento donationis totalis. Sic *naturali verbo,* quod reciprocam plenamque coniugum donationem *declarat,* conceptuum impeditio *verbum* opponit *objectivae contradictionis,* videlicet *nullius* plenae sui donationis alteri factae: hinc procedit non sola recusatio certa ac definita mentis ad vitam apertae, verum *simulatio* etiam *interioris veritatis* ipsius amoris coniugalis, qui totam personam dirigitur ad sese donandum."

"Cum coniuges, e contra, per usum temporum infecundorum observant nexum indissolubilem *significationum* unitatis ac procreationis, quae in sexualitate humana insunt, sese gerunt tamquam ministros divini consilii et utuntur sexualitate secundum pristianam virtutem dynamicam totalis donationis sine *fallaciis* aut mutationibus."

of what the act expresses of the internal disposition of the person acting.

2) Commitment to conjugal love is an element intrinsic to the sexual act (especially for those called to Christ by Baptism, but also universally).

3) Man and woman have an equal dignity which, in the conjugal act, as in all things, demands a respect for each other's rights and obligations, - - a respect essential to this conjugal love.

4) The conjugal act, in its physiological dimension, is designed by our Creator as a language for expressing this love.

It follows from the Pope's teaching, that the conjugal act is *counterfeited* and bereft of all moral dignity *either* because the physiological elements of its God-given language-nature have been subverted, *or* because these elements are being used physiologically while internal commitment to conjugal love has been, at least temporarily, revoked or made inoperable. Such a *counterfeited* act, we hold, is not subject to the moral solicitude which the Church extends to the *genuine* conjugal act in her repudiation of artificial contraception.

One final document of the era of Pope John Paul II, and indeed a document which, like *Familiaris Consortio,* has the 1980 Synod of Bishops as its context, comes, not from the hand of the Pope, but from the Irish Episcopal Conference on November 20, 1980. The document is a set of pastoral guidelines for priests issued by the Conference in view of recent civil legislation allowing in Ireland a somewhat limited sale of contraceptive agents.[90] Following an accurate review of theological principles for formal and material cooperation, as well as pastoral principles for dealing with recidivism and with invincible ignorance, the Irish Bishops then state:

> It sometimes happens that the use of contraceptives does not have the real *meaning* of a contraceptive act. This situation may be one of "quasi-rape", in which the husband forces intercourse on the wife, thereby *contradicting* the very *meaning* of married love. In these circumstances recourse to contraceptives by the wife would not appear to be an act of contraception in *the moral sense,* since this presupposes that intercourse is free, i.e., possesses the minimum degree of freedom necessary for a human act. In a situation of this kind there may be no moral objection to co-operation by a doctor or pharmacist in

---

[90]The guidelines were not issued in printed form or made available to the press, religious or secular. Each Bishop was to use his own discretion in making them availalbe to his priests. The paragraphs we shall quote appeared subsequently in *America,* February 7, 1981, p. 89. While we have been requested by an official of the Conference not to quote from the mimeographed copies of the guidelines which have come into our hands, there is no doubt as to their authenticity. Moreover, Irish priests visiting in Rome, including the chancellor of one diocese, inform us that, as might be expected, they have been made available not only to priests, but, in at least some dioceses, to physicians, nurses, and pharmacists.

providing a contraceptive (always provided, of course, that it is not an abortifacient in disguise).[91]

The Bishops do not give a detailed theological reasoning on which their teaching is based. We can note, however, resonances of the teaching found especially in *Gaudium et Spes, Humanae Vitae,* and *Familiaris Consortio* that: 1) the conjugal act has a *meaning* it is supposed to convey; 2) this meaning is a man's dedication to genuine *love* for his wife; 3) without this meaning's being present internally, the external physiological actions are *contradicted;* 4) this *meaning* is *contradicted,* when the act is forced upon the woman. While it is not clear what if any magisterial weightiness is to be assigned to a collaborative teaching effort of an individual national conference of Bishops, the guidelines certainly reflect the doctrine of a large number of bishops teaching within the confines of their own dioceses, where, in union with the Bishop of Rome, they do teach with true, even though not infallible, charism.[92]

SUMMARY

We began this chapter V with the clear evidence that a significant number of theologians, beginning in 1960, accepted as valid both the category of sexual oppression within marriage and the right of a wife thus abused to defend herself against the unjust imposition of a pregnancy which might ensue from a forced act. In spite of their awareness, expressed by several of them, of the possibility of distortion of this category and of abuses to which their doctrine would be vulnerable in practice, they argued that their position was based on doctrine which they found emerging with ever increasing clarity in the Church's teaching, including the official teaching. Four points in particular pointed in the direction of their teaching on sexual oppression within marriage:

1) That a genuine commitment to interpersonal love is one of the irreducible elements of the marriage bond.

2) That a wife has, with her husband, a basically equal right to this love, which of necessity includes a respect for her own rights and obligations.

3) That one of a wife's obligations is to defend her own personal dignity.

4) That an internal withdrawal of the commitment to love violates, not only the marriage bond, but, in some way, the conjugal act itself, whose physiological dimension, without love, ceases to have moral value and is, indeed, sinful.

---

[91]*ibid.* (emph. add.)

[92]*Gaudium et Spes,* n. 25.

The Magisterium in these 20 years did not explicitly address the issue in the strong terms of intra-marital rape; nor did it explicitly approve the use of artificial means for avoiding pregnancy in such circumstances. It did, however, officially make its own, in language more explicit than ever, the four principles on which the theologians rested their case. Moreover, it left the theologian's doctrine on this point unchallanged. As a matter of fact, with the exception of two, all of the theologians whom we cited would have to be listed as solid defenders of the doctrine of *Humanae Vitae*.

CHAPTER VI:
AN ENDING AND A BEGINNING

We began this study with two goals in mind: 1) to show that there has been true and, indeed, dramatic development of the doctrine of theologians regarding sexual oppression within marriage over the past 380 years; and 2) to show that it is at least a solidly probably opinion today that a woman who cannot escape sexual oppression from her own husband may, without going against Catholic teaching, licitly resort to artificial means to avoid a pregnancy resulting from sexual acts thus forced upon her. These goals have been clearly achieved, and we shall, in this closing chapter, show this in a summary way. We shall also indicate certain elements characteristic of the work of theologians of previous ages but which must be abandoned. And finally we shall indicate three elements necessary for any understanding of the conjugal act and for any theology of marriage.

A. Development of Theologians' Doctrine Regarding Sexual Oppression Within Marriage

We have shown in the preceeding chapters how dramatically the doctrine of 17th century thologians on sexual oppression within marriage differs from the doctrine of a number of theologians today who teach on this point in unchallenged harmony with the Church's Magisterium. In this section we shall summarize the evidence in these chapters.

DEVELOPMENT OF DOCTRINE: AN ECCLESIAL REALITY

First, however, we should emphasize that it is development in *theologians'* doctrine that we have sought to identify, not in the *Church's* doctrine. The distinction between these two is important. For theology is, in a certain true sense, "a private enterprise" within the Church, not an official corporate enterprise. Not that theology can claim "laissez-faire" privileges of "no interference" from the pastoral group which governs the Church as its bishops-pastors. For where the welfare of the whole Church within which theologians carry out their own enterprise is being threatened, authorities of the Magisterium have an obligation to put limits to what theologians may say. Such limits are reached when theologians, willy-nilly, begin to misrepresent what the Church is and stands for, and thus compromise the Church's deep knowledge of the person of Jesus Christ and the way of life to which that knowledge commits one. The Church is graced to possess and to share this knowledge and way of life with her members and indeed to discern when it is being basically distorted by anyone, including theologians.

The Magisterium, then, in contrast to the body of theologians, can teach officially, i.e., in a binding manner with and in the authority of the teaching Christ. Some of her doctrinal positions are permanent and, at least eventually, can be so identified, most easily in dogmatic definitions. Other positions, however, though binding, are only provisional. These latter, by the Church's own admission, are evidently such by reason of the formulae used and the circumstances involved, and represent only the best response the Church can come up with, in good conscience, at a given point of doctrinal development. An example would be the human and personal status of the newly conceived embryo in its first two weeks. Should sufficient embryological evidence accumulate in the next decades (a highly unlikely prospect, in the present writer's estimate), the Church might have to withdraw her absolute condemnation against aborting all such embryos.

The Magisterium could move, of course, in a positive and opposite direction from this: from seeing a position as perhaps provisional to seeing it clearly as permanent. The Church can, moreover, defend a formulation of theologians against its attackers, as the Council of Trent did in declaring the doctrine of transubstantion an evangelically useful *(aptus)* mode of expressing her belief in the Eucharistic Real Presence.

In regard to the theology of marriage, we would maintain that the Church, in the Magisterium of Pope John Paul II in *Familiaris Consortio,* has made a similar positive move with the affirmation of some theologians that the conjugal act is of its nature *language.* We would note also the 1980 moral doctrine guidelines of the Irish Episcopal Conference and, in a lesser vein, the pages of *Osservatore Romano* in the 1978 observance of the tenth anniversary of *Humanae Vitae.* While we cannot find the same Magisterial endorsement in these two documents for the main point of our thesis as we can in an apostolic exhortation, still these documents give at least some significant indication that the Church views with benignity the position we espouse.

Behind all evidences of development of the doctrine of theologians and the eventual use the Church may make of that for her own doctrinal development lies the issue of the very *possibility* of such development. That there is such development going on constantly (though at greater or lesser rates of acceleration at various times) is guaranteed, as Juan Alfaro points out in the quotation we have given from him in Chapter IV, by the necessarily limited attention the Church can concentrate on a particular time in history, etc. It is precisely in the limited questions with which theologians were previously addressing the subject of sexual oppression within marriage that we find an obvious explanation of how such a dramatic reversal of their common teaching could have taken place between 1600 and 1980. Theologians have to "feel their way" along at times shadowy sections of the passageways they explore.

So also must the Church in her Magisterium "feel her way". It is not always easily evident to her official teachers which expressions of doctrine must be ruled out, which should be tolerated, which encouraged, and which pronounced upon. One of the most important facts which has surfaced in this study is the unwillingness of the Church to pronounce on the issue we are examining (as also on many other important issues) because the issue was not clear to her. That the Church has issues - moral issues included - upon which she has taken an irrevocable stand is clear. That she mechanically pops out ready-made answers to every question facing her is a deceitful myth which should be laid to rest.

DEVELOPMENT ON SEXUAL OPPRESSION HAS TAKEN PLACE

Development of doctrine, then, is a real possibility for theologians and for the Church. And on the issue of sexual oppression it has actually taken place, at least in the area of such oppression *within* marriage. Regarding such oppression *outside* marriage, there was a lively camp of supporters for Sanchez' view right from the day he raised the issue. Not so, however, regarding rape *within* marriage! The liceity of artificial efforts to avoid impregnanion from such oppression was all but universally rejected from the day Sanchez broached the question. The question was, moreover, in effect dropped from discussion from Bossius in the 17th century to Schmidt in the 20th. Now, in the period immediately prior to Vatican Council II and, most significantly, in the wake of *Humanae Vitae,* we find one defender of the Church's traditional doctrine after another defending also the liceity of such pregnancy-prevention. The present writer was, moreover, able to find no recent opposition to the thesis at all.

As we still deal here with the dramatic change of theological opinion in this matter, I think it necessary in all honesty to recognize that, though not justifiable, much of the dissent from *Humanae Vitae* may be largely attributable to failings of the older moral theology which we have had occasion to examine in this study. Leaving to the Lord judgements as to the subjective motivations of dissenters and as to the objective damage done by the dissent (the latter enormous, unnecessary, and tragic, in the writer's opinion), must we not admit that the limitations of the older theology on conjugal life did much to provoke the dissent? Let us face it: That theology limped! Badly!

To say this is not to condone the *capovolgimento* – the turning of everything upside down – of which L. Ciccone speaks. It is to join him and other defenders of *Humanae Vitae* such as Christopher Derrick in condemning a legalistic approach which, for all their great, great value, so often hampered the classical moral manuals.

The present writer personally never dissented from *Humanae Vitae.* Quite the contrary! Yet I recall my reactions in my first quick reading of it practically as it came off the teletype in a newspaper editorial room. "How wooden! The Pope hasn't taken a step forward. Of course, how could he? The theologians haven't given him any place to step!"

But I was wrong about the Pope's teaching and about the theologians, – at least some of them. Enough to count.

B. A Solidly Probable Opinion Today

The second goal of this study was to show that it is a solidly probable opinion today that there may indeed be cases where a wife may use even artificial means of avoiding pregnancy without having to fear that she is thus going against the teaching of the Church regarding contraception. We shall give intrinsic and extrinsic reasons for defending this stance.

INTRINSIC REASONS

It is now clearly established in the doctrine of the Church that the conjugal act is, of the very nature given it by the Creator, a *sign* of the marriage commitment. It is thus constituted of an *internal message* (the marriage commitment) to which apt expression is given by *external manifestations* (the release of the male fluids on the part of the male and the acceptance of them into the vagina on the part of the woman.) Where the *external manifestations* are used, but the *internal message* is no longer intended, what is left is a lie, – a *locutio contra mentem*. Such a deceitful use of the external manifestations makes them part of a counterfeit conjugal act, and allows for none of the moral inviolability inherent in the genuine conjugal act. Therefore these physiological dimensions of the counterfeit conjugal act may be disposed of in whatever way is least dangerous to the party who has been or will be victimized by them.

A comparison with another human communication of the conjugal commitment may help clarify the argument. The *marriage vows* are also, in their integral nature, a *sign*, i.e., as *sign* they are composed of an *internal message* and an *external manifestation* of that message. If *either* the internal message *or* the external manifestation is absent, there are no vows. No one would pretend that we have marriage vows when either the man or the woman is both pronouncing the *words* of the vows and at the same time deliberately withholding *acceptance* of one of the basic elements of the vows. We rightly call such "vows" *simulatio* and in our Tribunals pronounce them invalid, i.e., non-existent.

The same is true when it comes to re-iterating the marriage vows, this time not in words and symbols called for by cultural (and ecclesial) convention, but in the *language* given for this purpose by the Lord Himself: the conjugal act. Where the basic *internal commitment* is mutually held to by both partners of a marriage, and the *external body-language* in the structure given it by the Creator is respected, then we have the authentic conjugal act which the Church wishes to defend as inviolable. Otherwise we have a counterfeit act basically divorced from human dignity and bereft of any moral value whatsoever.

Someone might object that the sperm and the ova are obviously intrinsically oriented towards procreation, and that any deliberate frustration of this orientation is against natural law as manifest in the very nature of these gametes. Obviously, however, such an argument is based on a purely physicalist theology which is utterly discredited in both theology and Church doctrine. As an argument, it is, for example, quite incompatible with the right of a rape victim outside of marriage to use artificial means to frustrate the semen of an attacker. Such a right has been universally accepted by theologians regarding contraceptive douches, and as it now is in the Belgian Congo Sisters' case also for anovulants. This acceptance, as we have seen, has been carefully reviewed by the teaching authority of the Church without any objections whatsoever.

EXTRINSIC REASONS

As is obvious from the preceeding chapter, a group of outstanding defenders of *Humanae Vitae* stand by an oppressed wife's right to defend herself from an unjust impregnation by an abusive husband. Several of them (Visser and Zalba) serve to this day as senior consultors for the Sacred Congregation for Doctrine. The addition of the Irish Bishops' Conference to this list, whatever Magisterial weight such a body may or may not have, certainly at least signals a defensibly respectable theological position. And not entirely without significance, as we have pointed out, is the fact that this position has been defended in the pages of *Osservatore Romano* precisely as part of the tenth anniversary observance of *Humanae Vitae*.

It is to be noted that among these theologians there remain differences as to the complete meaning and exact application of their doctrine on sexual oppression within marriage. We mention here only two such differences.

Should any act of complete sexual copulation be considered "the conjugal act" simply because it takes place between husband and wife? Ciccone expresses the views of a number of authors we have cited:

> It seems to us that one can say that a conjugal act stripped of love compromises the value of sexuality, which is lived at an animal level simply of copulation.[1]

De Margerie is even more explicit, as we have seen, saying simply that such forced acts should not be called "the conjugal act" at all. Nonetheless, all the authors do not make the point, and those who do do not work out its implications.

There is a difference also as to the frequency with which such intramarital sexual oppression occurs as would justify artificial intervention to prevent pregnancy. For example, Visser, it will be recalled, thought it would be most rare. Derrick, on the contrary thought it rather common. Ciccone, who does not treat specifically of the issue of artificial intervention, nonetheless believes that the sexual oppression of which *Humanae Vitae* speaks in its section 13 happens, at least on occasion, among some couples who are otherwise quite happily married.[2] It would seem that the later commentators on this issue favor the view that we have not yet faced up to the pastoral realities of how frequently, through ignorance or defective formation in sexual attitudes, if not always through real malice, sexual oppression within marriage occurs.

C. Elements To Be Abandoned

This study has convinced the present writer that three elements of moral theology prior to Vatican Council II must be abandoned. Although they are not found in the doctrine of the Church, these elements, it could be argued, were an

---

[1] Ciconne, *op. cit.*, p. 296.

[2] Ciccone, *op. cit.*, pp. 293-294.

obstacle to the Church's development of her doctrine in a way more adequate to her personal knowledge of Jesus Christ and to what He reveals to us about ourselves. The three elements are: 1) Physicalism; 2) A distorted view of the marriage *Jus ad corpus;* and 3) An inadequate grasp of the Magisterium's doctrine of Totality.

PHYSICALISM

Insight into the sacredness of the physical structure of our organs and their functions as a gift from God is hardly out of place in a Christian ethic. The "ism" suffix of "physicalism", however, is meant to indicate that we are dealing with an emphasis which amounts to serious distortion. From his general contact with parish priests, moreover, the present writer has the impression, indeed, that this distortion was rampant in theological formation.

The virtue in this erroneous physicalism was that it represented a deeply Christian insight that the body is indeed an aspect of the person. Truly what we do to his body we do to the human person himself. The Church through the ages has pitted this insight against every form of angelism, manicheism, and other cultivations of anti-body attitudes. This insistence on the sacredness of the physical structure of our lives was compatible with a Christian personalism which is developing in our time, though the exaggerations of physicalism retarded any consciousness of many of the personalist aspects of our physical structure.

Proponents of physicalism attempted, moreover, to face up honestly to the obvious fact that sexual activity is truly sexual only as long as it is respected in its procreational character. They opposed the present day world's mad flight from the most obvious of facts: Sex is about having babies. They also recognized that, in a *special* way not true of other human acts, the conjugal act is from the hand of God and admits of only a very limited "re-engineering" on the part of man's genius. And, finally, they saw the logical and inevitably actual connection between society's acceptance of contraception and acceptance of all the forms of sexual activity which the Spirit, as well as man's own rationality, has led the People of God to repudiate as sub-human and anti-Christian: homosexual actions, bestiality, masturbation, etc.

In spite of these strong points, however, this physicalism of the recent past nonetheless revealed certain weaknesses. First of all it saw as the *immediate* inherent end of the conjugal act the procreation of the child. This doctrine flew in the face of facts which are commonplaces of contemporary physiological science. For a married couple who have regular intercourse, say on a weekly basis, the majority of their conjugal acts cannot hope to produce pregnancy, since the woman is fertile only approximately four days out of the month. Moreover, the presumption that the *immediate* purpose of the conjugal act is procreation made it extremely difficult (and in the present writer's judgement, impossible) to defend the natural forms of family limitation which the Church has commended as compatible with the dignity of human sexuality.

A second problem with physicalism is that it reduced the conjugal act and, more important, one's self and one's spouse to a *physical*, i.e., a *material thing*, like a piece of land or a sum of money, which had been duly "contracted for" in the marriage vows. A husband who violated the stipulations of the *bimestre* law, as we have seen, was said by some authors to be guiltless because he was "only taking what was his". The husband, by legal contract, owned his wife's genital organs and the merely physical act of copulation which they made possible. The same was true, of course, of the "ownership" of a wife over her husband's body.

A DISTORTED VIEW OF THE CONJUGAL RIGHT

Concomitant with this concept of the conjugal act as a purely physiological action, was, in the older theology, a misdirected concept of *the conjugal right*, the *jus ad corpus*. As in the case of physicalism, so here also there is considerable and highly valuable truth in the traditional affirmation that there is a *jus ad corpus*. First of all, it keeps before the consciences of all in the Church the fact that there exists between husband and wife a true *right* to the conjugal act. The act is not to be subjected to the mere whims or moods of an individual. Nor is it a tool to be used to manipulate one's partner into giving in to one's own ideas on any of the many possible points of disagreement in marriage.

The true right to the conjugal act is based, at least in part, on the personal surrender which, in the marriage vows, each of the partners makes of his right to select someone else as a marriage partner. As a result of this mutual surrender, each one closes off for himself or herself the right to the genital expression of conjugal love with any other person for the duration of the marriage. Such a surrender, made in a supremely free, informed, and mutual consent, would make a later refusal of the conjugal act an injustice, and, as the manualists have pointed out, even a serious injustice.

Another virtue of the traditional insistence upon the *right* to the conjugal act was its emphasis on something truly physiological and procreational as the object of that right. It was not a right to just *any* physiological act, but to one which is genuinely *aptus ad procreandum*.

The weak points, however, of what we refer to as the older physicalism lay mainly in the answer given, often quite explicitly, to the question: To *what* does the conjugal bond give a right?

Does the conjugal bond in any sense give a right to an act of copulation which, in given circumstances, amounts to a repudiation of the *just* desires of one's partner (e.g., a wife's right to basic good health)? *Humanae Vitae's* section 13 seems to answer quite clearly that "the use of marriage forced upon a partner without regard for the other's condition and reasonable wishes. . . is a rejection of the conditions which the moral order rightly demands of the relationship between the married."

Does the conjugal bond give a right to acts, which, though physiologically complete copulations carried out with mutual consent, yet in their accumulated totality amount to a repudiation of any vocation to procreate (i.e., through the observance of the natural rythms of infertility when a couple has no justified reason to avoid pregnancy)? Pius XII in his 1951 discourse to midwives, pointed out the wrongness of such attempts to use the natural ovulatory rhythms "to evade the primary duty (of married life) without serious reasons. . ."

Does the conjugal bond give a right to copulation in which the wife is used without her free consent, merely as a physiological instrument duly "contracted for", for reproductive purposes (e.g., where the husband's *only* intent is to have his wife "give him a child")? A growing number of theologians, not at all out of harmony with the Christian personalism championed by Pope John Paul II, have warned us that *persons* may not be "used" simply as means to ends, however exalted.

Does the conjugal bond give a right to copulation primarily or even totally intended as a "remedy for concupiscence" (e.g., even where a husband is violating his own basic obligations)? Strüggl was only the first to raise eloquent protest against "using" a wife in such a way.

And, finally, does the conjugal bond give a right to an act which involves great physical pleasure and thus might – derivatively – create *some* kind of unity, through the mutual giving and receiving of pleasure, between two persons who have *de facto* renounced any kind of esteem for one another (e.g., the couple who hate and constantly hurt one another, but stay together "for sex")? As L. Ciccone made the point, the conjugal act is given by God as a celebration of a love which is *already present*, at least germinally, through the mutual consent of the couple.

To all these questions above, we would answer with resounding "No!" For the conjugal bond gives a couple a right, true enough, but a right to physical actions which are only the physiological dimension of a pluri-dimensional act, namely, the *sign* of mutual giving and acceptance of the totality of one's self and one's marriage partner, including always their procreational nature.

A FALSE AND TIMID INTERPRETATION OF THE PRINCIPLE OF TOTALITY

A third element found commonly prior to Vatican II in the moral theology of conjugal life must be rejected: an indefensibly narrow interpretation of the principle of totality. Like the physicalism and the juridicism of that era, so also the interpretation widely given to the principle of totality had its *forte*, but also its failings. We shall briefly examine both.

Among the strong points was an awareness of the sacredness of the concrete form of the body, its organs, and its function. There have been a variety of theories of material evolution proposed to explain scientifically how we have arrived at this point of history with the physiological realities typical of the human race. Whatever the value of these theories, efforts to uphold the principle of totality emphasized the divine and indeed Christic providence which has been, "from the beginning," at work in the forming of the human body. That body, the principle of totality bears witness, is gift, – yes, even in its details of natural form. These forms may not be manipulated by whatever mutilations may happen to recommend themselves to the latest demands of science and of the technology it spawns.

At the same time, theologian-defenders of the principle of totality did not cower from defending the body in a special way against propaganda favoring the mutilation of the genital faculties. In this, they bore witness (with what explicit consciousness I cannot say) to the special imaging of God which man shows forth precisely in his *sexual* nature. Any necessity for a fundamental destruction of the organic formations which result from and are the marks of that *sexual* nature the principle and its defenders clearly and rightly categorized as tragedy.

Finally, the principle of totality, no matter how misguided some of its explicators may at times have been, pointed out that, however justified one might be at times in having certain organs removed, there were limits to the right to mutilate, and those limits can be identified, formulated and applied.

The weak points, however, of the principle of totality as it was explicated by many showed themselves as this very identification, formulation and application was attempted. A number of theologians could bring themselves to allow for the removal only of seriously *diseased* organs. Some extended this to allow the suppression of a pathological *functioning* of an organ. When it was made abundantly clear in the Magisterium of Pius XII that even *healthy* organs, in certain circumstances, could be removed, many insisted, as Zalba points out, that this could be done only for the good of the *subject* who was going to *undergo* the mutilation. It could not be done for the sake of another, and thus homogeneous transplants *inter vivos* could not be justified. Removal of a healthy organ, moreover, could be done only for the overall *physical* well-being of the subject of such an operation, many maintained, and not for any *spiritual* or other *higher* good. Rome's tacit acceptance of the "Belgian Congo solution" was puzzling.

One by one these excessive limitations of the principle of totality came to be recognized and abandoned by such men as Zalba. He and many others are at the point now – and indeed were so before *Humanae Vitae*, as the "Belgian Congo Sisters" case shows – of recognizing that one may make whatever mutilations of the human body are necessary for the overall good of the individual as a *person* (and not merely as a body), when such mutilations are not otherwise avoidable either through less drastic interventions or by the person's exercise of his own free will in avoiding serious threats to his bodily, spiritual, or personal integrity. The present writer concurs in Zalba's position that this interpretation of the principle of totality is solidly rooted in the Magisterium of Pius XII.

D. Elements For A More Adequate Theology Of Marriage

In his intervention in the Bishops' Synod of 1980, Archbishop (now Cardinal) Joseph Bernadin of Cincinnati made a plea for advancement to a more adequate theology of marriage in these words.

> It cannot be taken for granted that people understand and accept a natural-law ethic, or that citing natural-law principles and formulas, as found in our traditional manuals, will be persuasive or even comprehensible to people unaccustomed to thinking in these categories. This does not mean that the natural-law tradition should be abandoned. It should not. But this tradition needs to be expanded, enriched.
>
> One way to do this is to work toward a more holistic approach to sexuality in conjugal love within the context of natural law. In such an approach, the body is understood not only in relation to the physically identifiable purposes of its parts (e.g., genitals for reproduction) but also as an expression of what it means to be made in God's image.
>
> The complementarity of sexuality (male and female) and its urgent inner dynamism toward union are seen as reflecting in human terms the dynamic unity within the triune God. Thus the difference between the sexes clearly is good, willed by God from the beginning as an integral part of his self-revelation; and light is shed on the need for both *physical* and *psychic* integrity in the act of sexual union through which spouses express and accomplish self-giving.[3]

Without pretending in any way to present in these closing pages an exhaustive treatment of elements necessary to be included in the truly "holistic approach to sexuality" which the Cardinal advocates, I would hope here to review briefly at least some of those elements as they have surfaced in the course of the present study. We shall, moreover, focus our consideration on the conjugal act as the supreme physical expression which is unique to those bonded in true marriage. We shall comment on that act as: 1) a *procreative* act; 2) an act of *justice;* 3) an act of *speaking*.

A PROCREATIONAL ACT

The conjugal act is a procreational act, i.e., it is inherently ordered to procreation. We would distinguish here between a *procreational* act and a *procreative* act, stipulating by the latter term an act which will *de facto* produce a procreative *effect*, i.e., a new human life. *Per se,* by an innate design and dynamism, the conjugal act is *procreative. Per accidens,* however, it may not be procreative. The lack of procreative *effect* will at times be due to controlling factors inherent to

---

[3] "Sexuality and Church teaching," in *Origins*, October 9, 1980.

our sexuality (i.e., the ovulation cycle) and quite according to nature. Or it may be due to some pathological deficiency which is the result of the damaged condition of the human race, whose very bodies cry out for redemption.[4]

Both *per se* and *per accidens,* however, i.e., *always* and *without exception,* the conjugal act will be *procreational,* i.e., oriented towards procreation. This orientation moreover is primarily and immediately located in the conjugal act, not as *effecting* an *actual procreation,* but as *expressing* the *procreational character* of the couple and of their union. In other words, on the one hand, the orientation of the act towards procreation is *ex sese* in the *intentional* order, i.e., the act, in its very God-given physiological components, *signifies* or *speaks of* procreation. On the other hand, the orientation of the act is only *per se* towards procreation in the *real* order; *per accidens* it may not, in a given instance, be so oriented.

Indeed, a couple may, for mature reasons, rightly make it their positive intention that the conjugal act, in a whole series of given instances, not be oriented towards procreation in the *real* order; or they may simply resign themselves to such a situation (as in the case of insuperable sterility). In both these cases, however, they are accepting the basic *procreational* nature of the act, i.e., its nature as a God-given *expression* or *sign* of what they are and of what their union is: *procreational.*[4a] This procreational nature, moreover, is of God's making, and consequently, in thus expressing themselves procreationally in the act, they are expressing their acceptance of their calling, which, in God's plan, is procreational. Thus, while they may have a moral obligation to intend, for a time, not to actually conceive new life (or even not to conceive at all, in at least some rare cases), or while they may disappointedly foresee that, due to pathological conditions, no child will be forthcoming, they nonetheless see these instances of sterility as modulations *(accidentia)* of their vocation to be open to the child God may want to give. In thus using the conjugal act to express their acceptance of their procreational character and calling as a couple, they avoid that indifferent attitude towards procreation against which Pius XII warned:

> The sole fact that the couple do not offend against the nature of the act and that they are willing to accept and bring up the child that is born notwithstanding the precautions they have taken,

---

[4]Romans 8: 23-24

[4a]Germain Grisez, in his most promising first volume of his series, *The Way of the Lord Jesus* (Chicago, Franciscan Herald, 1984), alludes to the procreational content of marital love (p. 892). Though he does not in this first volume treat *ex professo* the issue of rape (outside or inside marriage), he does seem to equate "contraception" and "conception-preventing behaviors... and techniques" (pp. 892-893). The language is imprecise, I believe, as, obviously, the Church has focused upon the theologians' advocacy of at least *certain* "conception-preventing behaviors... and techniques" and not found them morally reprehensible, i.e., in cases of rape outside marriage.

Moreover, I believe that Grisez is incorrect in saying that "the Church" has always "condemned doing anything to impede the fruitfulness of sexual intercourse by those who choose to engage in it." (p. 893) This would be true regarding married couples who intend to substitute a contraceptive act for the authentic conjugal act. Regarding single persons involved in fornicatory actions, however, only theologians, not "the Church," have spoken in this way. Bossius, as we have seen in Chapter 2, allowed for these "conception-preventing" actions for the woman who had consented to fornication out of fear. His opinion escaped condemnation in the otherwise sweeping decrees under Innocent XI in the 17th century.

would not of itself also be a sufficient guarantee of a right intention and of the unquestionable morality of the motives themselves.

The reason is that marriage binds to a state of life which, while conferring certain rights, imposes the accomplishment of a positive work which belongs to the very state of wedlock.[5]

Pius XII then immediately goes on in the same document to recognize that the obligation to the "positive work" of providing for the continuation of the human race has its limits, which can justify deliberate use of the anovulatory periods. Such a use, however, he has made clear, must never amount to a repudiation of or even an indifference towards the procreation to which they are called by the very nature of their human sexual selves and of their sexual union.

The use of artificial contraception, of course, *always* signals, in the *objective* order, *precisely* such a repudiation, even when the couple, in the *subjective* order, accept the overall procreational nature of their vocation. The deliberate ejaculation of the sperm outside the vagina (and even the use of the condom amounts to this), or its destruction within or casting out from the vagina (and, in effect, even the use of occlusive barriers do this) cannot, in the objective order, be *made* to *speak* of procreation. Such acts can in reality speak *only* of *rejecting* procreation. Their physiological structure can no more speak of procreation than can the physiological structure of homosexual acts, masturbation, or bestiality. As affirmations of one's procreational nature and calling, they are complete failures.

Even sterilization, temporary or permanent, aimed at eradicating beforehand the procreative character of the couple vitiates the procreational character of the conjugal act. It thus makes the act essentially impossible until the person who *willed* the sterilization sincerely repents of what he or she had done. Here the conjugal act is vitiated, not in its external physiological dimension (the semen is still physiologically given by the husband and genitally accepted by the wife), but in its internal, mental and volitional dimension. Until the contraceptive intention behind the operation is withdrawn, there is in the "conjugal act" no true *internal* giving and acceptance between the husband and wife, including their *procreational* nature. The external, physiological dimension of the act, therefore, complete as it may be, becomes as in the case of pre-marital acts, merely on empty shell which *could* express the conjugal bond, but *de facto* does *not*.

We must not hesitate here to be anatomically concrete in our analysis, for our human anatomical concreteness mirrors the God Who created it. Pope John Paul has spoken repeatedly of the "nuptial meaning of the body." Anatomically, then, the final (not the only) "significant" (sign-making and meaning-bearing) result of being a

---

[5]To Midwives, DISCORSI, p. 164: "Il solo fatto che i coniugi non offendono la natura dell'atto e sono anche pronti ad accettare ed educare il figlio, che, nonostante le loro precauzioni, venisse alla luce, non basterebbe per se solo a garantire la rettitudine della intenzione e la moralità ineccepitblile dei motivi medesimi.

La ragione è perche il matrimonio obbliga ad uno stato di vita, il quale, come conferisce certi diritti, cosi impone anche il compimento di un'opera positiva, riguardante lo stato stesso."

male is to be able to produce and release the semen. For a woman it is to be able to attract a man to herself and to be able to receive him and the fruit of his body genitally. The spontaneous concern of men and women about their reproductive integrity, functioning and even fertility can, indeed, be an exaggerated preoccupation. It is, nonetheless, rooted in a basically sound concern. It evidences that a person recognizes that, in a very definite way, the genital organs and products are a precious *sign* of what he or she *is* as a person. This attitude is found in the holiest of people who by no means abuse or are abused in the pleasure aspect of sexual orgasm.

The release into his wife of the semen, then, which, especially in its spermatazoa, represents *himself* is so deeply, psychically satisfying to a man (over and above the obvious considerations of the pleasure associated with orgasm) that his wife's allowing this from any other man is seen as the most profound violation of the husband as a person.

Again, the wife's accepting and welcoming into her body, and her being profoundly thrilled by the presence of her husband within her, both initially in coitus itself and subsequently in the abiding presence of his semen, must not be shied away from in any Christian analysis of marriage. Indeed, she, as a woman, is gifted with a naturally greater sensitivity to the *meaning* of this physiological presence of her husband within her, and finds it more difficult than he to let the absence or diminution of that *meaning* pass unnoticed. She is pained by failures far lesser than adultery in contradicting this meaning. Nor should her part in this making of their unique conjugal sign be seen as merely passive, as merely "receiving" her husband's genital presence. For it is only when she actively provides the ovum that the conjugal act can be transposed from its innate splendor to an even higher wonderousness,[6] so that the couples' love has a newly procreated person as a living sign of itself.

Marriage as a procreational bond, then, and marital intercourse as a procreational act are essential to any human and Christian understanding of what God has wrought in joining man and woman together in marriage.

AN ACT OF JUSTICE

In the judgement of the present writer, it would be a serious mistake in any future construction of a theology of marriage to ignore justice as one characteristic of the conjugal act. There is an obvious, pastoral reason for saying this. For, given the burdens, as well as the gradual and at times painful maturation, which are universally a part of married life, conscientious couples can be immensely helped over difficult periods by a strong, if stark, appeal to justice, an appeal which alone, at times, can restore equilibrium and perspective.

But we are by no means left only with a pragmatic argument as to the pastoral impracticality of abandoning the concept of the right in justice to the conjugal act.

---

[6]*Gaudium et Spes*, n. 50.

For the just right to the conjugal act is established *ontologically* in the nature of each person as *rational,* as *relational,* and as *procreational.* For man is unlike God Who in His love can create out of nothing objects not yet existent and make them worthy of His love (as, indeed, He creates each of us). Instead, each of us is presented with "given" objects for our love: the Creator Himself first of all, and our fellow-creatures as He has, by His prevenient action, made them to be loved by us. If we will not see, recognize and be in wonder at the goodness which God creates in another person without our collaboration, then we make it impossible for us to love that person. And loving that person as God presents him or her to us as a "given" is to love that person as *rational,* as *relational* and as *procreational.* There is no other way to truly love a person, either in marriage or outside it.

By reason of his *rationality,* each partner in a marriage has made a personal (knowledgeable and free) decision to enter into *this* marriage with *this* person and *no other.* As a result of this decision, he or she, "forsaking all others", knowingly and freely rules out the right of any genital expression of intimacy with any other person for the duration of this marriage. This surrender of *all other* possibilities of genital expression is made in view precisely of a mutual understanding that such genital expressions of their unique conjugal union will indeed be part of their life together. This "forsaking of all others to cleave" to the marriage partner alone is, then, a solemn exercise of personal sovereignty. Without a recognized right to the conjugal act and a concomitant obligation to enter into that genital act, this deeply personal exercise of rational choice is trivialized, and, with it, the person whom, allegedly, one has vowed to "love". This is to reject one's partner as God has "given" him or her: as one called to a life of certain basic and profound decisions.

Although a person is not free to take another person except on God's terms, as He creates that person, there is nonetheless an analogous kind of creativity which one is called to exercise towards his or her marriage partner. It is a creativity of helping one's partner (and thus helping one's self) to develop fully all the deeply human gifts which are the "given". Without recognition, however, of the right and obligation in justice to "rendering" the conjugal act, one's marriage partner could be habituated to a life of violations of serious commitments to him or her. Submission to such a pattern could only contribute to the atrophy of a person's own perception of himself or herself as one whose basic, conscientious and rational decisions have significant human worth.

Besides one's rationality, one's *relational* nature must be respected by a recognition that there is a right in justice to the conjugal act. This *relational* nature is also a "given" which comes from the Creator. By it one has a right to communicate the truth about one's self to other persons, and to share in the most human of all projects, the building of genuine human community. In marriage this revelation of self and cultivation of love between two persons has its special and unique language: the physiological dimension of the conjugal act.

To be unwilling, on the one hand, to use this language *when it can be used truthfully* is to refuse communication and thus violate the relational nature of one's partner. It is, in effect, to deny that the Creator has made one's partner with a right and a need to *communicate,* to *express* the most personal relationships to which he had committed himself, and to have those relationships willingly confirmed by his marriage partner.

Recognizing the right to the conjugal act, on the other hand, rules out two things: sexual oppression (outside or inside marriage) and whimsical refusals. And it rules them out precisely because of the relational nature of each of the partners in a marriage.

Sexual oppression is ruled out because, not only does one person involved not *want* to be involved in genital actions, but also and primarily, in these circumstances, the genital actions *cannot speak* of genuine conjugal love. They cannot be "intercourse," i.e., in the more fundamental sense of a willing and free exchange of personal thoughts, decisions, feelings, etc. These physiological acts by their very nature *express* a *reverence* for a person, a reverence which, when they are unjustly forced, is contradicted.

Whimsical refusal of the conjugal act is ruled out also. For recognition of the right to the conjugal act is simply recognition of the *kind* of relational persons the Creator has made by making us as we are. It is *His* choice that we be male and female, that we express ourselves always as male and female, and that we do this in marriage (and nowhere else) precisely by using the genital language of the body. This language He has built into our very persons in their physiological dimension. This language alone is designed by him to speak unambiguously of the conjugal union. To recognize a right to the conjugal act is to recognize, in a true sense, the right of one's marriage partner to speak of and to express what he or she is and what the bond is between them. To deny such a right is, in effect, to deny that God has made us as *relational* beings who are called by our very ontological nature to communicate ourselves, our convictions, our commitments, our deepest personal lives to another. In no relationship is this so true as in marriage, and the conjugal act is its climatic realization.

Finally, the *procreational* nature of each of the marriage partners demands that they recognize the right in justice to the conjugal act. For not only our rationality, i.e., our capacity to choose this marriage among many possible marriages, and our relationality, i.e., the call, built into our very being, to communicate unambiguously to our marriage partner our own nature and the nature of our bond, are part of us ontologically. For a call to be procreational is also ontologically built into our very being, and shows itself in the very physiological and psychological structure towards which our biological inheritance from the human race should propel us.

Failure of these structures to develop can only be regarded as a tragedy, a derailment of God's plan "from the beginning," and the result of the entrance of sin into our racial history. Such failure would include, among other things, hopeless sterility, various physical anomalies such as hermaphroditism, and homosexuality. These conditions call for both compassion towards those who bear such crosses, and, where possible, healing.

This procreational nature of ours requires, however, that we not be subjected or subject ourselves to acts which, in their very objective physiological structure, are repudiations of our procreational nature. Such acts would include the various forms of artificial contraception which the Church has always condemned, as well as various other forms of physiological perversion such as oral or anal ejaculations, masturbation (mutual or solitary), homosexual actions, bestiality, etc. It is to be noted that these actions are contradictory to our procreational nature regardless of what intention – even a heterosexual, conjugal intention – their perpetrators might wish to put upon them. In the objective order, these actions *cannot be made to say* what husband and wife are called to say to each other.

Our nature as *procreational* beings gives us a right, then, to those physiological actions which can beget children, *if* at a given time and in the given circumstances, the begetting of children is truly an expression of *conjugal love*. What must be recognized in any renewed theology of marriage, however, is that the right to the conjugal act is limited, and, indeed, not for extrinsic, but for intrinsic reasons.

An older theology saw the right to the act limited by an extrinsic reason, the right to have children. The reason for this was that the act was seen primarily an instrument for having children. Who has the right to the end, has a right to the means. When a husband lost his right to have children (e.g., because childbirth would kill his frail wife), he lost the right to the conjugal act.

By saying that the limitation of the right is from an *intrinsic* reason, however, we are appealing to the Church's teaching that the begetting of children and the physiological actions which make this possible are, by their very nature, a *sign expressive of conjugal love*. Because it is a *sign*, then, the conjugal act is not constituted only of an external *act*, but also of an internal *meaning*, as are the marriage vows themselves. Indeed, by saying that the limitation to the right to the conjugal act is *intrinsic* to the act, we are saying, more accurately, that the conjugal act, considered in its *essentials*, is *impossible* if its physiological dimensions cannot be, in the given circumstances, an expression of basic commitment to genuine conjugal *love*. Such an act, incapable of "signing love", is a counterfeit, with varying degrees of degradation for those involved in it. This conviction, as we have seen, has been expressed by Ciccone, Derrick, and de Margerie, as well as by others.

We are aware that such a position may present difficulties for the time-honored terminology of canonical jurisprudence, and wish to make it clear that we do not pretend to enter into that field. We present here only what we hold to be solid moral doctrine. Whether such doctrine has resonances in the field of canon law we leave to the discernment of the canonists.[6]

To say that there are intrinsic limits to the right to the conjugal act, then, is to say equivalently: "You can't ask for the impossible. And no one has a right to ask for the impossible."

---
[6]Renken, John, *The Contemporary Understanding of Marriage: A Historico-Critical Study of Gaudium et Spes (47-52) and its Influence Upon the Revision of the code of Canon Law*, Dissertatio ad Lauream in Facultate Juris Canonici Apud Pontificiam Universitatem S. Thomae de Urbe, Romae, 1981.

A KIND OF SPEAKING

The two previous points which we see as essential to any future theology of marriage – the conjugal act as a *procreational* act and as an act to which there is a strict *right in justice* – are closely tied to a point we have made throughout the study, but especially in Chapter V. For it was there, as we examined the Magisterially authenticated and most recent developments in the doctrine of theologians and of conciliar and papal teaching itself, that there emerged more clearly than in previous centuries the vision of the conjugal act as a form of *expression*, as, analogically, a kind of *language*.

We say "analogically", of course, because, obviously, we are not thinking of the conjugal act as being syntactically constituted. The conjugal act in the authentic sense is, however, according to Church teaching *(Familiaris Consortio)* a clearly recognizable, externally structured *sign* which, by reason of its very structure, is capable and indeed intrinsically ordered towards *expressing* the conjugal commitment. This conjugal commitment is to a love between two procreational beings who, in marriage, constitute a – indeed the *only* – procreational unity. The nature of the conjugal act as a *sign* – and indeed *the typical* sign – of this commitment we find to have been underplayed or even ignored by the dissenters to *Humanae Vitae* and, strangely enough, by many of its well-intentioned defenders, as Ciccone also has noted.

From this what we consider central truth about the conjugal act, it follows that the marriage bond gives a right to *an* act, but not to *every* act *per se aptus ad generandum*. We do not wish here to enter into the question of in vitro fertilization or other forms of artificial generation. We wish only to make the point that the only *actus per se aptus ad generandum* to which the marriage bond gives a right is an act which is inseparably *(inscindibiliter)* an expression of love *(verbum amoris)*. *(Familiaris Consortio)*

This concept of the conjugal act as language will, we hold, expose the foundations for at least several points of doctrinal development across the centuries. First it will show how the carnal genital act in cases of advanced age, of pathological sterility, and of the anovulatory phases of the menstrual cycle can truly be the conjugal act. For in all these cases, the couples can use the complete and God-given physiology of the conjugal act to *express* their acceptance of one another in a procreational union. This is true however much in certain cases the procreational nature of the couple may be de facto non-productive of a new human life or even pathologically frustrated. The presupposition is, of course, that even in these instances neither party has internally repudiated the procreational nature and calling of their life together.

This aspect of the conjugal act as language may also help us to see the foundation of the distinction between a marriage which is *ratum* and one which is *consummatum*. For in the *ratum* marriage the conjugal commitment is expressed in man-made, humanly conventional language. However lofty and at the same time humanly simple such language may be, nonetheless it cannot speak in words with the power of the language which wells up from our most profound orientation of psyche and physique: the language of physical genital union. This latter language is not from man, but from God. That is why it "consummates" as no merely human language can.

SOME CLOSING WORDS

The writer hopes that these explorations into the theological and doctrinal history of the treatment of the tragedy of rape within marriage have, nonetheless, brought into clearer light the great gift of God in creating marital love and its expression in the conjugal act. The physiological dimension of that act can never be bent to the purposes of sexual oppression without one's thereby effectively destroying the act's true and comprehensive nature. It is an act made for true conjugal love, and nothing less.

BIBLIOGRAPHY

I. SOURCES AND GENERAL REFERNCES

... "Address to International Congress of Equipes de Notre Dame," Paul XI, Pope, USCC, Washington, 1970.

... *Enchiridion Symbolorum*, ed. Denzinger, H. – Schonmetzer, A., Romae, 1974.

... *Enchiridion Vaticanum:* Vol. 1, *Documenti Ufficiali del Concilio Vaticano II:* Vol. 2-6 *Documenti Ufficiali della Santa Sede*, IIa ed., Edizioni Dehoniane, Bologna, 1979-1981.

... *Familiaris Consortio*, Pope John Paul II, Typis Polyglottis Vaticanae, 1981.

... *Gregorius IX, Decretals*, 1616, Lugduni.

... *Human Life in our Day: A Collective Letter of the American Hierarchy*, United States Catholic Conference, Washington, 1968.

... *Humanae Vitae*, in English translation by A. Durand, 1978, Bethlehem, PA.

... *L'Amore Umano Nel Piano Divino, Catechesi di Giovanni Paolo II nelle Udienze Generali*, Parte Prima, Libreria Editrice Vatican, 1980.

... *New Catholic Encyclopedia, The*, Washington D.C., 1967.

... *Pii IX Papae Acta*, Romae, 1854-1878.

... *Pius XII, Discorsi Ai Medici*, ed. S.E. Mons. Fierenzo Angelini, Roma, 1969.

... *To Live in Christ Jesus*, United States Catholic Conference, Washington, 1976.

... *Vatican Council II; The Conciliar and Post-conciliar Documents*, general editor, Austin Flannery, Northport, N.Y., 1975.

Sommervogel, A., *Biblioteque De La Compagnie De Jesus*, Brussels, 1890-1952.

II. MANUALS

Agnellus, Porpora, *Theologia Moralis*, Neapoli, 1851.

Aertnys, Josephus, *Theologia Moraiis*, ed. 1, Tornaci, 1913 – Damen, C., Roma, 1981; ed. Visser, J., Roma, 1969.

Antonelli, Joseph, *Medicina Pastoralis*, 5th ed., Romae, 1932.

Ballerini, Antonius – Palmieri, Domenicus, *Opus Theologicum, Morale in Busenbaum Medullam*, Prato, 1893.

Bassaeus, Eligius *Flores Totius Theologiae Practicae*, Venetiis, 1666.

Bossius, Joannes Angelus, *De Effectibus Contractus Matrimonii*, Lugduni 1655.

Bruschi, Joseph, *Cursus Theologiae Moralis*, Camerini, 1790.

Bucceroni, Januarius, *Institutiones Theologiae Moralis*, 6th Ed., Romae, 1914-1915.

Busenbaum, H., *Medulla theologiae Moralis*, Romae, 1676.

Cappello, Felix, *De Matrimonio*, Taurini, 1950.

Cassianus a S. Elia, *Arbor Omnium Opinionum Moralium, Ferrariae*, 1705.

Concina, Danielis, *Theologia Christina Dogmatico-Moralis*, Venetiis, 1751.

Cardenas, Joannes de, *Crisis Theologicus*, Venetiis, 1724.

Coppens, Charles, *Moral Principles and Medical Practice*, New York, 1887.

Craisson, D., *Notiones Theologicae Circa Sextum Praeceptum*, Parisiis, 1873.

Da Priero, Sylvester, *Summa Sylvestrina*, Venetiis, 1601.

De Avila, Stephanus, *Compendium Summae D. Navarri*, Venetiis, 1614.

De Moure, B., *Examen Theologiae Moralis*, Lugduni, 1628.

de Viva, Domenicus, *Cursus Theologico-Moralis*, Patavii, 1723.

Diana, Antonius, *Resolutiones Morales*, Venetiis, 1650.

Emanuele, SA. *Aphorismi Confessariorum*, Romae, 1607.

Escobar y Mendoza, Antonius De, *Universae Theologiae Moralis*, Lugduni, 1652-1663.

Fagundez, Stephanus, *In Decalogi Praecepti*, Lugduni, 1640.

Ferreres, Joannes B., - Mondria, Alfredus, *Compendium theologiae Moralis*, 17th ed., Barcinone, 1953.

Fuchs, Josephus, SJ, *De Castitate et De Ordine Sexuali*, ed. 2, Roma, 1959; ed. 4, 1963.

Gabrielis a S. Vincentio, *De Sacramentis*, Romae, 1656-1657 – *Summa Moralis*, Romae, 1657.

Genicot, Eduardus, *Institutiones Theologiae Moralis*, Louvain, 1896.

...*Casus Conscientiae*, Louvain, 1902.

...*Institutiones theologiae Moralis*, ed. 8a, Bruxelles, 1919; ed. 17a Bruxelles, 1951.

Gobatus, Georgius, *Opera Moralia*, Venetiis, 1670.

Grisez, Germain, *The Way of the Lord Jesus*, Chicago, Franciscan Herald, 1984.

Gunthor, Anselm, *Chiamata e Risposta*, Roma, 1979.

Gury, Joannes P., *Compendium Theologiae Moralis*, Romae, 1866; Tummolo, Raphaelis, 4th ed., Neapoli, 1928.

Haring, Bernard, CSSR, *La Legge di Cristo*, Brescia, 1957-1959.

...*The Law of Christ*, Philadelphia, 1959.

Iorio, Thomas *Theologia Moralis*, Neapoli, 1954.

Hurth, Franciscus, *De Statibus*, Romae, 1946.

Konigs, A., *Theologia Moralis S. Alphonsii*, N.Y., 1878.

Laymann, Paulus, *Theologia Moralis*, Venetiis, 1719.

la Croix, Claudius, *Theologia Moralis Antehac ex Probatis Auctoribus Breviter Concinnata a R.P. Herm. Busenbaum*, Parisiis, 1867.

Leander de Sacratissimo Sacramento, *Quaestiones Morales Theologicae in Septem Ecclesiae Sacramentis*, Lugduni, 1644.

Lehmkuhl, Augustine, *Theologia Morlis*, Friburg Brisgoviae, 1914.

Lessius, Leonard, SJ, *De Justitia Et Jure*, Venetiis, 1718.

Ligouri, Alphonsus, *Medulla Theologiae Moralis R.P. Busenbaum SJ theologi, cum adnotatione per Rev. P. Alphonsum Ligouri Rect. Maj. Congregatio SS. Salvatoris*, Napoli, 1748.

...*Theologia Moralis*, Torino, 1846.

Lopez De Texeda, Franciscus, *Controversia Theolog. Moralis*, Neapoli, 1646.

Lumbier, Raymond, *Observationes Theologicae Morales*, Barcinone, 1682.

Marc, C., *Institutiones Morales Alphonsianae*, Romae, 13 ed., 1906.

Marchantius, Jacobus, *Resolutiones Pastorales*, Coloniae, 1650.

Mausbach-Ermecke, G., *Katholische Moral-Theologie*, Munster-Westfallen, 1953-1961.

...*Teologia Morale*, Roma, 1956-1958.

Mazzotta, Nicholaus, *Theologia Moralis*, Neapoli, 1760.

Heinzel, Godfridus, SJ, *Summa Theologiae Moralis: Complementum De Castitate*, Oeniponte, 1961.

Merkelbach, Benedictus, *Summa Theologiae Moralis*, Parisiis, 1931.

...*Quaestiones de Castitate et Luxurio*, 3rd ed. Liege, 1929.

Milane, Thomas, *Exercitationes Dogmatico-Morales In Propositiones Praescriptas*, Neapoli, 1739.

Navarrus, Martinus, *Opera Moralia*, Romae, 1590.

Neyraguet, D., *Compendium theologiae Moralis S. Alphonsi*, Ratisbonae, 1841.

Noldin, Henricus-Schmidt, A., *Summa theologiae Moralis, Supplementum de Sexto Praecpto*, ed. 31, Oeniponte, 1940.

...Noldin, H., – Heinzel, G., *De Castitate*, Oeniponte, 1953,

Peeters, Hermes, OFM, *Manuale Theologiae Moralis*, Torino-Roma, 1963.

Pereyra, Benedict, SJ, *Summa Ex Universa Theologia Morali*, Ebura, 1707.

Pontius, Basilius, *Tractatus de Sacro Matrimonio*, Venet. 1645.

Raynaudus, Theolphilus, *De Ortu Infantium*, Lugduni, 1637.

Reginald, Valerius, *Praxis Fori Poenitentalis*, Moguntiae, 1617.

Renzi, Mattheus, *Encyclopedia Universae Theologiae Moralis*, Neapoli, 1671.

Sanchez, Thomas, SJ, *Disputationes de Sancto Matrimonio*, Antuerpiae, 1624; Venetiis, 1626 and 1645.

...*Opus Morale in Praecepta Decalogi*, Lugduni, 1621.

Schmitt, Martinus, *Epitome theologiae Moralis*, Lugduni, 1857.

Scavini, Petrus, *Theologia Moralis Universa*, Mediolani, 1847.

Strüggl, Marcus, *Theologia Moralis*, Venetiis, 1758.

Tamburinus, Thomas, *Theologia Moralis*, Venetiis, 1726.

Tancredus, Vincentius, *De Sancto Matrimonii Sacramento*, Panormi, 1640.

Trullenchus, Joannes, *Praxim Sacramentorum*, Barcinonae, 1701.

Ubach, Josephus, *Theologia Moralis*, Friburg Bisgroviae, 1926.

Vermeersch, Arthurus, *De Castitate et de Vitiis Oppositis*, Romae, ed. 2, 1923.

Viva, Domenicus, *Cursus Theologicus-Moralis*, Patavii, 1723

...*Damnatae Theses*, Patavii, 1737.

Voit, Edmundus, SJ, *Theologia Moralis*, Bassanensi, 1766.

Zalba, Marcellinus, *Theologiae Moralis Summa*, BAC, Madrid, 1954.

...*Theologiae Moralis Compendium*, BAC, Madrid, 1958.

III. BOOKS

...*Natural Family Planning: nature's Way – God's Way*, Collegeville, 1980.

...*The Future of Marriage As Institution*, ed. by Franz Böckle, Herder, 1970.

...*Principles of Catholic Moral Life*, ed. William E. May, Chicago, 1980.

Armstrong, R.H., *Primary and Secondary Precepts of Natural Law Teaching*, Hague, 1966.

Ashley, Benedict, OP and Kevin O'Rourke, OP, *Health Care Ethics*, The Catholic Hospital Association St. Louis, 1978; 2nd edition, St. Louis, 1982.

Billings, John, Dr., *Natural Family Planning*, 4th ed., Collegeville, MN, 1978.

Bihlmeyer, Karl, and Tuckle, Herman, *Church History*, Westminster, U.S.A., 1960.

Bonnar, A., *The Catholic Doctor*, 2nd ed., London, 1939; 6th ed., London, 1952.

Boyer C., *Cursus Philosophiae*, Roma, 1949.

Cappelmann, C., *Medicina Pastoralis*, ed. 9a, Aquisgrani, 1892.

Curran, Charles, *The Prevention of Pregnancy After Rape, Excerpta in dissertatione ad laurem, in Facultate Theologica Pontificiae Universitatis Gregorianae*, Rome, 1961.

Debreyne, P. – A. Ferrand, *La Theologie Morale et les Sciences Medicales*, 6th ed., Paris, 1884.

De Margerie, Bertrand, SJ, *Sacraments and Social Progress*, New York, 1974.

Derrick, Christopher, *Honest Love and Human Life*, New York, 1969.

De Rougemont, Denis, *Love in the Western World*, New York, 1950.

Ernest, Siegfried, *Man, the Greatest of Miracles*, Collegeville, 1976.

Jordan, Harvey Ernest, and Kindred, James Ernest, *Textbook of Embryology*, 4th edition, New York, 1942.

Good, Frederick L., and Kelly, Otis F., *Marriage, Morals and Medical Ethics*, New York, 1951.

Günthör, Anselm, OSB, *Kommentar Zur Encyklika Humanae Vitae*, Friburg 1. Br. 1969.

..."*Die Bishofe: Für Oder Gegen Humanae Vitae?*", Freiburg 1. Br. 1970.

Healy, Edwin F., *Medical Ethics*, Chicago, 1956.

Hughes, Phillip, *A Popular History of the Catholic Church*, New York, 1968.

Joyce, Mary Rosera, *How Can a Man and Woman be Friends*, Collegeville, 1977.

...*Love Responds to Life*, Kenosha, Wisconsin, 1971.

Kelly, J., and Ford, G., *Contemporary Moral Theology II*, Newman, Westminster, 1964.

Kippley, John *Birth Control and the Marriage Convenant*, 2nd ed., Collegeville, 1981.

Latourelle, Rene, SJ, – O'Collins, Gerald, SJ, *Problemmi e Prospettive della Teologia Fondementale*, Rome, 1981.

Le Compte, A., *L'Ovulation Spontaneè*, Louvain, 1873.

McFadden, Charles A., *Medical Ethics*, Philadelphia, 1955.

...*The Dignity of Life*, Huntington, Ind., 1976.

Martelet, G., *Amour Conjugal et renouveau conciliare*, Lyon, 1967.

May, William E., and Harvey, John F., *On Understanding Human Sexuality*, 1977.

...*Sex, Love, and Procreation*, Chicago, 1976.

...*The Nature and meaning of Chastity*, Chicago, 1976.

McCarthy, Donald and Bayer, Edward, *Handbook of Critical Sexual Issues*, St. Louis, 1983, The Pope John Center.

Mulligan, James J., *The Pope and the Theologians*, Emmitsburg, Maryland, U.S.A., 1968.

Noonan, John, *Contraception: A History of its Treatment by The Catholic Theologians and Canonists*, Cambridge, U.S.A., 1965.

O'Donnell, Thomas, *Morals, in Medicine*, Westminster, 1956; 2nd edition, 1959.

...*Medicine and Christian Morality*, Staten Island, 1975.

O'Mally, Austin, *The Ethics of Medical Homicide and Mutilation*, New York, 1910.

Ratzinger, Joseph, *Theological Highlights of the Second Vatican Council*, 1966, New York.

Renken, John, *The Contemporary Understanding of Marriage: A Historico-Critical Study of Gaudium et Spes (47-52) and its Influence Upon the Revision of the code of Canon Law, Dissertatio ad Lauream in Facultate Juris Canonici Apud Pontificiam Universitatem S. Thomae de Urbe*, Romae, 1981.

Speert, Harold, *Obstetrics and Gynecological Milestones*, New York, 1958.

Suenens, Leon Joseph Cardinal, *Love and Control*, Westminster, 1960, England.

Valsecchi, A., *Regolazione delle Nascite;* ed. 3, Brescia, 1967.

Wojtyla, Karol (Pope John Paul II) *Amore E Responsabilità*, Torino, 1980.

...*Fruitful and Responsible Love,* New York, 1979.

Vorgrimmler, *Commentary on the Documents of the Second Vatican Council,* New York, 1969.

Wiltgen, Ralph, *The Rhine Flows Into the Tiber,* New York, 1967.

IV. ARTICLES

...*Catholic Review,* Baltimore, MD. U.S.A., April 17, 1981.

Alfaro, Juan, "La teologia di fronte al Magistero," in Latourelle, Rene – O'Collins, Gerald, *Problemmi e Prospettive della Teologia Morale Fondamentale,* Roma, 1981, 413-432.

    Boissard, E., "Valeur moral d'un certain cas de sterilization temporaire," in *Angelicum,* 41, (1964) 167-209.

    Ciccone, L., C.M., "L'Encyclica Humanae Vitae: Analysi E Commento" in *Divus Thomas,* Piacenza, 1969, 3-58, 141-173, 267-311.

Davies, M.D., "Love and Contraception", *Irish Theological Quarterly,* 1966, 327-351.

De La Trinitè, Philip, "Un dibattimento morale relativo alle pillole anticoncezionali," *Palestra del Clero,* 41 (1962), 172-183.

De Margerie, Bertrand, "Some Aspects of Humane Vitae to Which Due Consideration Has Not Been Given," *Osservatore Romano,* May 25, 1978; 6-7.

Demmer, Klaus, "Die Moral-Theologische Diskussion Um Die Anwendung Sterilisierender Medikamente," *Theologie Und Glaube,* 1963, 145-436.

Grisez, Germain, "Catholic Faith and Intrinsically Evil Acts," in *Proceedings of the Fellowship of Catholic Scholars,* 1978.

Hellegers, Andre, "Some Aspects of the Use of Contraceptive Agents in the Mentally Retarded," *Jurist,* 1964.

Hurth, F., "Dubia Matrimonialia" in *Periodica de Re Morali Canonica Liturgica,* XXXVII, (1949), p. 220.

..."Il premunirsi rientra nel diretto della legitima difesa," *Studi Cattolici,* 27 (1961), pp. 64-67.

Janniere, A., "La differenciation sexuelle," in *Sexualitè Humaine,* Paris, 1966.

Kelly, Gerald, "Pope Pius XII and the Principle of Totality," *Theological Studies,* 1955, 16: 373-396.

Lambruschini, F., "È legittimo evitare le conseguenze dell'aggressione", *Studi Cattolici,* 27 (1961), 64-67.

Liebhardt, Von Leopold, "Sterilisierende Droge," *Theologische Quartel,* 1963, 188-203.

Malone, G.K., "Encyclical," *New Catholic Encyclopedia,* Vol. 5, 332-333.

McCarthy, Donald G., "Medication to Prevent Pregnancy After Rape," in *Linacre Quarterly,* 1977, 44: pp. 210-222.

McCormick, Richard, "Sterilization: The dilemma of Catholic Hospitals," *America,* Oct. 18, 1980.

..."Letter to the Editor," *America, Feb. 7, 1981.*

McGuckian, Michael C., "Moral Theology and Family Planning," *Furrow,* June-July, 1981, 546-549.

..."Letter to the editor," *America,* Feb. 7, 1981, 89.

Navarette, Urban, SJ, "Amor Conjugalis Et Consensus Matrimonialis," *Periodica,* Vol. 65, (1976), 619-632.

Novac, Michael, "Lust of the Eyes", *National Review,* Nov. 14, 1980, 1401.

Pallazzini, "Si può e si deve proteggere l'equilibrio della persona," *Studi Cattolici,* 27, (1961), 63-64.

Paquier, G., "Innocent XI", VII-2, 2006-14, *Dictionaire de Theologie Catholique.*

Riga, Peter, *"Humanae Vitae* and the New Sexuality," in Ernst, Siegfried, *Man the Greatest of Miracles,* Collegeville, 1976.

Vereecke, Louis, CSSR, "Alphonsus Ligouri," in *The New Catholic Enclycopedia,* 1967, Vol. 1, 340-341.

... ."Moral Theology, History of," in *New Catholic Encyclopedia,* 1967, Vol. 9, p. 119-1122.

Zalba, M., "La Portata del Principio di Totalità nella Dottrina di Pio XI e Pio XII e la sua applicazione nei casi di violenze sessuali", *Rasegna di Teologia,* IX (1968), n. 4, 225-237.

... "Media ad prolis generandam moderationem," *Periodica,* 1964, 201-259.

V. UNPUBLISHED DOCUMENTS

...Irish Episcopal Conference, *"Pastoral Guidelines for Priests",* November 20, 1980, Meath, Ireland.

INDEX

Abortion, 3, 23, 29, 33, 193, 102, 116, 122.
Absolute (exceptionless) moral terms, 10, 31, 32, 34, 56, 80.
Abuses of sound teaching, 77, 95-96, 101, 122.
Acts of man, 10.
Adultery, 1, 85, 116.
Aertnys, J., 55.
Aeterni Patris, 43.
Alexander VII, 22, 24.
Alexander VIII, 25.
Alfaro, J., 38, 125.
American bishops, 5, 8, 113-115.
Amplexus reservatus, 44, 79.
Anal copulation, 43, 74, 139.
Angelism, 129.
Anovulant drugs, 8, 9, 66, 67, 82, 84, 87, 88, 127.
Antoine, P., 110.
Antonelli, J., 56.
Aquinas, Thomas, St., 10, 27, 50.
Arcanum Divinae Sapientiae, 43, 58.
Armstrong, R., 10.
Artificial contraception, 25.
Ashley, B., 8.
Atheism, 26.
Azor, J., 13.

Ballerini, A., 48, 50, 54.
Barrier contraceptives, 87.
Baptism, 126.
Bayer, E., 9.
Bayley, C., 61.
Belgian Congo case, 12, 63, 82, 88, 90, 92, 115, 127, 132.
Benedict XV, 43.
Benedictines, 27.
Bernadin, J., Cardinal, 140.
Bestiality, 130, 140.
Biblical Commission Pontifical, 45.
Billmeyer, K., 26.
Bimestre, 13-16, 18-23, 30-33, 36, 35, 54, 130.
Biologism (physicalism), 51, 62, 78, 80 115, 117, 118, 129-131.
Bishops, 1, 3, 4, 6, 10, 11, 38, 123, 124.
Bismark, O., 42.
Body, 10.
Bona (goods) of marriage, 107-108.
Bonnar, A., 49.
Bossius, J., 21-24, 35, 37, 38, 44, 45, 82, 126.
Bourbon Restoration, 26.
Bruschi, J., 34.
Bucceroni, G., 55.

Canon law jurisprudence, 14, 38, 107, 139.
Cappellman, C., 35, 55.
Cappello, F., 56.
Cardenas, J., 23.
Cassian of St. Elias, 23.
Casti Connubii, 2, 43, 58, 60, 62-64.
Charity, 86-87.
Chastity, 121.
Christ, 58, 79, 106, 107, 120, 124, 126, 127, 132.
Church, 4, 11, 22, 58, 79, 106, 107, 120, 124, 126, 127, 132.
Ciccone, L., 109, 112, 126-128, 131, 139.
Communication of truth in conjugal act, 108, 118, 119, 137, 138.
Conception, human, 7.
Concina, D., 34.
Condoms, 39, 54, 57, 75, 87.
Congregation for the Doctrine of the Faith, Sacred Roman, (Holy Office), 22, 26, 38, 39, 44, 75, 113-115, 128.
Conjugal act, 4-6, 9, 37-39, 60, 113, 119, 120, 127.
Conjugal right, 96, 99-100, 105-108, 121, 127, 129-131, 133, 137.

Connery, J., 63.
Consent, 3, 5, 21, 23, 30, 32, 53, 118.
Consequentialism, 11, 63, 83.
Consummation of marriage, 16, 18, 19, 58, 140.
"Contraception" vs. "prevention of pregnancy", 4, 7, 9, 12, 39, 64, 108, 114, 140.
Contraceptives, artificial, 4, 7, 8, 99.
Contradiction in contraception, 119-122.
Contract, marriage, 94, 130.
Cooperation, material and formal, 121.
Coppens, C., 56.
Creator, 118, 119, 127, 135-138.
Culpability, 11.
Curran, C., 10, 28, 48, 49, 55.

Damen, C., 49.
Davies, M., 110.
Debreyne, P., 55.
Debt, marriage, 21, 30, 31-34, 48, 50, 32, 103. See also conjugal right.
Deceit in contraception, 120-121.
Defense, Self , 22, 91, 104, 122.
Definitions, dogmatic, 124.
Deism, 26.
De Margeire, B., 96, 100-102, 139.
Derrick, C., 96-97, 100, 102, 126, 128, 139.
Development of doctrine, 11, 25-28, 40, 43, 45, 51, 60, 77, 79, 93, 113, 115, 124-126.
Deus Scientiarum Dominus, 43.
Diana, A., 21, 31.
Diaphragm, 45, 46, 57, 84, 85, 87.
Disease, 14.
Dissent, 83, 127.
Divini Redemptions, 43.
Divino Afflante Spiritu, 43.
Divorce, 58, 983.
Dominicans, 27.
Dominus ac Redemptor, 26.
Douches, 57, 85.
Drugs, contraceptive, 51.
Drunkenness, 14, 84-86, 91, 101.
Duties and obligations, 102-104, 122.

Embryology, 25.
Ends of marriage, 44, 78, 79.
Enlightenment, 26, 40.
Episcopates, local, see bishops.
Ermeke, G., 56.
Eugenics and sterilization, 62, 63, 77, 78.
Expression of love, conjugal act as, 61, 80, 97, 99, 105-140.
Experimentation, medical, 69-72.
Expulsion of semen, 14, 17, 18, 20-23, 26, 29-31, 34, 45, 46 48, 52, 56, 82, 93.
Extrinsic authority, 6.

Fagundez, J., 23.
Familiaris Consortio, 53, 61, 97, 112, 116-121.
Family size, 104, 122, 125, 140.
Fear, 21-23.
Ferreres, J., 49.
Fertility, 9.
Fetus, 23, 33.
Force, 97, 111, 112, 138.
Forearming against rape, 92. See also Fuchs, J.
Formulations, theological, 54.
France, 42.
Frequency of rape in marriage, 128.
Friendship, marriage as, 105, 106.
Fuchs, J., 49, 56, 80, 82, 83, 96.

Gasser, 11.
Gaudium et Spes, 2, 4, 10, 11, 79, 80, 105-108, 112, 122.

Genicot, 45, 51.
Germany, 42.
Gobat, G., 21.
Gabriel of St. Vincent, 21.
God, see Creator.
God, image of, 4.
Good, F., 49.
Gregory IX, 13.
Grisez, G., 10, 134.
Günthor, A., 96-97, 101, 103.
Gunz, J., 35.

Hamer, J., Archbishop, 115.
Häring, B., 49, 83, 85, 86, 96.
Harvey, J., 10.
Health, wife's, 9, 62, 130.
Healy, E., 49.
Heinzel, G., 5, 45, 47, 54, 82.
Hermaphroditism, 138.
Hermeneutic, of Magisterial documents, 38, 40, 60.
   See also Alfaro, J.
Hermes, P., 47.
Holy Office, see Congregation for the Doctrine of the Faith, Sacred, 116, 129, 138, 139.
Homosexuality, 136.
Hospitals, Response of the Sacred Congregation for the Doctrine of the Faith Regarding Sterilization in Catholic, 61, 114-115.
Hughes, P., 26.
Human act, 6.
Human Life in Our Day, 115.
Humanae Vitae, 4, 5, 6, 10, 11, 53, 61, 62, 80, 83, 88, 96, 98, 108-115, 122-132, 140.
Humani Generis, 44.
Hurth, F., 56.
Hysterectomy, 110.

In vitro fertilization, 4, 140.
Incarnation, 11.
Infallibility, 11, 36.
Infertile periods, 110.
Injustice, see justice.
Innocent XI, 22-24, 35, 36.
Insanity, 14, 85.
Institute of Thomistic Philosophy, 44.
Institutiones morales, 13.
Instrument, sex as procreational, 139.
Intellect, 53.
International Theological Commission, 11.
Intrinsic evil, 4, 15, 17, 21, 31, 39, 63.
Iorio, T., 49, 51.
Irish Bishops, 3, 6, 116, 121, 125, 127.
Italy, 42.
Janniere, A., 110.
Jesuits (Society of Jesus), 26, 27.
John XXIII, 11, 102-104.
John Paul II, 1, 53, 75, 80, 97, 102, 125, 131, 135.
Jordan, H., 25.
Juridicism, 131.
Jus ad Corpus, 129-130.
Justice, 3, 23, 30, 33, 40, 49, 50, 53, 76, 77, 86, 87, 92, 94, 95, 99, 136.
Kelly, G., 63.
Kelly, O., 49.
Kippley, J., 110.
Königs, A., 34.
Kulturkampf, 42.

Lacroix, C., 23, 28, 32.
Language, conjugal act as, 109-110, 115, 116, 118-121, 125, 127, 140.
Latourelle, R., 38.
Lamentabili, 42.
La Rochelle, S., 49.

Laxism, 22.
Le Compte, A., 35.
Leander of the Blessed Sacrament, 21.
Legalism, 128. See also juridicism.
Lehmkuhl, A., 46, 48.
Leo XIII, 12, 27, 28, 42, 43, 58, 80.
Levada, W., 11.
Lewis, C. S., 96.
Life, wife's, 2, 9.
Ligouri, Alphonsus, St., 12, 13, 24, 27, 32, 33, 35, 40, 50.
Lopez de Texeda, F., 19-20, 31, 53.
Love, 6, 37, 38, 53, 57-61, 78-84, 97-101, 106-107, 109, 111, 112, 115-117, 121, 122, 139.
Lugo, 29, 30.
Lumbier, R., 23.
Lust, 91.
Lynch, J., 63.

Magisterium, 2, 4, 6, 10, 11, 12, 15, 25, 23, 25, 26, 35, 36-38, 40, 41, 44, 55, 56, 58, 61, 62, 72, 79, 81, 82, 89, 100, 102, 105, 112-115, 118, 122, 124, 127, 129, 132.
Malone, G., 43, 48.
Manicheism, 129.
Manuals, moral, 112, 128, 130, 135.
Marchant, J., 20.
Martelet, G., 110.
Masturbation, 2, 4, 8.
May, W., 11.
McCarthy, D., 7, 8.
McCormick, R., 61.
McFadden, C., 49.
Meaning in conjugal act, 5, 6, 79, 80, 109, 111, 119-122, 136.
   See also communication of truth in conjugal act.
Menopause, 110.

Napoleanic era, 26.
Natural family planning, see periodic abstinance.
Natural law, 4, 10, 11, 31, 58, 64, 80, 133.
Naturalism, 26.
Nature, see natural law.
Nazis, 75.
Noldin, A., 5, 54, 85.
Non-support, 14.
"Nuptial meaning of body", 135.

Obligation, see duties and obligations.
O'Collins, G., 38.
O'Donnel, T., 5, 8, 49, 63, 68.
O'Mally, A., 55.
Onanism, 21, 35, 36, 38, 39, 51, 54, 55, 57, 64, 74.
Oppression, sexual, see rape.
Oral copulation, 40, 139.
Orders, religious, 26, 27.
Organ donation, 63, 69, 132.
Original sin, 11.
O'Rourke, K., 8.
Osservatore Romano, 101, 125.
Ovulation, 7.
Ovum, 27.

Pacem in Terris, 103-104.
Palazzini, P., 83.
Palmieri, D., 48-51, 54.
Papal States, 42.
Paul, St., 52.
Paul VI, 10, 79, 100-102, 104-115, 119, 126.
Peeters, H., 84-87, 96-102.
Periodic abstinence, 4.
Person, 4, 107, 114.
Personalism, Christian, 34, 116-118.
Perversion, sexual, 19.
Pessary, see diaphragm.
Philosophical systems, see reason.
Physicalism, see biologism.

Physiological structure of conjugal act, 4, 36, 40, 46, 52, 61, 97, 107, 120, 121, 130-132, 135, 139.
"Pill, the", see anovulant drugs.
Pius VII, 36.
Pius X, St., 11, 42.
Pius XI, 2, 11, 27, 43, 58, 61-64, 89, 91, 94.
Pius XII, 5, 11, 43, 62-74, 83, 89, 91, 94, 101, 105, 114, 131, 132, 134, 135.
Pontius, B., 18-21.
Pope John Center, 9.
Popes, 10, 122.
"Pregnancy prevention" vs. "contraception". See "contraception"
Primacy of love, 59.
Probable opinion, solidly, 12, 125, 126-228.
Procreation as meaning of conjugal act, 109, 130, 131, 133, 138, 140.
"Procreational" vs. "procreative", 133-134.
Procreational nature, human, 39-40.
Property, sexual faculties as, 20, 30, 52.
Proportionality, 1, 7, 44.
Prostitution, 112.
Providentissimus, Deus, 43.
Provisional vs. permanent Church teaching, 125.
Psychological pressure, 99.
Punishment, sterilization as, 57.

Quadragesimo Anno, 43.
Quaecumque Sterilizatio, see *Hospitals, Response of The Sacred Congreation for the Doctrine of the Faith Regarding Sterilization in Catholic*.
"Quasi-rape", 6.

Race, continuation of human, 1, 3, 5.
Rational nature, human, 138.
Ratum et consummatum, 13, 18.
Ratzinger, J., 105.
Rape, extra-marital, 8, 9, 18, 22, 26, 27, 31, 32-35, 40, 45, 51, 56, 82, 84, 85, 96, 97, 127.
Reason, 11.
Refusal of conjugal act, 2, 3, 94.
Relational nature, human, 137.
Renzi, M., 21.
Reputation, 16, 17, 22.
Resistance to rape, 18, 87.
Respect, 39, 53, 107, 138.
Responsible parenthood, 2, 101.
Revelation, 11, 117.
Reverence, see respect.
Review, Baltimore Catholic, 4.
Rights, 53, 63, 76-78, 86, 94, 96, 102-104, 122, 136, 137, 139, 140.
Rigorism, 22.

Sacramentality, 11.
Salsmans, J., 49, 51.
Sanchez, T., 13-15, 19-24, 31-35, 39, 40, 48-51, 54, 55, 80, 82, 126.
Schmitt, A., 28, 44-46, 48, 54, 56, 79, 81, 82, 92, 102.
Semen, 136.
Separation, 85.
Sexual anomoly, 4.
Significance of conjugal act, see communication of truth in conjugal act.
Simulation of vows, 107, 119, 127.
Situation ethics, 44.
Sodomy, see anal copulation.
Sommervogle, C., 28.
Soul, 10.
Sperm, 27.
Spirit, Holy, 11.
Stagnation, theological, 12.
Sterilization, 5, 7, 8, 44, 57, 61, 63, 64, 65, 71, 75, 76, 87, 89, 114.

Strüggl, M., 33-34.
Synod of Bishops, Sixth, 53, 80, 97, 116, 121-133.
Tamburinus, T., 20.
Tancred, V., 20.
Theologians, 2, 12, 25, 28, 37, 38, 40, 83, 124, 126, 127.
Theology, 105, 127, 128.
Thomas, St., see Aquinas.
Thomism, 80.
To Live in Christ Jesus, 5.
Totality, principle of, 64, 65, 67, 70, 76, 81, 99, 129, 131-133.
Tradition, Catholic moral, 10.
Transplants, 132.
Trent, Council of, 125.
Tribunals, 127.
Truth of conjugal act, see communication of truth in conjugal act.
Tubal ligation, see sterilization.
Tuckle, H., 26.
Tummulo, R., 55.

Ubach, J., 50.
United States National Conference of Catholic Bishops, see American Bishops.
Unity (meaning of conjugal act), 109.
Universities, Catholic, 25, 27, 45.
Uterine isolation, 5.

Valsecchi, A., 89.
Vasectomy, see sterilization.
Vatican Council I, 11, 24, 26.
Vatican Council II, 12, 45, 79, 107, 113, 119, 126, 128, 131. See also *gaudium et Spes*.
Vatican Declaration on Certain Questions Relating to Sexual Ethics, 10.
Veneral disease, 85.
Vereecke, L., 25.
Vemeersch, 5, 46, 50, 52.
Violence, see force.
Virginity, 29, 86, 97.
Visser, J., 86-88, 90, 96, 102, 115, 127, 128.
Viva, D., de, 23.
Voit, E., 31.
Vows, 127.

Walsh, W., 8.
Will, see freedom.
Wiltgen, R., 105.
Withdrawal ("natural" onanism), 36, 40, 41.
Women (liberation, equality, rights, dignity), 101, 102, 103, 107, 116, 117, 118, 123.
World Wars I and II, 44, 65.

Zalba, M., 5, 48, 54, 61, 62, 63, 68, 82, 88-96, 101, 102, 115, 127, 132.

www.ingramcontent.com/pod-product-compliance
Lightning Source LLC
Chambersburg PA
CBHW070907160426
43193CB00011B/1390